Art in the Cinematic Imagination

Art in the Cinematic Imagination

SUSAN FELLEMAN

University of Texas Press ⋁ *Austin*

Requests for permission to reproduce material from this work should be sent to:
Permissions
University of Texas Press
P.O. Box 7819
Austin, TX 78713-7819
www.utexas.edu/utpress/about/bpermission.html

♾ The paper used in this book meets the minimum requirements of ANSI/NISO
Z39.48-1992 (R1997) (Permanence of Paper).

Library of Congress Cataloging-in-Publication Data

Felleman, Susan.
Art in the cinematic imagination / Susan Felleman.—1st ed.
    p.   cm.
Includes bibliographical references and index.
ISBN 0-292-70942-0 (cloth : alk. paper)—ISBN 0-292-70941-2 (pbk. : alk. paper)
1. Art in motion pictures.   2. Artists in motion pictures.   3. Women in motion pictures.
4. Art and motion pictures.   I. Title.
PN1995.9.A73F46   2006
791.43'657—dc22

                                                                    2005007256

To Joan Sharaf Felleman and in memory of Anne Halley Chametzky (1928–2004)

Contents

Acknowledgments

Although this is putatively a single-authored volume, many besides myself contributed to its realization. It seems it takes a village to make a book.

At Southern Illinois University Carbondale, where I have taught in the Department of Cinema and Photography since 1998, I have been the happy recipient of grants that supported my research from several sources, including the Office of Research and Development Administration, University Women's Professional Advancement, and the College of Mass Communication and Media Arts. For the support of my dean, Manjunath Pendakur; my department chairperson, Bill Rowley; the director of graduate studies, Tom Johnson; and many other colleagues, I am most grateful.

It is impossible to convey in list form the affection and respect I feel for a number of students (most of them graduate students) whose invaluable assistance—with tasks including clerical projects, photographic and videographic reproduction, translation, research, and the teaching assistance that always helped free me for research—I have benefited from during the course of this work. They are Farshad Aminian, Monica Bandholz, Marty Camden, Kurush Canteenwala, Rachael Carlson, Vaidehi Chitre, Katie Coleman, Phil Hastings, Jeffrey Hill, Eva Honegger, Virginie Lamarche, Nate Mahoney, Tom Mogle, Maria Richeva, Chris Sato, Anastasia Saverino, Rebecca Sittler, Anna Velitchkova, Ippei Watanabe, Tommie Xie, Wei Zhang, John Ziniewicz, and the positively heroic Michael McDonald (a mensch!), who lent expertise he had and time he didn't to helping solve a particularly sticky problem.

I thank my departmental support staff, Tommie Rayford and Rhonda Rothrock, for so much help over the years and am especially grateful to Kevin Koron, whose good-natured assistance and technical prowess have helped me out of many a fix. Colleagues at SIUC and other scholars who contributed thoughts, feedback, and vital information include David and Erin Desmond Anthony, Ed

Brunner, Kevin Dettmar, Liz Kotz, Cheryl Bray Lower, Eva Nikolova, Tina Wasserman, and Clarisse Zimra.

While most of the content of this book is the result of research undertaken in the past six years at SIUC, a couple of the chapters first appeared in somewhat different forms quite a long time ago, and before my first book, when I was in graduate school. It was back then, too, that I first saw more than a few of the films discussed herein and began to develop an analysis of them, often in the company of Glenn Korman and Beth Harris Ugoretz, the latter of whom I wish to acknowledge for the many passionate discussions with her that echo throughout this volume.

I wish to thank, too, the organizers of conferences, conference sessions, and colloquia and editors of journals and books who invited me to present and publish earlier versions of some of these chapters, or work preliminary to them. They include Peter Brunette and David Cast, organizers of sessions at College Art Association annual conferences (1991 and 1999, respectively); Dudley Andrew and James Lastra, organizers of "Painting and Photography in the Light of Cinema," University of Iowa, 1991; Paul Roth and Frank Grady, "Violence, Cinema and American Culture," University of Missouri–St. Louis, 2001; Noah Lopez and Tim Anderson, "Hollywood and Its Discontents," University of Arizona, 2001; Suzanne Daughton, who invited me to speak to the SIUC Speech Communication Proseminar in 2002; Paul Young and Devoney Looser, who invited me to speak to the University of Missouri's English Department Colloquium in 2003; and Kristi McKim, organizer of a session at the Society for Cinema and Media Studies in 2003. At these venues, various interlocutors contributed questions and comments that helped shape the future course of my study. I thank them.

Earlier versions of several chapters herein have been published previously, and I would like to thank all those involved for their permission to publish these materials in their present revised form. Earlier versions of chapters 1, 5, and 7 were published in *Iris, Camera Obscura,* and *Film Quarterly,* respectively. I remain especially grateful to Marc Vernet, who invited me to add my contribution to the special double issue of *Iris* that published proceedings of "Le portrait peint au cinéma," a conference he and Dominique Païni organized for the Louvre in April of 1991. I should also like to expressly acknowledge the very professional and personable Ann Martin, editor of *Film Quarterly.* A shorter, earlier version of chapter 6 appears in Steven Schneider, ed., *New Hollywood Violence* (Manchester University Press, 2004).

I have considerable debts to Brigitte Peucker, whose work I consider an important precursor of mine, and who generously identified herself as one of the University of Texas Press reviewers for this volume. Her feedback and her example are encouraging and inspiring to me. I am also indebted to the other, anonymous, reviewer of the manuscript, who contributed really helpful insights, criticisms, and leads, and to Jim Burr, Alex Barron, Leslie Doyle Tingle, Jan McInroy, Sue Carter, Nancy Bryan, Ellen McKie, and everyone else at the press who helped to bring this book to life.

I thank my friends for being my friends. I am lucky to have too many, I think, to thank individually. And I thank my family. The pleasures, emotions, and realities attached to the life beyond the page and the screen make work meaningful for me. My first book was dedicated to my unwaveringly insightful, supportive, good-humored, and wonderful husband, Peter Chametzky. My next book, should I be fortunate enough to complete another, will be dedicated to our two witty, talented, beautiful (of course!), and always inspiring children, Ben and Hallie. This one is dedicated to my mother, Joan Sharaf Felleman, and to the memory of my mother-in-law, writer Anne Halley Chametzky, whom we lost just as the book was to go to press. Both of these beloved mothers helped in many ways to make it possible for me to imagine and to manage this complicated, challenging, and incredibly fulfilling life I lead.

Art in the Cinematic Imagination

Introduction: Baring the Device

Art (and by this I mean the "other" visual and plastic arts: painting, sculpture, photography, architecture, etc.) has been reflected and represented in, thematized by and structured into narrative films in myriad ways throughout the history of cinema. This book considers a range of such incorporations, drawn from the postwar classical and contemporary narrative cinema—European and American. I am particularly interested in attending to patterns relating to the signification and symptomatization of sex, gender, sexuality, and psyche in the way art and artists figure in film, as I believe these to be the basic problems from which much else in human nature and culture derives. The "otherness" of the other visual arts has, to cinema, a significant, although rarely simple or directly correlative relationship to the way that other "othernesses"—primarily, but not exclusively gender difference—function in the larger culture and society within which cinema operates. Committed to no one methodology, I have found a complex of formalist, structuralist, poststructuralist, feminist, and psychoanalytic methods—those in which I was educated and am, for better or for worse, most fluent—necessary for pulling apart the tangled relationships I see around art and psyche in cinema.

If I employ no one single methodology per se, there is method here, however, and that method is essentially art historical. From the field in which I was trained, I inherit a tradition of close looking and close description—at and of form, structure, and style—and ways of approaching historical and cultural patterns in art and imagery: the iconography and iconology so aptly defined by one of art history's great innovators, Erwin Panofsky.[1] Panofsky, to the eternal surprise of many who think of art history as a conservative and stodgy discipline, was of course a rather early and very eloquent articulator of the cinema's close relationship to the other arts, who perceived the applicability of art historical method to cinematic objects.[2] But Panofsky was not my teacher. Among those who were, foremost for me are Linda Nochlin and Rosalind Krauss, from whom I learned that the disciplinary rigor of art historical method need not be abandoned under the influence of new intellectual paradigms. Nochlin's brilliant feminism and Krauss's incisive and protean critical insights are always rooted to the object and its problematic nature by investigation, fascination, and close regard. They are my exemplars. Methods and attitudes about seeing and interpreting objects learned from them and others have strongly influenced my viewing, teaching, and writing in the field of cinema studies. For me theory never precedes my interest in an object but always follows from it.

There is a small but significant body of scholarly work that has been done in and around this border area between cinema and the other visual arts in the past decade, including John Walker's *Art and Artists on Screen*, Brigitte Peucker's *Incorporating Images: Film and the Rival Arts*, Angela Dalle Vacche's *Cinema and Painting: How Art Is Used in Film*, Katharina Sykora's *As You Desire Me: Das Bildnis in Film*, and volumes of collected essays edited by Patrice Petro (*Fugitive Images: From Photography to Video*), Dudley Andrew (*The Image in Dispute: Art and Cinema in the Age of Photography*), Dietrich Neumann (*Film Architecture: From "Metropolis" to "Blade Runner"*), Linda Ehrlich and David Desser (*Cinematic Landscapes: Observations on the Visual Arts and Cinema of China and Japan*), and Angela Dalle Vacche (*The Visual Turn: Classical Film Theory and Art History*), as well as a number of landmark exhibitions. I hope and believe that my work contributes to this meaningful interdisciplinary trend in several ways.

My background in art history enables me not only to approach the film object art historically, but to comprehend and elucidate the art objects within it. I recognize art historical citations and investigate the particularity of the works that are shown, be those relatively minor elements of the mise-en-scène or deeply imbricated with the narrative. I hope that my knowledge of modern and contemporary art, in particular, has enabled me to represent the complexity of its representations on film with sensitivity. Another contribution I hope this study makes is in connecting this interdisciplinary project to one of the dominant paradigms in cinema theory: psychoanalytic feminism. I find the basic tenets of psychoanalysis deeply persuasive and I am a feminist: I believe gender is the foundational difference that has ordered human society, in many ways that must be exposed, understood, and often, if not always, dismantled. However, it is the more basic and pragmatic aims of psychoanalytic and feminist theory that I adopt. They are not ends in themselves but elements of a particular project: to uncover the meanings that the incorporation of art has for and in movies.

When a film undertakes the representation of "art" as a theme or engages an artwork as motif, it is, whatever else it is doing, also more or less openly and more or less knowingly entering into a contemplation of its own nature and at some level positing its own unwritten theory of cinema as art. Narrative films, then, can reveal much about their individual and collective undertaking and their sense of their own and their medium's origins through the incorporation or figuration of art. The particular film objects I discuss are ones that strike me as significant for the ways in which they, generally in relation to others, put these problems of art, origins, and difference into high relief, making somewhat clearer underlying conceptions, assumptions, and ideologies of the narrative cinema that tend otherwise to remain obscure and ambiguous.

Mainstream—that is feature-length, commercial, narrative—films that foreground art, as well as most that background it, can induce a rather curious tension, as the reflexive presence of art threatens the seductive flow of the fictional world within the film with a spasm of viewer self-consciousness. This is why we refer to such works as reflexive: it is as though a mirror has been held up to the beholder. The work of art *en abyme* (shown in-depth) reminds the viewer that she is viewing. It is interesting, then, to consider what is at stake in such potentially disruptive representations. For one, status: not only does the subject of "art" confer a certain stature; the reflexive use of art *en abyme* is a hallmark of modernist art, and therefore a nod (albeit an ambivalent one) to the "highbrow" viewer. Second, a claim: one knows that the film may have a (more or less articulate) contribution to make to the ongoing, unwritten theory of the art of cinema that the movies themselves are always telling, or to the ongoing, unwritten debate about cinema's sometimes uncomfortable and always shifting position among the worlds of art, commerce, industry, and mass media.

The meanings that arise from the heightened presence of painted portraits in a number of Hollywood films of the 1940s, discussed in chapter 1, "The Moving Picture Gallery," anticipate many of the closer readings that follow. Surveying more than a dozen films of various genres—from Hitchcock's *Rebecca* (1940) to Mankiewicz's *The Ghost and Mrs. Muir* (1947)—I observe not only the way in which objects of art are objects of desire, and the existential and psychological consequences of contemplating still images in relation to moving ones, but also the underlying problematics of mimetic representation generally and portrayal specifically. The painted portrait in these films often "represents" a dead person, but even when it does not, I demonstrate, it always stands for death, as well as art, two realities that the classical Hollywood film, it has been often argued, represses or disavows.

Many of the same issues around mortality, mimetic representation, portrayal, and desire are explored in greater depth in chapter 2, "A Form of Necrophilia (The Moving Picture Gallery Revisited)." Here, it is not merely the appearance of portraits—in this case photographic and painted—that is meaningful, but the narrative pattern in which they appear. In-depth analysis of five films that share a poignant narrative trope—men meet and fall in love with women who uncannily resemble their dead love objects in *Corridor of Mirrors* (1948), *Pandora and the Flying Dutchman* (1951), *Vertigo* (1958), *Obsession* (1976), and *The Last Tycoon* (1976)—demonstrates that the representation *en abyme* is a reification of a component part of the cinematic apparatus itself. The poignant theme is, in effect, allegorical.

Chapter 3, "The Birth, Death, and Apotheosis of a Hollywood Love Goddess," considers the way that sculpture—as three-dimensional object of art—fleshes out (as it were) problematics of corporeality, carnality, and embodiment, adding to the morbid and aesthetic mix around the classical cinema. Analyzing the intriguingly symmetrical relationship between two films starring Ava Gardner and featuring statuary—*One Touch of Venus* (1948) and *The Barefoot Contessa* (1954)—I describe the paradigmatic aspect of Gardner's stardom in relationship to an iconology that sheds light on inherently allegorical aspects of these films, as well as problematics around eroticism and moviegoing.

Two of the films discussed in chapters 2 and 3, Lewin's *Pandora and the Flying Dutchman* and, especially, Mankiewicz's *The Barefoot Contessa*, are meaningful sources, I argue, for the two European art films that are explored in considerable depth, both independently and in relation to each other, in chapter 4, "Survivors of the Shipwreck of Modernity." Jean-Luc Godard's *Contempt* (*Le Mépris*, 1963) and Jacques Rivette's *La Belle Noiseuse* (1991), as "art" films and, moreover, as adaptations of modern literary landmarks (Alberto Moravia's *Il Disprezzo* and Honoré de Balzac's *Le Chef d'oeuvre inconnu*, respectively), claim an artistic heritage much more readily than even the most self-conscious of the more "hollywoodienne" films discussed previously. But the art film's readiness to bare its own devices comes to seem predicated on its insistence on baring the female body, too, and preserving, indeed naturalizing, a sexist ideology of culture for which the nude is emblematic. This chapter explores each film's complex engagement with its literary sources and with the other plastic arts, as well as with the distinct architecture of its location, and uncovers a veritable archaeology of the myth of the feminine in modern Western culture.

It is not only veterans of a movement of arguably preconscious (or should that be precocious?) sexism—Jacques Rivette and the New Wave—who perpetuate retrograde myths in contemporary films, though. The mythology bodied forth so elegantly in Rivette's "masterful" contemplation of artists and models is uncannily similar to that I uncover in two very different contemporary films from the 1980s in chapter 5, "Out of Her Element." In most respects, *Splash* (1984) and *Children of a Lesser God* (1986) could not seem more different from *La Belle Noiseuse*. Certainly, neither is an "art" film; these were two very commercial films made in the very commercial climate of Hollywood in the mid-1980s. Indeed, art is a mere diversion, or detail, in these movies, not a central theme. But art objects emerge as symptomatic of the construction of a mythic femininity in both films, which share an image of woman as elemental, immanent, fluid . . . an image that psychoanalysis brings to the surface.

There is an elemental aspect to the representation of women, too, in three other American movies of the 1980s, those I discuss in chapter 6, "Playing with Fire." *After Hours* (1985), *Legal Eagles* (1986), and *Backtrack* (1989) all manufacture an incendiary mix of women, art, money, and danger in stories set in and around the contemporary art world. Perplexity and suspicion swirl around art, particularly around the new, conceptual, and performative forms that proliferated in the art world of the 1980s and that are here associated with women. I explore the ways in which these three films frame this association, and expose the symptomatic ways in which their scorn and suspicion of both (seemingly) nonremunerative, noncrafted art forms and women artists reflect upon their own sense of viability (never mind virility).

Craft, gender, and virility are all themes, too, in chapter 7, "Dirty Pictures, Mud Lust, and Abject Desire: Myths of Origin and the Cinematic Object," which focuses on three other contemporary films—*Artemisia* (1997), *Camille Claudel* (1988), and *Life Lessons* (1989). In these films, the theme of the heterosexual artist couple is employed to embody a myth of the origins of art—as the outcome of the art act's inherently erotic aspect—and at the same time to perpetuate a gendered view of art in which what is great and virile in the male artist is pathological in the female.

The films considered in these chapters range from ones in which statues, figurines, photographs, or portraits are metonymic images of larger thematic preoccupations (*Suspicion*, *Splash*, or *Children of a Lesser God*); to ones with structurally significant art objects, artist characters, or settings related to the art world (*One Touch of Venus*, *Legal Eagles*, or *After Hours*); to others entirely pervaded by art and artiness (*Pandora and the Flying Dutchman* or *Contempt*); to those wholly concerned with art, the lives of artists, and art making (*La Belle Noiseuse*, *Artemisia*, or *Life Lessons*).

This is not an encyclopedic endeavor, though: I make no claim to considering every film in which art is a theme; that would be an unwieldy and probably boring undertaking, even if limited by country or period. Neither is my selection arbitrary. I attempt to cover a range of Anglo-American and European narrative films from the postwar period to the present and to discuss films' representation and incorporation of a wide range of art forms and media: painting, sculpture, photography, and architecture, as well as performance, installation, and conceptual art. I had originally intended a final chapter on the contemporary artist biopic, focusing on a number of recent films about twentieth-century artists: *Carrington* (Hampton, 1995); *Basquiat* (Schnabel, 1996); *Love Is the Devil: Study for a Portrait* (John Maybury's 1998 film about Francis Bacon), *Pollock* (Harris, 2000); and *Frida* (Taymor, 2002). But I have decided that this is really the subject for another book, perhaps my next, especially since more biopics are in the offing, including a soon-to-be-released movie starring Andy Garcia as modernist painter and sculptor Amadeo Modigliani.

To a greater or lesser extent, the films that I am considering are exceptional. That is, to the degree that they make art part of their explicit subject matter, they tend to skew toward the self-conscious end of the narrative cinematic spectrum. Most of them have received at least a modicum of critical attention and praise. A few of them are controversial, a few obscure. Some were successful at the box office, some not (*Splash* was the tenth highest grossing film of 1984, for instance,[3] while *Backtrack* was never released theatrically). They are all, in some way—and perhaps this goes without saying—fascinating to me. It is my conviction that films such as those examined here offer a privileged view into a complex of overlapping and interlocking cultural and industrial problems, assumptions, and attitudes, in which issues of sex, gender, identity, and psychology generally—group and individual—entwine with those of art, commerce, class, and power. Some of these complex relationships might be fruitfully introduced by means of a particularly suggestive case study.

Artists and Models

All you very lovely ladies in your very fancy frocks,
And you fellows with the palettes, in your most artistic smocks,
Use your thumb to get perspective of a world that's drab and gray,
Add a lot of color and frame it just that way . . .[4]

Among the many weirdly revealing images in the musical comedy *Artists and Models* (Frank Tashlin, 1955)—in which Jerry Lewis plays Eugene Fullstack, a gifted dreamer whose nightmares (he talks in his sleep) are converted into lurid, rather surrealist comics by his painter roommate, Rick (Dean Martin)—is one found in the title production number, staged for an on-screen audience at the "Artists and Models Ball." In it Martin and Lewis sing a song of artists and their models as women (showgirls) emerge from heaps of colored chiffon fabric representing daubs of paint on an oversized painter's palette.

The production and the song's lyrics (see the first verse, above) graphically define artists as male and models as female (a profoundly typical formula in Western culture—see the discussion of *La Belle Noiseuse* in chapter 4), despite the film's strong homoerotic overtones and artist-characters of both sexes: Dorothy Malone plays Abigail Parker, a successful comic book artist who uses Bessie Sparrowbrush (Shirley MacLaine) as a model (!) for her successful "Bat Lady" character. The title number also echoes the dichotomy between male

Artists and Models (Frank Tashlin, 1955; photo courtesy of Jerry Ohlinger's Movie Material Store).

sexual confidence and insecurity usually displayed in the dynamics of the popular comedy team of Martin and Lewis: while the daubs toward which the suave Rick (Martin) gestures as he sings—red, blue, green, and yellow—magically produce women who fawn over and embrace him, those that the puerile Eugene (Lewis) selects—violet, lime, gold—contain mere material. This part of the number ends as Eugene sings, "you will never hear me knocking any pink that's really shocking," as from the last daub of paint emerges a woman who just keeps on emerging, even after reaching normal height (a mechanical pedestal and prodigious lengths of pink fabric permit her to achieve monumental stature); "I think we're going color blind," the two "artists" exclaim finally in unison.

In the second, instrumental, part of the number, Eugene and Rick leave the stage and take their brushes into the audience, where they use the skin of scantily clad models (showgirls) as canvas, sketching amusing figures (and love letters) on exposed flesh, sometimes transforming it into the support for what are rather like animated motion pictures, as when—rather uncannily—one blonde's supple knees are turned into cartoonish heads for dolls dressed just like herself (although it might be more accurate to say that she is dressed like the dolls, in a farcical, short blue gingham frock and petticoat).[5]

In the first part of the number, the female body (gob of paint) was the painter's medium, or vehicle; now she is the ground, or support. So, represented as

Animated flesh in
Artists and Models.

the very stuff of which art is made, in this one colorful musical scene the female body is an ambivalent medium—simultaneously figure and ground, object of desire and ridicule, and source of inspiration and anxiety.

This spectacular equivocation in which women are elevated as material muses and also reduced to mere material is powerfully suggestive. In *Artists and Models,* through the use of comedy, travesty, and pop cultural forms—elements of the "bricolage" Paul Willemen says is most characteristic of Tashlin's method of "assembly and disassembly (dismantling)"[6]—various aspects of the relationship between cinema and other visual media are vividly exemplified, embodied, and, along with other cultural problems, satirized. As some of the complexities of this relationship—generally more obscure or subtle, indeed often repressed in movies—are the subject of my study, perhaps this unsubtle film can be used to expose and introduce the problem of figures and themes relating to art and artists in the classical narrative film and the always gendered scenarios in which these are framed.

It is for reasons having to do with history, genre, and perhaps even authorship that *Artists and Models* lays bare such complexities more nakedly, as it were, than most movies. Made in the very middle of the 1950s, in the waning days of the studio system, it revels in flaunting possibilities that had been typically denied or suppressed by the classical Hollywood film. As Henry Jenkins and Kristine Brunovska Karnick have noted in the context of this kind of postwar "formalized" comedian comedy—a genre already characterized by a high degree of reflexivity—this was a period that spawned some other rather "baroque" subgenres (i.e., the adult Western, the self-reflexive musical, the excessive melodrama, and film noir), "marked by a blurring of previous genre distinctions, increasingly flamboyant visual and performance styles, self-conscious acknowledgement of their own construction and destabilized identities."[7] And although most American auteurists (with the notable exception of Peter Bogdanovich) have been reluctant to treat the sublimely silly Tashlin as a major figure, certainly there are those who would attribute any such notably self-conscious and constructed qualities to this director's singular sensibility(among them the French in the 1950s—e.g., Jean-Luc Godard and the critics of the French postsurrealist journal *Positif*—and some associated with the British journal *Screen* in the 1970s).

Contrary to the image conjured by its title, *Artists and Models* takes sex, violence, popular art, mass culture, and their psychosocial intricacies as its basic subjects, not high art, which is marginalized and to some extent lampooned. This is all vividly summed up in the opening scene of the film: Rick and Eugene are working on (and in) a huge animated billboard advertising Trim Maid cigarettes. The first shot is an extreme close-up of what, when the camera zooms out, turns out to be the hand of Rick, on a scaffold several stories above the New York City sidewalk, painting the red upper lip of a colossal woman's open mouth. As the client and his employer look on from below, the artist is putting the finishing touches on the visage of a sexy, oversized, female smoker. Rick tells Eugene, who is inside the mechanical billboard, to turn on the smoke machine, but Eugene is too passionately wrapped up reading comics to attend properly to his job ("Wait," he insists, "I'm on the third murder. It looks like the Bat Lady's gonna blow one of the Rat Man's heads off!"). He then neglects to connect the smoke tube to the aperture of the open mouth and absently flips the switch the wrong way. The big tube starts sucking instead of blowing. First it sucks up all Eugene's comic books, putting him into a panic, and then, when he scrambles after them, it sucks him in (in a cutaway shot, we see him struggling in what is a virtual birth canal). When Rick finally sets things straight—rescuing Eugene, reconnecting the tube, and flipping the switch—tattered comic books spew out of the open mouth of the Trim Maid girl. "She's not smoking;

"She's not smoking. She's spitting!" (from *Artists and Models*).

she's spitting!" complains the dismayed client. It doesn't take a psychoanalyst
to grasp the sexual innuendo of material like this.

Tacitly homoerotic relationships are another nonnormative feature of *Artists
and Models*' plot that stands out in high relief, as one Internet Movie Database
"user's" comments underscore:

> Lewis and Dean Martin play "roommates" who met each other way back when
> they were Boy Scouts, sleep in separate twin beds in the same room, take baths
> with the door open, and at one point talk about getting a divorce. At one point
> the semi-retarded Lewis (and he admits as much himself) says to Martin: "I
> can't keep my dickie down, Ricky." Um, he's putting on a tuxedo I think. Simi-
> larly, Dorothy Malone lives in the apartment directly above them, unmarried
> with thick, black glasses and earning a good living on her own. She spends her
> time dressing the barely adult Shirley MacLaine, who has a cute little butch
> cut, up as the Bat Lady. The homosexual content seems to me almost too obvi-
> ous to be meant. It's usually much subtler in Hollywood movies of the era.
> Then again, it's impossible to miss it, even if you're a 1950s housewife. Even-
> tually, the two gay couples meet and change partners, Martin getting Malone
> and Lewis MacLaine.[8]

As Frank Krutnik notes regarding an almost identical plot pattern in another
Martin-Lewis vehicle, *Sailor Beware* (1951), "The two female partners . . . mirror the terms of difference inscribed in the Martin-Lewis partnership . . . Like is
paired with like, and this serves to minimize the importance of heterosexual differences when measured against the familiar differences between the two men."[9]
Thus the essentially homoerotic terms of the relationship are not genuinely disrupted. As Krutnik additionally notes, the entire genre of comedian comedy
is characterized by a strong undercurrent of misogyny and sexual hostility, as
it "repeatedly offers controlled assaults upon, or inversions of, the conformist
options of male identity, sexuality and responsibility."[10] The misogyny in the
genre is typically enhanced in the work of the male comedy duo, as Molly Haskell has noted, which "from Laurel and Hardy to Abbott and Costello, is almost by definition, or by metaphor, latently homosexual: a union of opposites
(tall/short, thin/fat, straight/comic) who, like husband and wife, combine to
make a whole."[11]

But there's nothing latent about the marital qualities of the relationship between Rick and Eugene in *Artists and Models*. The first scene set in their apartment—they've come home after being fired for the billboard debacle, we learn—
begins with Eugene, a dishrag tied around his waist, asking Rick how he'd like
his dinner prepared. As the ludicrous dinner scene continues, Eugene sets up a
virtual (there's virtually no food) romantic dinner for the two of them, complete

with candlelight (real) and wine (imaginary). After dinner, he plays an imaginary piano and serenades Rick, singing to him ("When You Pretend"), even sitting in his lap briefly. Before the scene is over, Rick has spoken to Eugene of divorce. This explicit travesty of marriage is a kind of cover for the underlying reasons for the homosocial bond between the two males, though. Its raison d'etre is to maintain the partnership and ward off the potential disruption of women: "within the genre, women tend to signify the demands of integration and responsibility for the male."[12] The relationship between two men only mimics marriage, while it in fact protects the men against economic and sexual maturity. Rick may castigate Eugene for his inability to hold down a job and Eugene may play at the dutiful and loyal "wife" to his philandering ladies' man roommate, but they really stick together out of a mutual commitment to warding off the financial and conjugal obligations of marriage and family.

Here, then, what might appear a wholly transgressive attribute is really more of a generic one, along with most of the film's other "inversions," including the very amusing image of female sexual initiative offered through Shirley Mac-Laine's performance. Again, it is the dynamic of the comedian-couple that necessitates this. If Martin's character is dominant, sexually confident, suave, and seductive, then Lewis's must be passive, sexually insecure, klutzy, and coy, which he is, in uproarious contradistinction to the aggressive MacLaine. The delightful inversion of her characterization notwithstanding, most of the many female parts in *Artists and Models* seem to be the products of a very misogynist imagination, comprising a range of carping and castrating types—emasculating wife, scolding mother, nagging landlady, mannish masseuse—and more than the usual array of seductively clothed, seemingly dimwitted, nubile beauties ("models"), along with a campy dose of femme fatale (Eva Gabor as Sonia, an Eastern bloc agent—this is the height of the cold war, after all—and the comic book vamp, the Bat Lady). The credit sequence alone features—in twelve shots—twenty different eye-popping "models" (these look much more like fashion models or, again, showgirls, than artists' models), although six of them are only shown from the hips down, as a row of six sexy pairs of bare leg.

One of *Artists and Models*' silliest and most symptomatic conceits is that a comic book artist would require live models. What at first looks like a gag turns out to be a more motivated device, though. It is the source of one major thread of the movie's romantic farce: because Abby draws from life, Eugene encounters Bessie dressed as the Bat Lady and is smitten—in a paralytic, abject sort of way. But Eugene—despite opportunities and hints—refuses to recognize Bessie out of costume as the same alluring, fatal creature of his fantasies (and Bessie wants to be desired for herself, not for her two-dimensional associations, so doesn't pull her trump card to secure his interest). The "gag" actually instantiates, then, not only the relationship between two- and three-dimensional representations, and between still and moving images, two formal conundrums of pictorial arts generally, but also the relationship between model and image, or performer and role—that is: the intriguing puzzle of portrayal and portrayed. Eugene, in this respect, is a mere exaggeration of the prototypical moviegoer: caught in the web of illusion, he cannot or will not extract himself, even enough to see what Bessie continually throws under his nose—that she and the Bat Lady are one and the same. So, in fact, Tashlin's *Artists and Models* peppers with laughs the very same cinematic trope that is bathed in melancholy in Hitchcock's *Vertigo* and the other films I discuss in chapter 2.

Indeed, although wholly lacking in seriousness, *Artists and Models* manifests many if not most of the traits that I find meaningful and analyze in the coming chapters. In addition to giving form to the seemingly magical propensity of representations to seduce and perplex viewers—a propensity I analyze throughout, especially with regard to the use of portraits and statues *en abyme*—Tashlin's film, like those discussed in chapters 3 and 4, also regards the female body—excessively—as simultaneous object of desire, source of anxiety, and cipher of cultural meaning. (Frank Tashlin himself was co-author of the screen adaptation of *One Touch of Venus*, the first in a "trilogy" of Ava Gardner films discussed in chapter 3). And, as with two deceptively different films, *La Belle Noiseuse* and *Splash*, femininity is associated with animality in *Artists and Models*. Bessie Sparrowbrush is both Bat Lady and, by virtue of her name, bird woman. Women are treated as predatory and carnal.

The comic book and nightmare themes of Tashlin's film permit bold expression of the obscure but powerful connection between women, art, and violence that I observe in chapter 6. Most symptomatically, *Artists and Models,* like the films I discuss in the final chapter, assumes that the practice of art—at any and every level, from comic books to high art—is infused with psychosexual energies. A scene in which Abby substitutes herself for a female model with whom she is posing Rick in a clinch, and is then aroused, seems a mere comical variant of the scene in Agnès Merlet's *Artemisia* in which the lustful young painter puts down her brushes and inserts herself (sexually) into the scene in which she has posed her fellow painter Tassi as Holofernes. Of course, one ought not forget that one of the meanings of "art" to American moviegoers of 1955 was precisely "sex," since this was the period when the more mature fare produced abroad was increasingly being seen in the United States, usually in "art houses" under the rubric of "art film."

Thus sexuality constitutes a source of slippage between the terms of art and film, at least in the (English) language of movie going in the postwar period. But this is obviously no vernacular accident. Although maybe "foreign" to the movies in America (in a somewhat naïve, simplistic reading of the classical

Hollywood film), sex is always already a component of all art, along with death and other basic human preoccupations. This study explores the ways in which art, when taken up by cinema, becomes its speculum, revealing at many levels the psychic, social, and cultural components of the apparatus . . . returning the repressed . . . baring the device.

CHAPTER 1

The Moving Picture Gallery

You die, and yet your doubles captured in the fragility of the celluloid survive you and continue to carry out your ephemeral actions.
ROBERT DESNOS, TRANSLATED IN WILLIAMS, *FIGURES OF DESIRE*

We cannot remain unaware of this aspect of moving pictures. The flesh of Katharine Hepburn and Gregory Peck has now gone to earth, yet their beautiful traces haunt our movie screens and fly as signals out into the universe.[1]

This death-defying magic wrought by moving pictures is not strictly a function of technology. It is representation itself that can raise the dead, as was observed long before photography by Leon Battista Alberti: "Painting has a divine power," he wrote in "Della Pittura," "being not only able to make the absent seem present, as friendship is said to do, but even to make the dead seem almost alive after many centuries."[2]

Portraits, the very sort of painting that Alberti was invoking when he wrote of the reanimation of the dead, seem in many Hollywood films of the 1940s to have poignant and sometimes magical properties.[3] These portraits function as analogical representations of the power of movies themselves, and register a degree of sensitivity to the mortality that is inherent in both forms, as a function of the mimetic representation of "real" corporeal bodies. That they are able to do so, given the much theorized propensity of "classical" Hollywood cinema to construct its narratives in a manner that disavows death, would appear to be a paradox worth exploring.

In *Camera Lucida*, Roland Barthes notes the inscription of death in every photograph as "*a catastrophe which has already occurred. Whether or not the subject is already dead, every photograph is this catastrophe.*"[4] Barthes's claim that this catastrophe does not depend on a human subject as referent only serves to underscore the emphasis that he places throughout his book on the photographic portrait. It is no accident, then, that the two other modes of representation that Barthes invokes in contrast to photography are cinema and painting.[5]

The painted portrait, the photographic portrait, and the narrative cinema (excepting animated narratives) are each constituted by the two-dimensional traces of "real" corporeal bodies. When Alberti wrote of painting's ability to "make the dead seem almost alive," he was focusing on mimetic portraiture. For other genres and modes of painting, be they landscape, still life, history painting, icons, or nonrepresentational works, do not require, even if they imply, a specific, singular subject who *has been*.

More than any other representational practice, the painted portrait may depend, as Michael Fried has indicated, upon a subject's presentation of self.[6] But it depends equally on an artist's re-presentation of the portrayed—thus involving implicitly a tension, or ambiguity, between the portrayed as subject and as object, between self-presentation and re-presentation. In the cinema, we are confronted with an ambiguity comparable to that of the painted portrait. Here, we register a tension between actor and role. This tension registered by the beholder of a portrait or a movie, which seizes the body of the portrayed as both subject and object, in Lacanian terms, is another echo of the mortality inscribed in mimesis, since it invokes the basic revelation of the mirror stage—of the reflexive otherness of self beheld as image—which is the initiation of the subject into a universe of gendered sexuality and death.[7]

But part of the force of narrative cinema as generally theorized is precisely its insistent disavowal of the mortality inscribed in representation through its attempted repression of and compensation for "the actual discontinuities between representation and the world, and between the self and the image."[8] This repression of discontinuity and concomitant disavowal of death is supposed to be an inherent function of the enthralling flow of moving pictures and particularly of narrative cinema at its most seductive: the classical Hollywood cinema produced under the auspices of the studio system. In contrast to the Hollywood movie, the painted portrait engages far fewer techniques of disavowal; in fact, inasmuch as we understand it as intended not only to enhance the status of its living subject but also to persist beyond its subject as a commemoration of the ancestral and honored dead, the portrait must not deny death's hand in the same manner as the motion picture.

The paradoxically heightened appearance of portraits in Hollywood films, then, testifies to a far from totalized disavowal. In quite a number of motion pictures produced between 1940 and 1950, portraits do not simply appear—as elements of the set, or focal aspects of the mise-en-scène—but indeed act; they move. And the narratives in which they move are more or less explicitly involved with the very morbidity and uneasiness that are underlying structural, if rarely acknowledged, facets of portraiture and mimetic representational practices generally. Indeed, these films are exceptional only in degree; and, as has been argued, while Hollywood cinema, like other classical and academically constrained forms, may have aspired to create a seamless, satisfying universe of narrative and imagistic wholeness and plenitude, it is important to recognize the various ways in which what it repressed returned.

Portraits in Alfred Hitchcock's *Rebecca* (1940) and *Suspicion* (1941), for example, play small but significant roles that anticipate their more heightened appearances in later films. In *Rebecca,* a portrait of a de Winter ancestor, Lady Caroline, provides the unnamed protagonist's (Joan Fontaine) only visual point of identification with the dead and inexorably absent Rebecca, whose absence defines the film's narrative. This has been well described by Tania Modleski, who relates the second Mrs. de Winter's overidentification with the absent Rebecca to a girl's Oedipal relationship to the mother. "The horror of the moment of the masquerade ball," Modleski writes of the scene in which the second Mrs. de Winter unwittingly costumes herself as the first, based on the portrait of Lady Caroline, "derives from the fact that though the woman substitutes her body for her mother's she must believe . . . 'she is herself.' Neither hero nor heroine (not to mention spectator) must become aware that in presenting herself the woman does nothing but re-present another woman, the mother. The film, however, not only announces the submergence of the heroine's identity into that of the mother's, but twice equates her predicament with death."[9] Thus the portrait of Caroline de Winter functions as a screen onto which is projected what Modleski calls "one of [Hitchcock's] 'proper' subjects—the potential terror and loss of self involved *in* identification."[10]

Oedipal anxieties can also account thematically for the charged portrait of the father in Hitchcock's 1941 *Suspicion.* In three scenes, the absence and, later, death of General MacLaidlaw is belied when the characters of Lina (Joan Fontaine) and Johnnie (Cary Grant) actually speak to, almost interacting with, his portrait. In the first such scene, Johnnie's remonstrations with the portrait induce it to jump, or fall, quite literally from the wall, as if alarmed at Johnnie's proposition. These scenes employ the portrait as a kind of externalized emblem of the internalized father, as Stephen Heath has noted in his analysis of the last scene in which the portrait plays a part: "The scene finds its center in a painting: the massive portrait of Lina's father which bears with all its Oedipal weight on the whole action of the film—this woman held under the eye of the father (the name as crushing as the image: General MacLaidlaw)."[11]

The dynamic by which these portraits embody the Oedipal identifications and misidentifications of the characters in Hitchcock's films, and move them, or engage them in psychic process, suggests, indeed almost literalizes, the effect of the narrative cinema on its viewers that has been called "suture," that is, its

Suspicion
(Alfred
Hitchcock,
1941).

propensity to secure the imaginary identification of the viewer with and in its narrative. But by virtue of mirroring that very process, the portraits threaten to disturb the smooth working of the narrative. The portraits, too inert and nonnarrative to realistically inspire such identification within a realist scenario, threaten the viewer with awareness of the magic of the mimetic and narrative devices employed by the film itself to engage him or her. This is very much a danger in a number of movies in which the portrait assumes a more explicit role and is incorporated into narratives whose realism is strained by, if not abandoned to, psychological or supernatural treatment of mortal desire.

In Otto Preminger's *Laura* and Fritz Lang's *The Woman in the Window*, both from 1944, the male protagonists fall in love with portraits of beautiful women. In *Laura*, it is ambiguous, at first, when Detective McPherson (Dana Andrews) falls asleep beneath the portrait of Laura (Gene Tierney)—his desire for which has been established—and then awakens to the "real" Laura, presumed dead, whether or not he is dreaming. This ambiguity is a function, as Reynold Humphries has indicated, of the uncanny: "The irruption of Laura the woman into the privileged space of Laura the portrait is not just a question of a return from the dead but rather of a return of the repressed."[12] Humphries aptly relates this to the even more explicit scenario of *The Woman in the Window*, in which the entire narrative, stemming from Professor Wanley's fascination with the portrait, is revealed—only finally—as a dream: a dream in which mortal terror and death are conceived as the inevitable outcome of his desire.

Film noir's peculiar amalgam of sexual angst, morbidity, and the portrait may well find its apogee in another Fritz Lang film, *Scarlet Street* (1945), in the painfully ironic scene in which the defeated and dispossessed portraitist (Edward G.

Laura (Otto Preminger, 1944; photo courtesy of Jerry Ohlinger's Movie Material Store).

Robinson) witnesses the sale of what might be called his "self-portrait as femme fatale," that is, the portrait Chris painted of Kitty (Joan Bennett) that was exhibited as her self-portrait. The cadaverous image of the woman who stole his meager self-respect, along with the authorship of the painting, and whom he murdered in a fit of sexual jealousy, is borne, funereally, out of the gallery and past the painter, as he shuffles past in a schizophrenic oblivion. The pathological possibilities of mimesis and its subject-object confusions reach so fevered a pitch in *Scarlet Street* that it's hard to imagine a sicker scenario.[13] But, as we shall see, sicker the portraitist will become in a related genre of the 1940s, that of the "paranoid" woman's film.

Mary Ann Doane has discussed a number of films of this genre, including Hitchcock's *Rebecca,* George Cukor's *Gaslight* (1944), and Peter Godfrey's *The Two Mrs. Carrolls* (1945, released 1947), in all three of which the female protagonists (Joan Fontaine, Ingrid Bergman, and Barbara Stanwyck, respectively) tend to fuse with the dead female subjects of portraits. According to Doane, these films establish "the portrait and disturbances in the mimetic process as the dominant and structuring figure of [their] narrative[s]. What is at stake is the play of identity and difference, the breakdown of that dialectic, and the resultant fusion, which is presented as specifically feminine."[14] But it should be noted that male "fusion" is not wholly missing from films of the 1940s. Masculine identity is disrupted by portraits of women in *Scarlet Street*, as noted above, as well as in George Cukor's *A Double Life* (1947), in which Ronald Colman plays an actor who tends so extremely to identify with his roles that he becomes murderously jealous while preparing to play Othello. The etiology of his identity crises is unambiguously located by the tyrannical presence of a portrait of the actor's deceased mother, who had been the most admired Shakespearean actress of her day. It seems that Doane might be overlooking a parallel disturbance in the constitution of the male protagonist and his implicated beholder.

After all, in both *Gaslight* and *The Two Mrs. Carrolls*, the husbands who persecute their wives (Charles Boyer and Humphrey Bogart) are quite mad. *The Two Mrs. Carrolls* is a particularly interesting film in this context, because Mr. Carroll is the portraitist. Doane's analysis of the role of the portraits in this film depends on a somewhat inaccurate stylistic assessment. She argues that "Humphrey Bogart plays an artist whose psychosis is signified by a tendency toward an abstraction that can only be understood, within the confines of the classical Hollywood text, as *mis*representation."[15] But it is not abstraction that is characteristic of Mr. Carroll's portraits of his wives. A very recognizable likeness of Barbara Stanwyck is distorted not by abstraction, but by corruption of the movie star's youth and beauty.[16] This employment of a kind of speculative or magic realism is also used for the portrait in *The Picture of Dorian Gray*, both the novel and the 1945 Hollywood film version, which is discussed below.

The portraits that the crazed Mr. Carroll paints of his wives are portraits of their mortality. Rather than tending toward the abstract, the portrait of the second Mrs. Carroll registers, in a hypertrophic way, as Mr. Carroll works on

The portrait of the second Mrs. Carroll, from *The Two Mrs. Carrolls* (Peter Godfrey, 1945).

it secretly over time, the very passage of time itself, embodied in the degradation of his wife's body.[17] Mr. Carroll's attempt to ward off his own implication in this process of decay can be construed from his pattern of ridding himself of the "real" body and searching out a new, and younger, wife. In this sense, while it does reinforce the to-be-looked-at-ness of the feminine, *The Two Mrs. Carrolls* also implicates the possessor of the gaze, whose pathology stems from the fact that possessing it does not protect him from the mortal implications of the portrait.

In a sense, *The Two Mrs. Carrolls* is engaging the same trope as Edgar Allan Poe in his story, "The Oval Portrait," in which a painter portraying his young bride "*would* not see that the tints which he spread upon the canvas were drawn from the cheeks of her who sat beside him." Upon applying the last perfect stroke, the portraitist turns from the image to its subject and finds her dead.[18] "His fervid obsession to re-present her," as Elisabeth Bronfen has eloquently put it, is the very "condition of her death."[19] Poe's conception of exchange between living subject and artwork, like the Pygmalion myth, is inherently cinematic, as was beautifully explored by Jean Epstein, who incorporated that element of "The Oval Portrait" into his film version of *The Fall of the House of Usher* (1928), along with elements of Poe's related tale of love and death, *Ligeia*.[20] The effectiveness of "The Oval Portrait," as Françoise Meltzer has noted, relies in large part on inducing "an uncanny sentiment in the reader by playing on the lingering belief in a prohibition against overly mimetic art."[21] As in Poe's story, Mr. Carroll's mimetic accomplishment is constructed as murder, but in *The Two Mrs. Carrolls* it is construed as the result of psychopathological, not ineffable, supernatural forces.

Not so in *The Picture of Dorian Gray*. Albert Lewin's 1945 film version of Oscar Wilde's novel in fact enhances the supernatural aspect of the force that converts Dorian's wish that contrary to fate, he should remain ever young, while the portrait should grow old instead. In the scene in which the wish is uttered, Dorian stands enthralled before the completed portrait as if before a mirror. Embodied in this one scene are the infantile "omnipotence of thoughts, instantaneous wish-fulfillments, secret power to do harm and the return of the dead," which Freud connected to the uncanny,[22] as well as Lacan's mirror stage, when the child first identifies itself as a subject through an illusion of corporeal coherence.

The critic Parker Tyler's reaction to the transformed portrait of Dorian Gray, painted by Ivan Albright for the film and shown in color insert, is interesting: "One wonders," Tyler writes, "if Wilde's imagination, feverish as it might be on such a point, would sanction this horrible example of a dracula to end all draculas. Moreover, . . . after Dorian's assassination of the portrait has rendered it young again and rendered him the old and repulsive image of the portrait, the glimpse we are permitted of Dorian is provided by a dummy—the full-length dummy rigged up by the Albright brothers to pose for their painting. The Hollywood skeleton cannot be kept in the closet: *it must fall out.*"[23] Tyler's criticism seems misplaced. At the very heart of the film, after all, is a "moving picture," a portrait that changes and moves along with the narrative. Indeed, *The Picture of Dorian Gray*, even, and perhaps especially, in its divergences from the Wilde novel, is a distinctly reflexive consideration of the hazards of visual thralldom and specular seduction. And although it is not exactly a horror film, the revelation of the horrible Albright portrait, in lurid Technicolor, and in contrast to the neat, stylized, black-and-white beauty of the body of the film, is an unforgettable moment of cinematic terror.[24]

Supernaturalism, an element of *The Picture of Dorian Gray*, is at the very heart of several ghost films from the 1940s that feature portraits of the restless dead. *The Uninvited*, directed in 1944 by Lewis Allen, is an elegant little ghost story about the battle between two female ghosts over a young woman (Gail Russell) who is the daughter of one of them, but who mistakenly believes her mother to be the other, malevolent, ghost, two enormous portraits of whom, painted by her artist-husband, dominate several scenes. *The Uninvited* can be interpreted rather easily in the psychoanalytic terms of object-relations theory as an allegory of a girl's perilous sexual maturation as she struggles with conflicting imagoes of a "good" mother and a "bad" mother. Her "cure" is finally effected by confronting these ghosts, or imagoes, abandoning an ego ideal based on a misapprehension of the bad mother's perfection, freeing herself for marriage (to Ray Milland). As in *Rebecca*, the portrait functions as a screen onto which the female protagonist's identifications and misapprehensions are projected.[25]

The Time of Their Lives, an Abbot and Costello comedy directed by Charles Barton (1946), features what is undoubtedly one of the screen's most aerodynamic "moving pictures." A ghost (Marjorie Reynolds) makes her presence known by carrying her portrait about. René Clair's *I Married a Witch* (1942) complicates the exchange between the living and dead. The very presence of Veronica Lake, as a witch bent on revenge, induces a portrait of Frederic March's "dead" ancestor, who was responsible for her trial and burning, to slip from the wall, as if alarmed (rather like the portrait of the father in Hitchcock's *Suspicion*). In Preston Sturges's *Sullivan's Travels* (1941), too, a deceased patriarch's portrait is animated by affronts from the living. In such films death is not denied, but rather robbed of its horror and ineffability by the relative facility with which the living and the dead interact. The portrait functions almost as a hinge between the two realms, which rather confirms the role of portraits as memento mori.

These and other ghastly stories relate to other products of the horror genre, which Dana Polan has described as undergoing during the 1940s "a secularization in which figures of menace lose their ties to forms of irrationality and become accessible to an all-too-earthly discipline and control: horror narrative becomes the successful narration of a successful cure."[26] But contrary to Polan, I do not see this secularization as comprehensive. In his analysis of the function of supernaturalism in such films of the '40s as *It's a Wonderful Life!*, *Luck of the Irish*, and *Miracle on 34th Street*, as well as two other films that concern me here, *The Ghost and Mrs. Muir* and *Portrait of Jennie*, Polan suggests that rather than employing a sense of the "marvelous" that moves "toward the fantastic or toward horror," these films subordinate the supernatural "to a new faith in the psychological self. The marvelous becomes an aid that mediates the sacred and the de-sacralized—an aid by which humans can fulfill human ends and tasks."[27] Although this is more or less characteristic of some of the films I have discussed, and perhaps most of Polan's other examples, Joseph Mankiewicz's 1947 *The Ghost and Mrs. Muir* and William Dieterle's 1948 *Portrait of Jennie* retain a strong sense of the marvelous. These two supernatural love stories embrace the morbidity and desire occasioned by their portraits and are perhaps the most poignant indices of the marriage of portraiture and cinema in the 1940s.

In Dieterle's *Portrait of Jennie*, Joseph Cotton plays a struggling artist who meets and falls in love with Jennie (Jennifer Jones), a young girl who, it evolves, has returned from the dead to find the lover to whom she was fated. The supernatural romance is enhanced by the elusiveness of Jennie's comings and goings; each time she reenters Joseph Cotton's world, she has aged disproportionately to the "real" time that has passed. When she reaches viable adulthood, she is reclaimed by death before the romance can be consummated, although not too soon for a portrait to be completed. Art is the progeny of the spiritual union. The film's third reel, with its monochromatic tinting of black-and-white footage, enhances the sense that its events are occurring in another, other-worldly register. The final Technicolor insert of the (really rather prosaic) portrait being admired by romantic schoolgirls in the Metropolitan Museum of Art recalls the use of color insert in *The Picture of Dorian Gray*. The naturalism of these black-and-white films is gravely undermined by the sudden shock of Technicolor, which enhances the supernatural properties of the portraits.

Joseph Mankiewicz's *The Ghost and Mrs. Muir* is an even more fascinating supernatural love story, since we must suffer the sad images of the long, loveless, and relentlessly mortal existence that Mrs. Muir (played by Gene Tierney) must endure after magic and the ghost of her desired sea captain (Rex Harrison) have abandoned her. "He expresses regret for the marvelous life that they could have had together," as Mankiewicz himself later said. "There is the wind, there is the sea, there is the search for something else . . . And the disappointment that one meets."[28] As in *Portrait of Jennie*, the supernatural romance results, if not in physical love, at least in art. Mrs. Muir publishes a novel based on the life

The Ghost and Mrs. Muir (Joseph Mankiewicz, 1947; photo courtesy of Jerry Ohlinger's Movie Material Store).

and adventures of a sea captain. In a most interesting twist here, the portrait, of a man, and the inspiration it provides a woman, reverses the usual formula of artist and muse. The manner in which the portrait and a whole complex of representational issues are integrated into a bittersweet story of love and death is more subtle than in *Portrait of Jennie*, and more moving. In a beautiful cinematic movement, the painting of Captain Grey initiates the relationship: while inspecting the haunted house, Mrs. Muir glances into the darkened parlor, sees what appears to be a living, moving man—the Captain—does a double take, then sees she has mistaken a painting for a person. The last scene of the film, in which a spectral image of the young Mrs. Muir emerges from her own dead and elderly body to disappear into eternity with her ghostly lover, does not disavow the explicit morbidity of the entire scenario. This moving picture is as disturbing as it is beautiful, and its disturbances arise from its distinct comprehension of the basic hand that death has in art as well as in love.

The moving picture is not an invention of the 1940s Hollywood studio film. Indeed, as a motif that explores the magic of mimesis and the mortality of the human subject, the moving, or haunted, portrait predates the cinema itself by centuries. As a literary motif such images proliferate in Gothic romances and their legacy from Walpole, E.T.A. Hoffmann, Hawthorne, Novalis, and Poe, of course, to Zola and Oscar Wilde.[29] And the cinematic possibilities of the portrait were explored earlier, more fully, and in other cinemas, including Epstein's, Jean Cocteau's (*The Blood of a Poet*, 1932), as well as in the Italian and Russian silent cinema.[30] Neither does the morbid thralldom of movie characters to portraits cease with that troubled decade. In the 1950s, although perhaps not with the regularity they had in the 1940s, portraits continue to emerge *en abyme* in particularly self-conscious Hollywood films and they persist in signaling a kind of cultural unconscious exploration of the nexus of mimesis, identity, sexuality, and death in cinema's ancestral forms. Two such films, Albert Lewin's *Pandora and the Flying Dutchman* (1951) and Alfred Hitchcock's *Vertigo* (1958), are central to my next chapter, in which an obscure wing of the "moving picture gallery" is explored. Others engage portraits in profoundly Oedipal narratives: Nicholas Ray's *Born to Be Bad*, 1950, for instance, or *Elephant Walk* (Dieterle, 1954).

Morbidity is very much at issue in all of the films I have considered here, be it as an explicit theme or as an implicit subtext. In these films portraiture plays a distinct role in imbuing the characters' identity, anxiety, longing, and desire with a morbid sensibility. But these are qualities generated by alternative devices in many other (Gothic,[31] noir, etc.) films of the period that defy the traditions and techniques held by many theorists to be standard for the industry. Thomas Elsaesser has neatly summarized the "host of associations" activated by portraits in films such as these: "partly historical (they often connote a period setting and a genre: the gothic); partly social (in a world of objects and people, a painting is always excessive in that it is both object and person); partly economic (whoever owns a painting has surplus value to display, which means it can also function as a signifier of class); and finally, the connotations are inescapably sexual (Beauty and Fatality, Perfection, Woman, the Unattainable Object of Desire)."[32] To Elsaesser's host, though, must be added basic existential and intertextual associations. It must not be forgotten that, whatever we now think of the classical Hollywood film industry, there were always individuals involved in it who thought not that they were but cogs of an apparatus, but that they were involved in making art. The portrait, then, hangs as an index of Art and Death on the walls of the moving picture gallery and its movement there should remind us that this gallery is anything but static.

CHAPTER 2

A Form of Necrophilia
(The Moving Picture Gallery Revisited)

To put it plainly, the man wants to go to bed with a woman who's dead; he is indulging in a form of necrophilia.
ALFRED HITCHCOCK

In this remark, made in an interview with François Truffaut and discussing the plot of his 1958 film *Vertigo*,[1] Alfred Hitchcock casually mentions what is not only *Vertigo*'s rather unsettling central proposition, but also, I shall argue, an important psychosexual characteristic of the cinematic experience generally. Using Hitchcock's observation as a starting (and perhaps ending) point, I shall examine several films, including *Vertigo*, that share a peculiar narrative theme: in each, men encounter—or reencounter—women who are uncannily like the dead women on whom they remain erotically and guiltily fixated—doppelgängers of their dead love objects. An analysis of similarities and differences between these films—one conscious of both diachronic and synchronic relationships—suggests a paradigm of cinema itself, or at least the classical narrative cinema.

In the previous chapter, I considered the appearances and function of painted portraits in a number of Hollywood films of the 1940s and found them to be symptomatic of a propensity of the film form—in a medium occasionally sensible of its genealogical relationship to other media, photographic and mimetic —affectively to limn the fragile boundary between eroticism and morbidity. The films that are the primary objects of this chapter, too, foreground problematics of representation through, among other means, the motif of the portrait. *Corridor of Mirrors* (Terence Young, 1948), *Pandora and the Flying Dutchman* (Albert Lewin, 1951), *Vertigo* (Alfred Hitchcock, 1958), *Obsession* (Brian De Palma, 1976), and *The Last Tycoon* (Elia Kazan, 1976) meet at the crossroads of representation, eroticism, death, and return. I take as some secondary objects, in a sort of postscript, three more contemporary films that complicate the theme of return by reversal of the gender pattern: *Dead Again* (Kenneth Branagh, 1991), *The Majestic* (Frank Darabont, 2001), and *P.S.* (Dylan Kidd, 2004).

It should not be necessary to add that this short list by no means exhausts the films in which the theme is prominent. Men encounter doppelgängers of their dead love objects in a striking array of films from around the globe, including *Angelo Bianco* (Raffaello Matarazzo, 1955), *Solaris* (Andrei Tarkovsky, 1971, and its remake, Steven Soderbergh, 2002), *Iruvar* (Maniratnam, 1997), *Suzhou River* (Ye Lou, 2000), and *Marie et Julien* (Jacques Rivette, 2003), as well as two black comedies that bring the morbid psychosexual implications of this theme to the fore in the context of generic supernaturalism and horror: *Blacula* (William Crain, 1972), and *Dellamorte, Dellamore/Cemetery Man* (Michele Soavi, 1994).[2]

These films share not only a basic narrative conceit but also a complex of other common preoccupations. They suggest a common syndrome; or, possibly, a myth. Discerning the symptomatology of this myth is a multilayered endeavor. Melancholy, the most pronounced symptom, is the preeminent mood of each of the five films I discuss here, a mood one is naturally somewhat tempted to attribute to their rather pitiable, impotent male protagonists. As Elisabeth Bronfen notes in her comparative analysis of Hitchcock's *Vertigo*, Edgar Allan Poe's "Ligeia" (1838), and Gustave Rodenbach's *Bruges-la-Morte* (1892), two literary texts that share a similar theme,

> the man's initial response to the loss of his beloved is a form of melancholy—he withdraws from the world, his desire is invested in the dead. The world of the living regains his interest only when he sees that he can retrieve his "lost" love object by falling in love with a second woman who resembles the first. Because she is used as the object at which the lost woman is refound or resurrected, the second woman's body also functions as the site for a dialogue with the dead, for a preservation and calling forth of the woman's ghost, and for the articulation of a necrophiliac desire.[3]

This well describes the situation of the male protagonists of each of the films under discussion here. Eric Portman plays the stiff, effete, stone-faced Paul Mangin in *Corridor of Mirrors:* a man who suffers from a catastrophic sense of belatedness and a horror of laughter akin to a vampire's of the cross. The lugubrious Hendrick van der Zee, Lewin's "Flying Dutchman," played by James Mason, is based on legend's and Heine's "eternal Jew of the Sea,"[4] "eternally blown back and forth between Death and Life, neither of the two willing to claim him; his sorrow as deep as the sea upon which he drifts, his ship without anchor and his heart without hope."[5] Scottie, of Hitchcock's *Vertigo*, as played by James Stewart, as has been often enough observed, is certainly a case: phobic, obsessive, clinically melancholic.[6] Michael Courtland (Cliff Robertson), the morose, guilt-ridden protagonist of De Palma's *Obsession*, suffers from a paralytic nostalgia and remorse. And Monroe Stahr—frail, sickly, and remote, based on Irving Thalberg and played by Robert De Niro, in Kazan's version of Harold Pinter's adaptation of F. Scott Fitzgerald's unfinished novel—exudes a profound sadness, too.

But the diagnosis cannot be restricted to these protagonists. More fundamentally, the films themselves are melancholic.[7] All proceed with funereal languor and have elegiac musical scores (by Georges Auric, Alan Rawsthorne, Bernard Herrmann, and Maurice Jarre).[8] Each dwells morbidly on an often paradoxically hollow image of the beloved and her subsequent reincarnations and representations. Indeed, the presence of portrait paintings and photographic portraits in these films must be seen as part of the larger syndrome, invoking the memorial aspect of those forms and foregrounding repetition, return, and reproducibility—signal and structuring properties of their narratives. "Love," as Bronfen puts it, "because it involves the repetition of loss, is intimately bound to the production of images; . . . love for images implies an exchange with revenants that places the lover in the position of the mourner."[9]

An oppressive sense of belatedness is characteristic of these films, too. This is true at the level of scenario—several characters manifestly suffer it—but also beyond. Three of the films are period dramas. *Corridor of Mirrors* is set in the prewar period, but its setting often seems more historically remote, as its protagonist suffers from a profound case of antimodernism. Indeed, Paul Mangin is convinced that he and his beloved belong to an earlier time—the Renaissance, a conviction the film does nothing to refute definitively. This is true of *Pandora and the Flying Dutchman*, as well. Although made at the dawn of the 1950s, the film is set "twenty years ago" (i.e., circa 1930) and, like *Corridor,* its narrative reaches back to prior Renaissance lives. *The Last Tycoon,* which dates from the period of the Hollywood Renaissance, is set in the "golden age" of the studio system—the 1930s—but implicitly looks back a bit further to the silent era. *Vertigo* is set entirely in its own present but relies on a disquieting and uncanny fascination with the past and with the inexorable, annihilating *durée* of time— historical (Carlotta Valdez) and prehistoric (the rings of the ancient Sequoia). *Obsession,* obsessed with Hitchcock and *Vertigo,* is set in *Vertigo*'s time (1959, to be precise) and its own, but its mise-en-scène, as with *Corridor* and *Pandora,* reaches back to the Renaissance. It is hard to avoid the connotations of the very word Renaissance (rebirth) in this context. A disturbed and disturbing relationship to time—historical, durational—is deeply imbricated with the appearance of art and artifacts in all of these films. And throughout this sequence, which commences in the immediate postwar period (1948), narrower (World War II) and broader (modernity itself) problems with the historical past and present, as well as problems with film's own history, are revealed. And a nostalgia for the silent cinema is betrayed through analogy.

Ultimately, through the problematic established by return, repetition, re-production, desire, art, and history, these variations on a theme of uncanny love point to the incorporeality, the irreality, the absence, the nothingness of the object of desire—not the films' protagonists', though: ours. The melancholic mood—or is it mournful (Freud's distinction is distinctly relevant to my thesis[10])?—is about cinematic regard itself, the apparatus's and industry's for their fantastic objects, but also the film audience's regard for it. By the time Monroe Stahr turns to the camera to address us directly at the denouement of *The Last Tycoon*, this has become painfully obvious.

"You Are Someone Entirely Different"

If the plastic arts were put under psychoanalysis, the practice of embalming the dead might turn out to be a fundamental factor in their creation. The process might reveal that at the origin of painting and sculpture there lies a mummy complex.

ANDRÉ BAZIN[11]

Corridor of Mirrors is a strange and now largely forgotten British "prestige" production directed by Terence Young (who would go on to become well known for a cycle of James Bond films) and filmed in Paris studios in black and white.[12] The film is framed by a contemporary (circa 1948) narration of a prewar story told by the film's female protagonist, Mifanwy Conway (played by Edana Romney, also one of the film's writers), now a lovely, young, prosperous country matron and mother of three. She has received a mysterious and disturbing communication that has caused her to swiftly pack for a trip to London. On the train, by means of a voice-over narration relating her inner thoughts, she tells us that she is going to meet her lover, at Madame Tussaud's wax museum! There, before the wax effigy of an elegantly clad, infamous murderer named Paul Mangin, we are borne by the narration back to Mifanwy's meeting with Mangin at a prewar London nightclub. Young Mifanwy is gaily carousing with a circle of friends when the stone-faced, lordly, imposing figure of Mangin (hardly more animated than he appeared in effigy!) enters; he is manifestly taken with Mifanwy—he asks the band to play a waltz and then more or less sweeps her off her feet, as they (and the camera) spin erotically around and around the floor (cf. spinning and dancing in *Vertigo* and *Obsession*). Later, Paul assists her in removing an irritant from her eye, as Mifanwy and her party are being photographed.[13] Mangin is introduced as very mysterious, and something of an eccentric: Byronic, "a painter, art critic, connoisseur." He dons extremely formal, rather anachronous garb, dominated by a regal cape. His seemingly preternatural interest in Mifanwy, who herself appears rather antiquated in her full-length, flowing evening gown, is disturbing and seductive. When he encounters her again, he persuades her to visit his home, and they proceed there in his horse-drawn carriage.

Mifanwy's entry into Mangin's house is represented as an utterly fantastic experience, much like Beauty's entrance into the Beast's castle in Cocteau's film of a couple of years earlier, an obvious source for the oneiric atmosphere of *Corridor*'s extravagant, almost surrealist, middle section.[14] The grand doors seem to float open on their own power, revealing a vast, awesome, and luxurious interior, much more like a Renaissance Venetian palazzo than a London townhouse. Mifanwy soon becomes a fixture there—a regular visitor—and the living mannequin for the dazzling collection of Renaissance costumes and jewelry that is housed in a mystifying "corridor of mirrors." Uncannily, all the vestments fit her perfectly and she revels, albeit somewhat uneasily, in this *marvelous* game of dress-up. Paul fixates on this pastime, which is clearly not a game to him. He deplores all manifestations of Mifanwy's contemporaneity, in speech or behavior, particularly her cigarette smoking. And he reacts with dreadful antipathy to her laughter. He presses his morbid belatedness on her, expressing contempt for the present and romance with the past.

One night when Mifanwy stays over at Mangin's house (in a guest room; the passion he feels for her is strangely reticent), she is disturbed by a strange white cat and a shadowy figure associated with it. Following the shadow, Mifanwy has a classic gothic encounter with Veronica, a theretofore unknown and spooky housekeeper who describes herself as a prematurely aged victim of Paul's prior fascinations. Alarmed at the possibility that she is but one in a series of sexual objects and models for his collection of finery, Mifanwy staggers away, but in her inchoate attempts to escape finds herself in Paul's study, where they have a confrontation. When Mifanwy objects to "becoming one of those dolls in your cupboards," Mangin refutes Veronica's story, insisting that there have been no others and that he has been waiting for Mifanwy alone; he must tell her something "puzzling and strange . . . a miracle." To Mifanwy's avowed disbelief in miracles, Paul replies, "Then what is this?" Drawing aside a black drapery, he reveals a monumental painted portrait of Mifanwy, dressed exactly as she is in the scene. "It's wonderful!" exclaims its seeming model. "When did you do this of me?" He indicates a brass plate at the base of the picture, which she reads aloud. "*Portrait of a Lady*, attributed to Cristofano Lori, 1486! . . . I don't understand," she murmurs. Paul explains:

> I was in a castle in Italy after the last war, wounded. . . . All the time I lay in bed, she looked down at me. At night, I dreamt about her. She filled my imagination. After the war, I went back to England. I found no peace and no happiness. That girl's face haunted me. She drove me back to Italy. I had to

possess her. The day I bought her, an infinite peace and happiness enveloped me for the first time in my life. I was determined to find out who she was. They let me search through the archives at the castle. And I discovered her name: Venetia. Then something very strange happened. I became conscious of knowing events in her life before I'd even read about them. I felt that somewhere, somehow, I'd known her before . . . that mirror in her hand, I thought I'd given it to her myself. I'd always laughed at the idea of reincarnation, but this had happened to me, so I was bound to believe it. By now, I was convinced that I had lived four hundred years ago, that I had been Venetia's lover.

"You're Paul Mangin!" insists Mifanwy, "living here and now. How could you believe that you are that man?"

"Yes, how could I believe?" Paul echoes. "One part of the puzzle was missing."

"That part," she pauses, "was me."

Distressed by Paul's Svengali-like intentions and his supernatural claim upon her—its challenge to her very subjectivity ("you are someone entirely different," he has paradoxically maintained)—Mifanwy seems suddenly horrified at what she has become: Galatea to his Pygmalion, a mere actress for a part, or worse, a simulacrum, a revenant (one who has returned from the dead). She distances herself from Paul and embarks upon a relationship with an associate of her distinguished father's, the naturalist Hugh Sinclair. But she is lured back once more by an invitation from Paul. The film's climax begins with the extravagant Venetian costume ball he throws. This wholly fantastical scene unfolds like a dream, with fluid camera work, romanticist score, and little dialogue. It begins with fireworks, and the camera wanders past nymphs dancing and commedia performers miming, as Paul takes Mifanwy, garbed like a glittering, antique bride (in a costume designed by him), on a gondola ride through makeshift canals. As the party nears its end, the two go indoors and waltz magically through the corridor of mirrors. Paul gives Mifanwy a ring of engagement that is exactly like the one worn in the portrait. Mifanwy rebuffs him. "It was my vanity which made me take part in all this madness," she insists. "But when you showed me the picture of this woman and told me that I was her, then things became a bit too complicated, Paul." She laughs derisively. "She laughed, too," is his bitter reply. "I should have known that four centuries cannot change a woman's soul. A pity, Mifanwy, that you inherited not only her beautiful body, but also her worthless soul."

Mangin reveals that their prior affair (the fifteenth-century one) ended with the murder of his mocking mistress by his strangling her with her own beautiful hair. In a hallucinatory scene strangely like the dénouement of Orson Welles's *Lady from Shanghai* (made in 1946 but released the same year), images of Mi-

Corridor of Mirrors (Terence Young, 1948).

fanwy, chased through the corridor of mirrors, are multiplied. A mannequin falls out of one of the doors she opens. She turns and dozens of images of her turn. When it seems there is no escape, and as a demented looking Paul closes in on her, she laughs. Her laughter wounds him like an arrow. He is stunned; his face loses focus and Mifanwy escapes the house.

In the aftermath of this episode, Paul, still reeling, encounters Catherine, a singer at the nightclub at which he and Mifanwy met and evidently a spurned lover (or admirer) of his—drunk, bitter, and still in costume after the other party guests have departed. She passes out and he carries her to the bedroom that Mifanwy has previously occupied. Ominous signs foretell the dénouement. When the next morning Catherine is found strangled and the *Portrait of a Lady* is found ripped to shreds, Mangin is arrested for the murder and neither denies the crime nor defends himself. Mifanwy later visits the condemned man in prison. Paul, resigned, tells her: "Before, I was searching for someone. I know I must have seemed mad and frightening to you. But have you ever thought that everyone from the very minute he is born is searching for something. Most people die without even knowing what it is. I knew. So, I'm one of the lucky ones. All sorts of people before me tried to live outside their time, quite futilely."

These remarks very poignantly describe not only Paul's outlook, but, in a sense, that of all the films I'm here concerned with. They articulate Mangin's extreme romanticism, his melancholic sense of belatedness, and his nostalgia for a woman he may never have known, a nostalgia occasioned by a picture, which is at best a trace, an echo, but is also always already a memento mori. As Jacques Lacan has remarked of Aristophenes' myth of the origins of love, it is "moving" but "misleading" to suggest "that it is the other, one's sexual other half, that the living being seeks in love. To this mythical representation of the mystery of love, analytic experience substitutes the search by the subject, not of the sexual complement, but of the part of himself, lost forever, that is constituted by the fact that he is only a sexed living being, and that he is no longer immortal."[15] Love ultimately *is* death, then, according to Lacan, but also a fiction that obscures it.

From the moment of Paul's execution, *Corridor*'s narration returns to Madame Tussaud's, where a none too elegant expository scene establishes the demented housekeeper, Veronica, as both the reason for the mysterious letter that summoned Mifanwy and the murderer of Catherine (whom she had taken for Mifanwy). Paul is posthumously exonerated; finally, he is "guilty" only of his romantic eccentricity and arcane belatedness. A perfunctory happy ending has Mifanwy reunited at the station platform with her quite ordinary, forgiving, and doting husband, Hugh, and her irritatingly exuberant twentieth-century children.

But this rather forced happy ending, this return from a dark, disturbing, dreamlike journey, does little to disavow the extravagant, romantic morbidity of the central story of *Corridor of Mirrors*, several moments from which warrant further discussion. The wax figure of Paul at Madame Tussaud's may be a stock horror film cliché, but at the same time, in this context it signals the film's preoccupation with likeness. The dummy of Paul, and the mannequins that momentarily frighten Mifanwy both when she first sneaks a peek into Paul's corridor of mirrors and when she attempts to escape him at the end, multiply and expand the mimetic problems associated with the portrait that is so uncanny and that is at the film's narrative heart. The uncanniness these likenesses are meant to invoke is subtly underscored through other details of the scenario. The mimetic anxiety of the moment when Mifanwy and her friends are photographed at the nightclub is emphasized by her complaint after the flash of the first shot that she's got something in her eye, the something that Paul seemingly magically appears to remove just as the camera flashes for a second picture. Another scene finds Mifanwy returning home from Paul's one evening to find her father looking at films with Hugh (who will become Mifanwy's suitor and husband). Struggling to thread the projector, Sir David Conway disparages it as an "infernal thing"—a minor detail that advances the film's exaggerated interest in the look and in mechanisms and mediums of vision and representation (cameras and projectors, paintings and mirrors). "Infernal" things, literally, are those that belong to the nether world, the world of the dead. Yet another echo of *Corridor*'s interest in the magical properties associated with representations is its assault on the portrait. When Catherine (mistaken for Mifanwy) is strangled, the picture is simultaneously slashed. This reflects an atavistic animism that may be no insignificant part of the magical relationship between representation and death. As with practices like voodoo, and also taboos against mimetic representation (Mosaic and Islamic, for instance), a fear or conviction that the human spirit inheres in its visible form seems part of the murderer's motivation here. This psychological source of supernatural aura is similar to that in tales of the "double," or of exchange between living and nonliving, as in some of the creepier tales of E. T. A. Hoffmann, Edgar Allan Poe, Oscar Wilde, and others.[16]

"It Was Her Face. It Was Still Her Face"

> I can never see or see again in a film certain actors whom I know to be dead without a kind of melancholy: the melancholy of Photography itself.
> ROLAND BARTHES[17]

Another strange pastiche about love, death, and past lives, *Pandora and the Flying Dutchman*'s scenario is couched in the top-heavy literary, mythological, and aesthetic trappings that Albert Lewin (writer-director) derived from sources as wide ranging as classical Greek (Pandora) and Germanic legend (the Flying Dutchman), Elizabethan drama (references to Othello), Romantic poetry (Coleridge et al.), and surrealist painting (especially Chirico and Delvaux).[18] The film retells the myth of the Dutchman with an added focus on the woman who redeems him. Ava Gardner plays beautiful but cold-blooded chanteuse and expatriate Pandora Reynolds. She is an unhappy object of ubiquitous desire; men will do anything in the hope of having her. Early in the film one spurned suitor commits suicide; another pushes his cherished race car off a cliff and into the sea at her behest; and a third, a toreador, attempts murder. She is unmoved, seemingly heartless, until she meets her destiny, the very man who murdered her in a prior existence. While *Pandora*'s plot does finally posit reincarnation and a kind of supernatural inevitability as the explanation for the return of the never repressed (the death of the love object), it uses sculpture, painting, and photography—ancestors of the cinema—to reveal this uncanny return. At the narrative level, Pandora's indifference is considered a sickness, parallel to Hendrick's (the Flying Dutchman's) immortality—they represent in the end each other's cure, as they prepare ecstatically to drown together at sea. At a metacinematic level, however, she exemplifies the prototypical Hollywood sex goddess, a construct dependent on an image of narcissistic plenitude, a woman whose subjectivity must always diminish in proportion to the aura of objecthood she projects. Metacinematically, too, Hendrick's sickness expresses a fundamental problem associated with cinema. The figures therein, like the captain of the ghost ship, are neither alive nor dead. They are traces of living beings but traces that can be preserved beyond death.

In this sense, one can read *Pandora*'s plot—even more explicitly than that of *Corridor of Mirrors*—as an allegory of cinema. Hendrick can die but he cannot stay dead—not until he is redeemed by love. Pandora achieves her desire to desire—she desires Hendrick—and is redeemed from her cold prison house of narcissism. She is able to love but must die . . . die again, that is. Because, of course, as the reincarnation of the long-dead beloved, she is dead *again*, she is *already* dead; she has been *always* already dead. Her reincarnation is really no more uncanny than Ava Gardner's own, when *she* is born again after dying (twice) in *Pandora*, to die again in *The Barefoot Contessa* (Mankiewicz 1954), and to live on and on in *On the Beach* (Kramer 1959); even after she is dead, even after the end of human life on earth; that is to say: her reincarnation is *just* as uncanny as moving pictures themselves.[19]

Pandora conveys this paradox with art. The setting, a Spanish fishing village on the Mediterranean coast, is also an archaeological site, according to its narrator, Geoffrey Fielding. Antiquities, especially fragments of Greco-Roman sculpture, abound, and key scenes find the protagonists watched by the "gods," and even interacting with them. Another scene shows a man in Oedipal conflict with his dead father by way of a portrait of the patriarch. And the scenario confronts the contemporary Pandora with her own representations. When she first encounters the Dutchman, having been inexplicably lured to swim out to his anchored yacht, she finds him painting her portrait—in the form of a rather surrealist tableau.[20] The ensuing scene revolves around the uncanniness of this narrative puzzle—that someone she's never met would be portraying her, moreover as the legendary Pandora. Mystified and provoked by this conundrum, Pandora

Pandora and the Flying Dutchman (Albert Lewin, 1951; photo courtesy of the Museum of Modern Art Film Stills Archive).

lashes out at the picture and literally defaces it (this makes her the second of three female iconoclasts discussed in this chapter). But the painter is strangely unperturbed by her assault, even welcomes it—in worthy surrealist fashion—as an improvement, one that introduces chance. The kind of "objective chance" that Breton and his friends extolled understood coincidences as meaningful, as signs of the power of unconscious thought in a universe governed by desire, and Hendrick alludes to this ethos in asking Pandora, whom he immediately recognizes as his fate, "coincidence, what is coincidence?"

The Dutchman's previous connection to Pandora, or to the Renaissance bride whose revenant she is, is proved by a picture, too. one that is also presented as a paradox. This second picture is a miniature portrait of Ava/Pandora in Renaissance costume, and seems based on the type of Northern Renaissance painted portraits exemplified by Hans Holbein's. Of course, such paintings are themselves often uncanny, due to their extraordinary verisimilitude and protophotographic aura (as David Hockney and friends have recently discussed).[21] This miniature is obviously not a painting, but rather a photograph—a chronological impossibility, since the story locates the primary romance over two centuries prior to the invention of photography. The anachronistic photograph (made for the film by the director's friend Man Ray)[22] collapses time, foregrounding the temporal impossibilities that period films typically repress. And the photograph and the painting, as portraits, point to the genealogical background to cinema's complex relationship with mimesis and the representation of the human subject, who in the fiction film is always seen "as"—Ava Gardner "as" Pandora Reynolds—and whose mortality is poignantly inscribed in pictures—painted, still, and moving—as has been expressed quite eloquently by, among others, Edgar Allan Poe, André Bazin, Susan Sontag, and Roland Barthes.[23]

It is telling that when Hendrick (Mason) speaks yearningly of Ava Gardner's beautiful visage, "It was her face, it was still her face," he is not speaking of a portrait, or of the reincarnated face of his beloved in the form of Pandora Reynolds, but of the marmoreal face of his original dead bride, in the first lines of a dirge-like scene: a flashback, the sound of which is a recitation of a memoir written hundreds of years ago, while the visuals begin with a fluid camera movement revealing the yet mortal Dutch seaman standing at the bedside of his murdered bride. This lyrical scene recalls Poe's proposition that "the death of a beautiful woman is, unquestionably, the most poetical topic in the world," a proposition beautifully deconstructed by Elisabeth Bronfen in *Over Her Dead Body*.[24] The repetition of "still" invokes the uncanniness of death, the enigma of

Man Ray's color photograph as painted miniature portrait in *Pandora and the Flying Dutchman* (photo courtesy of the Museum of Modern Art Film Stills Archive).

"It was her face. It was still her face," from *Pandora and the Flying Dutchman* (photo courtesy of the Museum of Modern Art Film Stills Archive).

the relationship between body and life, but also death's stillness, which is always unwittingly preserved in those very portraits that come into being to defy it.

"It's as Though I'm Walking down a Long Corridor That Once Was Mirrored"

> The painter stood entranced before the work which he had wrought; but in the next, while he yet gazed, he grew tremulous and very pallid, and aghast, and crying with a loud voice, "This is indeed *Life* itself!". turned suddenly to regard his beloved:—*She was dead!*
> EDGAR ALLAN POE, "THE OVAL PORTRAIT"

A painted portrait is also key in *Vertigo*, a film I hesitate to discuss, as almost anything I might say about it has probably already been said. But I don't think its possible reference to *Corridor of Mirrors* has been noted. Gavin Elster (that is to say, Hitchcock) might have hatched *Vertigo*'s particular contribution to the reincarnation plot in the afterglow of Young's 1948 film, though.[25] When Madeleine first attempts to explain to Scottie about her "absences," she seems to borrow the film's central metaphor. "It's as though I'm walking down a long corridor that once was mirrored," she begins, with hesitation. "And fragments of that mirror still hang there. And when I come to the end of the corridor, there's nothing but darkness. And I know that when I walk into the darkness, I'll die."

Here, as with *Corridor* and *Pandora*, the function of a picture is part of (among other things) an allegorization of the operations of the fiction film generally, and the Hollywood movie specifically. But fraud, not reincarnation, is the source of the relationship in *Vertigo* between the portrait and the already dead woman, the uncanniness of which is not based on a striking physical resemblance but on a seemingly supernatural identification. The painting is employed by the fraud; thus, as with *Pandora*, a cinematic progenitor suggests something of cinema's nature. But notably, a photographic portrait does not. Of course, in *Vertigo*'s diegesis, an actual photograph of Elster's wife would not show Kim Novak, and Elster could not have provided Scottie with a counterfeit photograph of Judy/Madeleine (whose "striking" resemblance to herself is ultimately *not* uncanny) without considerable risk, as he would be conveying physical evidence of his deception. *Vertigo*'s plot, in fact, must evade the evidentiary role of photography in favor of the somewhat more metaphysical claims of painted portraits. Numerous commentators, including Elisabeth Bronfen, Tania Modleski, and Brigitte Peucker, have explored how Carlotta's portrait (or, if we count Midge's travesty of the picture,[26] portraits) functions as more than an index of the fiction film's fraudulent tendencies.[27] The portrait stands for the many different psychic turns, from identification to castration, that the narrative invokes. And it reinforces the film's use of Scottie, who (re)constructs the image of Madeleine from the clay of Judy, to represent the power and pathology of the artist/director. He is Pygmalion, who falls in love with the figure that his art has brought magically to life, but also the painter in Poe's parable, who kills his beloved by imitating, reproducing her.[28]

"The Same"

> It is the living image of a dead thing.
> ROLAND BARTHES[29]

Brian De Palma's *Obsession* bespeaks, of course, his own obsession with Hitchcock; it reprises scenes and mixes plotlines from a number of the "master's" movies. *Vertigo* is its particular touchstone, although it is much indebted to other Hitchcock films, notably *Rebecca*. It is, in fact, to *Vertigo*, rather what Judy is to Madeleine in *Vertigo*'s scenario, or what Sandra is to Elizabeth in its own story—an uncanny repetition, a return. *Obsession* reorients the viewer in terms of the film's psychic relationships, though. *Obsession,* written with Paul Schrader, opens in New Orleans in 1959 and through a diffusion filter shows the idyllic world of wealthy real estate developer Michael Courtland (Robertson), his beautiful wife, Elizabeth (Genevieve Bujold), and their nine-year-old daughter, Amy, as well as their social set, including Michael's partner, Robert LaSalle (John Lithgow). This idyll comes to a sudden and violent end with the double kidnapping of Courtland's wife and daughter and their fiery deaths in a car crash, when the kidnappers, having discovered that Michael cooperated with police and substituted a hidden radio transmitter for the demanded ransom money, attempt to escape capture. Sixteen years later, on a business trip to Florence, Michael (or Court, as his partner calls him), stops in at the church where he had met his wife some twenty years earlier (it is San Miniato al Monte) and is stunned to encounter Sandra Portinari, who is working on restorations of the church's frescoes and who bears an uncanny resemblance to his dead wife. They talk, interestingly, about the restoration of the pictures (by "Bernardo Daddi," a name, like Portinari, not without associations that portend important plot developments). The restoration element functions metaphorically, as Robert C. and Grace A. Cumbow have noted:

> Metaphorically, the Madonna is Sandra. . . . The painting underneath is ambivalent: in Court's apprehension of the spontaneous symbolism, it represents Elizabeth: in Sandra's, her own true identity. . . . The implication that it's sometimes better to be content with what one sees than to peel away appearances to seek the truth beneath is borne up by the council's decision—concurred in by both Court and Sandra—to restore the Daddi and explore the hidden older painting no further.[30]

But as Jonathan Rosenbaum has noted, the restoration theme allows De Palma and Schrader to relate the film's narrative problematic to its own metacinematic anxieties of influence.

> Pondering over her restoration work . . . Sandra wonders aloud to Michael whether she should risk removing a painting's surface to see what lies beneath it, or else restore only the first layer. "Hold on to it," Michael replies, giving voice not only to his surface obsession but to De Palma's cool strategy—to reconstruct or "restore" the mood and manner of Hitchcock's *Vertigo* some eighteen years after the fact.[31]

When he returns to LaSalle, who awaited him outside the church, Court is asked how it was. "The same," is his meaningful, understated response. Michael

Obsession (Brian De Palma, 1976).

is instantly obsessed with Sandra, whom he follows around Florence in a scene reminiscent of the one in *Vertigo* where Scottie follows Madeleine around San Francisco. Sandra, however, seems a sincere, genuine, living person, not a somnambulist. Ultimately she dates Michael, agrees to marry him, and returns, engaged, with him to New Orleans.

We learn of Sandra's (Amy's) duplicitous nature much later in *Obsession* than we do of Judy's in *Vertigo*, only shortly before Michael himself does. And meanwhile, we see "evidence" that Sandra is genuinely fascinated with her predecessor, Elizabeth. While Madeleine's reverie before the portrait of Carlotta in *Vertigo* is soon revealed as a performance of Judy's (directed by Elster), similar scenes in *Obsession*—in which Sandra stands rapt and worshipful before Elizabeth's memorial (a replica of the Florentine church itself) and, especially, in front of her portrait [32]—are unwitnessed by anyone within the narrative. Rather, they are only for the viewer's benefit. The mystified viewer is suspended between Michael's credulous, hypnotic investment in the uncanny revenant and guesswork (there are hints) as to whether the nature of this likeness is "natural" or "supernatural." This reorientation is very much concerned with pictures. Unlike in *Vertigo*, a photograph is used to prove the uncanny resemblance, but again, here only for our benefit: we see Michael privately studying a wallet photo of his dead wife shortly after he has met Sandra, as if to confirm to himself (and to us) the remarkable likeness. But when soon after he tells Sandra that she is like Elizabeth and she asks if he has a photograph to show her, he says no.

In mystifying the viewer—stringing us along with Courtland for longer, but also involving us with Sandra's fascination—rather than disclosing the conspiracy to us as Hitchcock has, De Palma implicates us more directly. And his film, in a sense, goes to the psychoanalytic heart of the problem, since the expla-

nation for the resemblance is genetic and the fascination psychoanalytic: Sandra
is Amy, Elizabeth's and Michael's now grown daughter, who was not in fact
killed with her mother. She has participated in the fraud for money, but also
for revenge, since she (only somewhat mistakenly) blamed her father for her
mother's death, and as a way (at least unconsciously) to live out her own taboo
fantasies. Her relationship to the image and memory of Elizabeth is Oedipal.
So is her relationship to Michael. Sandra's pre-Oedipal fantasies of symbiotic
plenitude, her identification with an imaginary "phallic" mother, and contradictory Oedipal fantasies of taking the mother's place with her daddy are all mixed
together and played out alongside Michael's equally disturbing obsessions and
delusions. Here the dilemma Sandra described to Court, as to whether to remove the Madonna (Mother) or to restore the Daddi, takes on another level
of meaning. Disturbingly, through the film's delayed disclosure, these fantasies,
obsessions, and delusions are implicitly extended to the viewer. Robin Wood describes "the emotional force of the extraordinary final moments," as Courtland

> rushes toward the woman who is the seeming reincarnation of his romantic
> ideal (explicitly, the Beatrice to his Dante . . .) armed with two objects—the
> suitcase of money that proves the greatness of his love for her, and the gun with
> which he means to kill her for betraying that love. As the suitcase bursts open
> and the banknotes are dispersed, she reveals in a word that she is his daugh-
> ter. The ensuing reunion—ecstatic on her side, profoundly troubled on his—
> is modeled on the famous climactic moment of *Vertigo*, the moment (circling
> lovers, circling camera) of simultaneous fulfillment and disillusionment. Here,
> however, what is expressed [is] . . . the celebration of her identification with
> the mother, ironically fused with the destruction of romantic illusion.[33]

The destruction of romantic illusion is a function of exposure of the psychology that underlies the various fantasies that are interconnected in this and the
prior films. As this series has proceeded from the equivocal, surrealist romanticism of *Corridor of Mirrors* and *Pandora and the Flying Dutchman*, to what Wood
calls a "ruthless and uncompromising critique" of the male power drive in *Vertigo*, to *Obsession*, one can detect the progressive exposure of male psychosexual
mechanisms.

But the mechanisms associated with the male power drive and its concomitant romantic illusion may not be the only ones exposed in *Obsession*, whose
obsessions are manifold. Many aspects of the film suggest the problematics associated with a parallel, feminine fantasy. In a scene in which the two visit a
tower associated with Dante, Sandra tells Court about Dante's great love of
Beatrice. "Here, in between, sat the lady of the screen: the lady Dante pretended
to love so that Beatrice would not be embarrassed by his continual gaze." Only

a short pause separates this rather cinematic allusion from Sandra's next line, "You still love Elizabeth, don't you? That's why you want me." As Robert and Grace Cumbow have noted,

> There is an obvious parallel between this story . . . and the motif of the two paintings [the superimposed Church frescoes] . . . Court pretends to love Sandra, who actually stands as a screen between him and the unattainable dead Elizabeth, masking the unspeakable reality of necrophilia; and Court truly loves Sandra, who stands as a screen for the equally unspeakable incestuous love between father and daughter, a passion which is nakedly apparent by the end of the film.[34]

"I Was Just Making Pictures"

Photography is the inventory of mortality.
SUSAN SONTAG[35]

The Last Tycoon, based on F. Scott Fitzgerald's unfinished novel, repeats the theme of uncanny resemblance in the context of a film about the quintessential moviemaker. This offers an opportunity to test and confirm this trope as a metaphor for a component part of the nature of movies themselves. In *The Last Tycoon,* the resemblance between Kathleen Moore (Ingrid Boulting) and Minna Davis, a deceased movie star and wife of production executive Monroe Stahr (Robert De Niro, playing a character loosely based on MGM's Irving Thalberg), is simply that—a resemblance: its uncanniness is attributed neither to supernatural nor fraudulent forces; it may not even be so uncanny. Stahr himself seems to be the only character overwhelmed by it. And significantly, even as he immerses himself in an obsessive pursuit of the preternaturally iconic Kathleen, he goes on making pictures. A key scene is that in which a celebrated British author (à la Aldous Huxley) is called into Stahr's office, along with a couple of staff writers assigned to the same project, and given a practical lesson in screenwriting. The scene is taken almost verbatim from Fitzgerald's novel, and initially *seems* totally unconnected to the parallel story of obsessive love.[36] In it Stahr acts out the different parts he imagines:

> STAHR: Do you ever go to the movies?
> BOXLEY: Rarely.
> STAHR: Because people are always dueling and falling down wells?
> BOXLEY: And talking a load of rubbish.
> STAHR: Listen . . . has your office got a stove in it that lights with a match?

BOXLEY: Er . . . yes I think so.

STAHR: Suppose you're in your office. You've been fighting duels all day. You're exhausted. *He sits.* This is you. *He stands.* A girl comes in. *He goes to the door, opens it, comes back in, shuts it.* She doesn't see you. She takes off her gloves, opens her purse and dumps it out on the table. *He mimes these actions.* You watch her. *He sits.* This is you. *He stands.* She has two dimes, a nickel and a matchbox. She leaves the nickel on the table, puts the two dimes back into her purse, takes her gloves to the stove, opens it and puts them inside. *He mimes all this while talking.* She lights a match. Suddenly the telephone rings. She picks it up. *He mimes this.* She listens. She says, "I've never owned a pair of black gloves in my life". She hangs up, kneels by the stove, lights another match.

He kneels, mimes lighting another match, then quickly jumps up and goes to the door. Suddenly you notice there's another man in the room, watching every move the girl makes . . .

Pause.

BOXLEY (*intrigued*): What happens?

STAHR: I don't know. I was just making pictures.

BOXLEY: What was the nickel for?

STAHR (*to* JANE): Jane, what was the nickel for?

JANE: The nickel was for the movies.

BOXLEY *laughs:* What do you pay me for? I don't understand the damn stuff.

STAHR: Yes you do. Or you wouldn't have asked about the nickel.

Ultimately, Pinter's screenplay and Kazan's mise-en-scène reprise this scene so that what was initially a clever illustration of movie mechanics becomes deeply and meaningfully entangled with the problems of obsessive love and pictures of the dead. Many critics, including some of Kazan's admirers—even, to a certain extent, Kazan himself—have complained that the love story in *The Last Tycoon* has something wrong with it, is missing something, and is "not related to the rest of the film."[37] But I would argue that few films better explicate the connection between desire and moviemaking.

In *The Last Tycoon*, as with the other films that share its theme of return, portraits, whether painted or photographic, confirm a resemblance between the dead and the living objects of desire. One prominent portrait—shown in the film's opening scene—is hand-tinted and is thus in fact both a photograph and a painting; the two forms combine, collapsed, superimposed, in a manner that confirms the genealogical relationship between painting and photography, even as it hints at the differences between the two media. Painting obscures the documentary aspect of the photograph, diminishing its evidentiary potential, but preserving its trace and enhancing its aesthetic aura. Images of Minna Davis,

The Last Tycoon (Elia Kazan, 1976).

Monroe Stahr's dead wife-goddess, reinforce what the film and the characters within it wish us to believe — what Stahr himself seems to believe: that he worshipped Minna, that theirs was a grand, passionate love, that he has never, will never get over her. It is really rather a shock, then, albeit an understated one, when, after Stahr and Kathleen have finally made love (they are the only lovers in any of these films who do!) — in the skeletal, incipient house he is building on the sea — she induces him to speak of his grand passion. The film is faithful to Pinter's screenplay:[38]

> KATHLEEN: I know why you liked me at first. Edna told me.
> STAHR: What did she tell you?
> KATHLEEN: That I look like Minna Davis.
> STAHR: Yes.
> KATHLEEN: You were happy with her?
> *Pause.*
> STAHR: I don't remember.
> KATHLEEN: You don't remember?
> STAHR: No. (*Pause.*) I remember her face, but I don't remember what we were like.

How is one to make sense of a lover who cannot remember what it was to love? This is not *Memento* (although it should be remembered that *Memento*'s conceit — backward narration — was employed previously in *Betrayal*, a 1983 film adapted by Harold Pinter from his own play). Stahr's amnesia is connected to the film's allegorization of movies; one must, after all, forget who a movie star played in her last movie to believe her in this one, although one mustn't forget how beautiful she is, or how desirable. The amnesia, then, derives from cinema's emphasis on the look (this is interesting, too, in reference to *Memento,* which employs and implicates photography in reference to memory). The obsessive, repetitive beholding of Edana Romney, Ava Gardner, Kim Novak, and Genevieve Bujold in *Corridor, Pandora, Vertigo,* and *Obsession,* along with Ingrid Boulting here, reminds us that scopophilia's objects are, after all, experienced visually. We know that these women are loved and desired from the manner in which the film regards them, as much as or more than from the way that the narrative establishes any other, less purely visual, basis for love. It is only her appearance that motivates Paul Mangin's fatal attraction to Mifanwy; it's not her scent. It's not Pandora's home cooking or intellectual depth that draw men to her. Neither is it Madeleine's tennis game or lively sense of humor that fascinate Scottie; he is hopelessly in love with her before he's heard her utter a word. And nothing more than Sandra's and Kathleen's uncanny resemblances to women who are recalled or characterized only visually is established in *Obsession* or *The Last Tycoon* as the motivation for Court's and Stahr's obsessions. Both films show scenes of those "original" love objects — De Palma's at some length in its opening, Kazan's only fleetingly in what appears to be a kind of hallucination — but they are more (Elizabeth) or less (Minna utters a short sentence) mute. And to the extent that behavior and personal style can be separated from other visual cues, they induce a kind of awful cognitive dissonance: Paul, Scottie, and Court, for instance, are each unnerved by such symptoms of human agency in their revenants as Mifanwy's cigarette smoking, Judy's sartorial vulgarity, and Sandra's walk.

The Last Tycoon concludes with a puzzle that hints at the connection between the themes of necrophilial desire and moviemaking. Stahr has a particularly bad day. He receives a wire from Kathleen, with whom he had planned to spend the weekend, informing him of her marriage, and he then, as a result of his despair, becomes uncharacteristically drunk and behaves quite badly with the writers' union representative (played by Jack Nicholson), unwittingly setting himself up to be deposed by the studio from his previously unassailable position. Stahr returns to his office and the lesson in screenwriting scene is repeated, word for word, but this time there is no Boxley in the scene. Indeed, Stahr is alone in the room (but for us). The dialogue that had been addressed to Boxley is now delivered as direct address to the camera.[39] When the "girl" enters, the scene changes and she is Kathleen, in a domestic location we assume to be her home. Stahr's address is now voiceover, played as written in Pinter's screenplay:

KATHLEEN *comes into the room. She puts her purse on the table.*
STAHR (*voice over*): A girl comes in.

KATHLEEN *opens her purse.*
(*Voice over.*) She doesn't see you.
KATHLEEN *takes a blue envelope out of her purse.*

157. Stahr into camera.
STAHR: She takes off her gloves, opens her purse and dumps it out on the table.
He mimes these actions. You watch her. *He sits.* This is you. *He stands.* She has
two dimes, a nickel and a matchbox. She leaves the nickel on the table, puts
the two dimes back into her purse, takes her gloves to the stove, opens it
and puts them inside. *He mimes all this while talking.* She lights a match.
Suddenly the telephone rings. She picks it up. *He mimes this.* She listens.
She says, 'I've never owned a pair of black gloves in my life.' She hangs up—

158. Interior. Kathleen's house.
KATHLEEN *is kneeling in front of the fireplace, which is full of ashes. She picks up a
box of matches.*
STAHR (*voice over*)—kneels by the stove, lights another match.
KATHLEEN *lights the envelope. She place it on the ashes. It burns.*
A MAN's *back comes into foreground. His hair is blond.*
STAHR (*voice over*): Suddenly you notice there's another man in the room,
watching every move the girl makes . . .
KATHLEEN *looks up, sees the MAN, stands, goes to him, smiles, embraces him.*
BOXLEY (*voice over*): What happens?
STAHR (*voice over*): I don't know. I was just making pictures.
KATHLEEN *stands back to look at the MAN. The camera becomes the MAN. She
looks into the camera. The MAN's hand touches her face.*

159. Stahr into camera.
STAHR: I don't want to lose you.

The camera becomes the MAN.

So, addressing the camera directly, Stahr not only instructs us how to make pictures. He inserts his beloved into the scene (it's key here to note that it has been
established that Kathleen is not an actress, avows no aspiration to become one,
and claims little knowledge of or interest in movies, so this is not her playing
a role; it can only be understood as a projection of Stahr's imagination). Here,
finally, the love story is connected to the moviemaking, albeit obliquely, with
rather subversive implications. The image of Kathleen is incorporated into a
scenario already established as entirely arbitrary, mechanical, and more or less
meaningless ("I don't know . . . I was just making pictures"). Also incorporated,

"I don't want to lose you," from *The Last Tycoon*.

along with the image of Kathleen, is a location, a context for her, that has been shown previously in the film, but with a more uncertain or unexamined relationship to the question of whether she exists there in fact or is placed there by Stahr's imagination. Now, in a flash, Kathleen's status within the diegetic world of the film dissolves from real, if enigmatic and ineffable, object of desire, to mere projection or image of desire. The scene shows how the lens of the camera becomes the surrogate of both the moviemaker (Stahr) and the moviegoer (us) and how, in pictures, an object *must* become an image. In repeating to the camera a line uttered earlier to Kathleen, in the context of a love scene we thought was sincere—"I don't want to lose you"—the entire orientation of the scenario shifts. It is no longer Kathleen whom the quintessential moviemaker does not want to lose. It is us, his audience, for whom he makes pictures, whose nickels are forfeited repeatedly, endlessly in a quest for something to be gained by the endless repetition of an insubstantial image of desire. This repetition (doubling, or multiplication) is morbid; as Freud notes in his essay on the uncanny, it betokens the death instinct.[40] The reappearance of stars in role after role, the reproducibility of the cinematographic image, the inevitable experience of seeing in motion pictures dead objects of desire: these attributes of cinema are the structuring facts of this oft-told tale.

As with spirit photography, which is a kind of ghostly ancestor of these scenarios, as observed by Tom Gunning, "we find an extraordinary conjunction of uncanny themes, the visual double, the 'constant recurrence of the same thing,' and the fascination with death and its overcoming through the technical device of mechanical reproduction."[41] Hitchcock's Scottie is not the only one who indulges in a form of necrophilia. This form of necrophilia, a form without cadavers—this specular necrophilia—we all suffer from it: all cineastes, anyway.[42]

P.S. (Afterthoughts on Gender and Medium)

It would seem from the commonalities of these five films that this "form of necrophilia" is gendered. All of the objects of necrophilial desire are women; all of their morbid lovers, men. And the gender biases of the classical cinema and its preferred objects are overdetermined by cultural and psychic forces. Elisabeth Bronfen has thoroughly analyzed the imbrication of death, femininity, and the aesthetic in modern literature and art. But it must be added that the cinema can and sometimes does offer up male objects of desire, too. If these five films (1948-1976) date from an era in which the silent cinema and the prewar classic cinema were being "mourned," what stories relating to these themes, if any, can be found in the contemporary, post–Hollywood Renaissance narrative cinema? And might the sexual and gender roles of such a scenario possibly be more fluid or variable in a cinematic universe informed at least indirectly by postmodernism, feminism, and academic film theory of various stripes? Two films, both of which are powerfully engaged in a kind of Bloomian romance with the classical Hollywood cinema, raise problems related to gender and return: *Dead Again* (Kenneth Branagh, 1991) and *The Majestic* (Frank Darabont, 2001).

In *Dead Again*, Branagh revives the reincarnation theme, with not one, but two contemporary characters who bear uncanny resemblances to the couple at the center of an infamous murder case of the forties. Although the scenario might have included the kinds of presentiment (or should it be postsentiment?) that led Paul Mangin, in *Corridor of Mirrors*, to conclude that he and Mifanwy both were reincarnations, it does not.[43] Indeed, Branagh's contemporary private eye, Mike Church, seems uncannily ignorant of his prior existence until he is induced to recall it under hypnosis. Even then, his attraction to the amnesia victim he calls Grace seems unmotivated by the past. As a plot element, amnesia itself represents a sort of affront to the perverse romance with the past that is so characteristic of *Dead Again*'s predecessors. Even as a film excessively caught up in film history, patently indebted in story and style to Hitchcock, Welles, and countless classic melodramas, as Marcia Landy and Lucy Fischer have detailed in an excellent consideration of the film, this pastiche does not, in fact, so much mourn the classic cinema as "valorize itself through re-vision" of it. And, as Landy and Fischer also note, the film's bizarre gender-reversal conceit (under hypnosis, Church discovers that he is not the reincarnation of Roman Strauss, but rather, Roman's wife, Margaret) not only creates illogical gaps and inconsistencies in the scenario, but also is ultimately gratuitous and fraudulent as a postmodern reconsideration of gender roles in the classic film: "At a time when deconstruction, postcolonial discourse, and queer theory have sought to undermine certain forms of psychological and behavioral identification, *Dead Again* resorts—its assignment of murder, violence, and blame to the figure that conjures up the spectre of same-sex sexuality—to traditionally pernicious characterizations. . . . The film rehearses, rather than revises, gender and sexual conventions."[44]

Lacking a protagonist who recognizes the image of the beloved in her (or his) revenant, then, *Dead Again* evades the raison d'etre of many of the scenarios from which it derives inspiration. No one looks at another across time with melancholic desire in *Dead Again* (in fact, no one even dies "again" in *Dead Again*), and this reflects its own lack of genuine feeling for the films it pastiches, or travesties.

"You Remember Movies, but You Don't Remember Your Life?"

More provocative in its relation to the necrophiliac tradition, and in its use of amnesia as a plot element, is *The Majestic* (directed by Frank Darabont, 2001).[45] Set in 1951, it features Jim Carrey rather against type as Peter Appleton, an up-and-coming Hollywood screenwriter who goes on a drunken spree in response to first being subpoenaed to testify before the House Committee on Un-American Activities and then being suspended by the studio that employs him. He has a car accident, loses his wallet and his memory, and is rescued and embraced by a small-town California community, to many of whose residents he appears strangely familiar. His familiarity is pinned down when the owner of the now-defunct local movie theater (the Majestic of the title) recognizes the amnesiac as his own son Luke Trimble, one of the brightest and shiningest of over sixty youths in Lawson, this small town, who were killed or listed as missing in action during the Second World War. Luke was among the missing, presumed dead on D-Day, posthumously awarded the Purple Heart for his valor. The seeming resurrection of Luke helps to revive and uplift the dispirited town. Although they wonder about where he might have been and what he might have been doing in the intervening nine or so years, the residents of Lawson push their foreboding aside and celebrate. Luke's father determines to renovate and reopen the Majestic theater, describing to his amnesiac son the wonders of the movie palace of old: "It was like a dream, like in heaven . . . they were gods."

Meanwhile, Appleton, despite his amnesia, doubts that he is Luke, as does Luke's erstwhile fiancée, Adele, who is the only lover in this or any of the films under consideration who seems reluctant to equate visual resemblance with identity. She is not sure she recognizes Luke's character in his doppelgänger's body, although she does warm to his kisses. But for reasons both obvious and obscure, Adele and Appleton both go along with the presumption that he is Luke and join in the renovation of the Majestic and other joyous civic undertakings. The last act of this exceedingly (and admittedly) Capraesque story explodes the happy scene, as Appleton recalls his real identity just as Luke's father suffers a fatal heart attack in the screening booth, and federal agents acting on behalf of HUAC (which has been demonizing him for his seeming flight from testimony) soon track down the fugitive screenwriter and expose him as a fraud to the disappointed community. Adele, a lawyer and idealist, admits to him that she had already concluded that he was not Luke, and urges Appleton—who is being given the opportunity to exonerate himself by naming names—to live up to Luke's image and honor the First Amendment by refusing to cooperate. Appleton, who was implicated in Communist front activity by having once in his youth attended a meeting to pursue a girl, betrays his cowardice and his political naïveté, and determines to do whatever it takes to get back his life and career. But after much soul-searching, inspired in large part by reading Luke's uplifting last letter to Adele from Europe, tucked inside a copy of the U.S. Constitution, Peter Appleton ultimately does the right thing, defying the congressional committee by invoking the First Amendment, vindicating himself and honoring the righteous dead, and thus earning himself the right to return to the embrace of Lawson, where he trades in his nascent career as a screenwriter for the management of the Majestic Theater!

Gross sentimentality, hokey patriotism, and political simplification notwithstanding, *The Majestic* is interesting for the way it engages the issues of representation, moving pictures, love, and death through the theme of return, and for the unusual reversal of gender with which it does so. "He's even more handsome than I remembered," gushes Irene, the local music teacher and keeper of the Majestic's candy concession. Luke's (or Appleton's, or is it Carrey's?) embarrassed reaction to Irene's admiration exemplifies the film's discomfort with the way that its plot demands that the gaze (women's, men's, and community's) be focused on this male object. The camera does not revel in beholding the visage of Jim Carrey as it did Ava Gardner's or Kim Novak's, or even as it sometimes did with matinee idols and male movie stars such as Valentino, Gary Cooper, or Tyrone Power. Yet the scenario demands a relentless beholding and celebration of his presence.

It is probably no accident, however, that the gender reversal corresponds to the most notable differences between the plot of *The Majestic* and those of all its predecessors. One is a strong distinction between the character and voice of the original and those of his reappearance. Indeed, this difference throws into sharp relief how lacking in character and voice the women who constitute the original objects of desire in the other films were: how irrelevant they are/were as subjects.

Near *The Majestic*'s ending, when Peter Appleton reads a letter written by Luke Trimble, the voice-over narration that imparts it to us is not Carrey's voice (it is, in fact, Matt Damon's), which underscores the film's conviction, indeed its moral: that you can't judge a book by its cover. This relates to another distinction that must be made between this plot and the others. Although the film tells a resuscitated love story—that of Luke/Peter and Adele—Luke's restoration to Adele is not of primary importance. His return is dramatized and celebrated much more in terms of Oedipal, civic, and even mercantile relationships, echoing the powerfully gendered ethos of the filmic society that *The Majestic* itself honors in its various homages (through citation or paraphrase): to Capra especially, but also Preston Sturges (*Sullivan's Travels*), King Vidor (*The Big Parade*), William Dieterle (*The Life of Emile Zola*), William Wyler (*The Best Years of Our Lives*), and others.

The more complex web of social and familial relationships in which the male object is located in this story relates to fundamentally different conceptions of gender. It is informative, with regard to this inversion of formula, to make note of a trio of other contemporary films that center on the theme of the return of a male object: *The Return of Martin Guerre* (Daniel Vigne, 1982), its American remake, *Sommersby* (Jon Amiel, 1993), and *Olivier, Olivier* (Agnieszka Holland, 1992). As with the absent Luke Trimble in the *Majestic*, the men who claim to be Martin Guerre (Gérard Depardieu) and Sommersby (Richard Gere) can be believed or doubted because they had gone to war (the One Hundred Years War and the American Civil War, respectively) as young men and "returned" many years later, older and changed. Olivier, in Holland's film—like *The Return of Martin Guerre*, based on a historical incident—was only nine years old when he disappeared. The fifteen-year-old who returns (Grégoire Colin) cannot be uncannily like him, as he has been subject to the inexorable transformation of male puberty.

Masculine identity, in all four films, is problematized in terms of its relationship to the body and to character. Tempted by physical resemblance, the community and family are more alert to differences in character. Whether he is "the same" or not is disputed (and, unlike the female revenant, he is always, finally, not). The returned male object of affection is tested against "reality." Memories, shoe sizes, appendectomy scars, musical abilities, and character traits are investigated and cited by credulous and incredulous relations and acquaintances. Such tokens of distinct character and identity were either irrelevant or distracting to the obsessive, mournful lovers of female revenants or doppelgängers in the films with which this chapter began. In those films the woman's return took place within the confines of an exclusive, erotic dyad and was meaningful to the male protagonist alone, while tensions arise within the family or community about the verity of the man's return, as he is not merely an erotic object, but also a societal, economic, and familial agent. Agnes Varda, in *101 Nights of Simon Cinema* (1995), her irreverent and helter-skelter synopsis of and homage to a century of cinema, recognizes and recapitulates this inherently cinematic trope (along with many dozens of others), including a plotline about the fraudulent "return" of Vincent, M. Cinema's grandson and sole heir—missing ten years—that nods to *Martin Guerre, Vertigo,* et al.[46]

The Majestic's deeply nostalgic romance with "the movies" and a bygone society clearly relates to this more complex narratological background of the theme of return. Appleton's magical transposition from Hollywood to Lawson is foreshadowed by the strains of "Over the Rainbow," a jazz instrumental version of which is playing in the bar as he knocks back whiskeys prior to his accident. The scenario is unabashed—despite its "critique" of HUAC and the industry's complicity with it—in constructing a vision of Hollywood that derives from Hollywood: the glamour and sophisticated cynicism of the movie milieu, the wholesome virtues of small-town America, the patriotic self-sacrifice of citizens during the Second World War, the splendor and fantasy of the movie palaces and the stories that unfolded within them. So happily two-dimensional is this vision that the film's credit sequence (after a witty precredit parody of a script conference) opens with a perfect, literal figure of it: a picture postcard of Grauman's Chinese Theatre that comes to life.

Its immersion in the Hollywood myth lends *The Majestic* an aura more of pastiche and homage than of allegory. But representation *en abyme* figures in it, too. Photographs of Lawson's war dead are displayed in storefront windows all over town. And—talk about the return of the repressed—one of Luke's (Peter's) civic deeds is to bring up from the courthouse basement, where it has been hidden beneath a drop cloth, and publicly unveil a memorial sculpture given to the town by President Roosevelt in honor of its disproportionate sacrifice. These images are not implicit mementi mori; they are explicit memorials, and yet their ancestral relationship to the movies that are celebrated in *The Majestic* is still inarticulate. This element of the film's plot describes its own relationship to Hollywood's so-called golden age, to *Meet John Doe* or *It's a Wonderful Life.*

"I'm Some Guy Back from the Dead! Is That What You Think?"

But suddenly, to add a welcome answer in this echo chamber of love and death, there is now a film that treats a male object (revenant?) of female desire with almost exactly the same type of morbid and erotic fascination that his female equivalents have received, and situates him in a narrative that fixes him in the glare of the desiring female gaze, dissociated from the Oedipal, civic, and economic relationships that such gender reversals—I have just argued—necessitate.

It even preserves the age disparity typical to the "genre" without inducing the uneasy and vaguely derisive aura that usually surrounds movie representations of "older" women with young men, using actors just about exactly the same ages as the characters they play.

P.S. (Dylan Kidd, 2004) was adapted, with her contribution, from Helen Schulman's novel of the same name.[47] The film tells the story of Louise Harrington (Laura Linney), a thirty-nine-year-old Columbia University admissions officer and recent divorcée, who meets, seduces, and becomes romantically involved with F. Scott Feinstadt (Topher Grace), a twenty-four-year-old MFA applicant who bears an uncanny resemblance in name, voice, and person to her first love, her high school boyfriend, Scott Feinstadt, who died twenty years earlier in a car crash. The two Scott Feinstadts are/were both painters. Scott the first died shortly after breaking up with Louise to date her best friend Missy (Marcia Gay Harden), now a married mother of twins, who insinuates herself into the narrative to impel jealousy and to confirm that F. Scott resembles "the original" Scott to an extent uncanny enough to deem him a likely revenant ("I touched him. . . . It's him, Weezie!"). Other than Missy, none of the film's other major characters—Louise's mother (Lois Smith), brother (Paul Rudd), and ex-husband (Gabriel Byrne)—are privy to the return of Scott or the "mystical" vortex of rejuvenated lust and confusion into which Louise is drawn.

P.S. has much of the eerie eroticism, mystery, and uncanniness of the earlier tales of necrophilial desire. Louise is not quite so melancholic a character as her male prototypes but she's no bon vivant. The film (and Linney) effectively establishes the sudden reawakening of her languishing sexuality in a manner that, remarkably, retains confidence in Louise as subject and agent and in Grace's F. Scott Feinstadt realizes a consummate object of mature feminine desire: evidently real; beautiful but not vain; egocentric maybe (like many young people), but not egotistical; direct; sensitive; and—in his relative youth and inexperience—vulnerable and honest.

And tellingly, P.S. seems to comprehend the essential relationship between the visual arts and its theme of resemblance and return. An abstract magnum opus of Scott the first's is prominently displayed in Louise's apartment. A maelstrom of thick swirls of deep blue, beyond its narrative role, the painting comes to function both as a manifestation of Louise's unresolved past and as a projection of her current emotional turmoil. She seduces F. Scott in its shadow. F. Scott's work, seen in the form of slides he submits with his MFA application, is very different; it is figurative, not abstract. This discrepancy seems to cause Louise some discomfort; unable to perceive him as independent of her own ghosts, she is disarmed by the distinctness of his hand. But subtly, the forms in which this art is seen reinforce the existential equivocation around the second coming of Feinstadt. While the dead Scott's painting—large, texturally and chromatically intense—is resolutely concrete, hanging heavily above Louise's sofa, F. Scott's work is seen only in transparent, ghostly, immaterial reproduction. And in an apt bit of pictorial casting, his works are played by those of Bryan LeBoeuf, many of whose cryptic, rather academic paintings—including a couple of those shown here—are like freeze frames of double exposures, with tableaus featuring somehow ghostly doppelgängers.[48]

Strangely, and perhaps significantly, the evidence Louise seeks of the two Feinstadts' resemblance to one another, and uncovers in a shoebox filled with letters and other memorabilia in her old room at her mother's suburban home, is a drawing: a self-portrait done in pen on a little scrap of paper; it is not a photograph, though the room (seemingly preserved in its adolescent state) has numerous snapshots pinned to the wall. And the drawing is revealed only to us, the audience. Louise does not produce it to persuade F. Scott, when he is—understandably—incredulous, that he is "some dead guy" (as he puts it). The drawing, which does indeed resemble him, does establish, however subtly, that the late Scott Feinstadt, like the new one, had mimetic talents. P.S.'s decision to shun the evidentiary aspect of the photographic in favor of mimetic facture points to the common subjectivity of art and memory, knowledge, recognition.

"The Whole Thing Is Just Too Fucking Mystical for Me!"

Indeed, for all its similarities, P.S. is no more a mere return, or recycling, of a familiar narrative from the past—or a straightforward reversal of its gender structure—than is F. Scott, who we learn at the film's climax is really called Fran (his entire name is Francis Scott Key Feinstadt!), a return, a reincarnation, a revenant, or "extension" of Louise's dead love. Like Fran, P.S. is alive, and skeptical of such morbid fancies. The film describes the bad fit between the romantic vestures of Louise's nostalgia and Fran's living self and, significantly, the sexual interference it causes. Mifanwy Conway was torn between the marvelous romance of Paul Mangin's obsession and her own ego. Pandora sacrificed herself to Hendrick's myth. Judy struggled futilely against Scottie's compulsion to render her in the image of the dead one. P.S. takes a further step in the deconstruction of the parable that began with Obsession and, especially, The Last Tycoon. The gender reversal is but one element that enables the sexual object to refuse reduction to objecthood.

A remarkable scene illustrates this. On the excited verge of their second sexual encounter, Louise orders F. Scott to undress, and he does, with a winsome mix of self-consciousness and kinky complicity. But then she tells him to "go to the mirror and look at your reflection," and he does. "You're forty years old," she says, and proceeds to paint a mortifying picture of the physical and emotional indignities of aging. In this sad scene—in which she comes up behind him and, looking over his shoulder into the mirror in rather a (gender-reversed) allusion to the classic image of Death and the Maiden—Louise's own disillusionment and disappointments, her resentment of lost youth, are projected cruelly onto her young lover, whom she imagines by having died young to have avoided this fate! But F. Scott/Fran, after going along with her inexplicably mean-spirited game, and who does not know or believe himself to be dead, simply rejects it. He tells her that he knows she's doing this because she's been hurt (because it's been done to her) and insists that she look at him when he makes love to her. This deconstructs the transcendental possibilities suggested in both the dialogue and imagery of the previous scene, when out on their first "date," Louise and F. Scott kiss in a bar, surrounded by mirrors, and the camera catches their embrace in an infinite series of reflections, a self-reflexive "corridor of mirrors."

The disarmingly frank role of sexuality in *P.S.* betrays its ideological difference from the necrophilia that has long been cinephilia's mirror image. This explains the narrative raison d'etre of Louise's ex-husband Peter disclosing to her—later the very day of her first meeting and ravenous sex with F. Scott—that throughout their marriage he suffered from an addiction to sex. While their conjugal life was fallow, he reveals, to Louise's utter shock and dismay, he was compulsively seeking out sex, with hundreds of partners. *P.S.* contrasts this pathological sexuality with the miracle of mutual sexual desire, fulfillment, and love that Louise's incipient relationship with F. Scott promises, if she could only free herself of twenty-year-old ghosts, guilt, and resentments. When Louise and Fran have their climatic confrontation, he counters her necrophilia with his own "healthy" desire.

"F. Scott," she exclaims, in self-defense, "the whole thing is just too fucking mystical for me!" "You don't think this isn't mystical for me, too?" Fran replies incredulously, and proceeds to describe the experience—emotional and sensual—of falling in love. The corporeal currents of such love—the tactile sensations, smells, hormonal surges—are missing from the cinema (can only be invoked metaphorically): movie love always threatens to become necrophilia. But, strangely, Fran refuses finally to acknowledge that he is in a film. His vivid desire, for art and love, overcomes both Louise's mystification and the cinema's: inverts the allegory and dispels it.

CHAPTER 3

The Birth, Death, and Apotheosis
of a Hollywood Love Goddess

Ava Gardner—as an actress who becomes aware, from one part to the next, of the quasi-divine character she is and assumes—is indeed the most fascinating of all stars in the history of cinema. Enunciating herself rather than merely speaking lines, filming her life and living her films, she is the only actress who can with all seriousness be raised to the imperial, imperious, inaccessible level of the three greatest screen actors, namely Charles Spencer Chaplin, Erich von Stroheim and Orson Welles.

CLAUDE GAUTEUR, "PORTRAIT D'AVA GARDNER"

The objects and persons of the screen universe are images, doubles; the actor's role as hero divides him into two beings; the projection of the spectator onto the hero corresponds to a doubling action: these triple doublings, as one may call them, promote the mythic ferment. Their combination brings the star into being by investing the real actor with magic potentialities. . . . It is when the mythic projection focuses on her double nature and unifies it that the star-goddess is produced.

EDGAR MORIN, *THE STARS*

Ava Gardner's stardom is fascinating. Although, as Richard Lippe points out, she appeared in more than twenty-five films during the 1940s, "her screen identity did not really emerge until the 1950s." Under long-term contract at MGM in the early 1940s, she played minor roles before winning acclaim in Robert Siodmak's *The Killers*, and, Lippe notes, "she is a radiant presence in *The Hucksters, Singapore, Pandora and the Flying Dutchman*, and *Showboat*, among others. To an extent, the studio succeeded in promoting her as a sex goddess because of her extraordinary beauty and sensuality."[1] And, indeed, despite uneven reviews of her performances, by the mid-1950s, Gardner was quite frequently described in deific terms. The French, in particular, were rhapsodic about Gardner then, and for many years after, especially in response to her embodiment of the "eternal feminine" as Pandora, characterizing her as force of nature, femme fatale, *beau-monstre*, goddess, and even auteur, whose influence on the films in which she appeared was compared to such authorial screen presences as Chaplin, Stroheim, and Welles.[2] A dialectical and intertextual analysis of three films that bridge the period in which Gardner evolved from contract player to veritable Goddess suggests not only some of the reasons for her peculiar star trajectory, but more importantly points to some aesthetic and social problems related to and symptomatized by the postwar Hollywood film, problems having to do with fetishization, corporeality, and desire.

This topic first suggested itself to me, embryonically, some years ago, in the context of my researches into *Pandora and the Flying Dutchman*. In my book on Albert Lewin's films, I noted that the treatment of Gardner in *Pandora* worked

> to dissolve any difference between a movie goddess and an actual deity. It should be noted that Ava Gardner had already blurred this particular boundary: three years before, in the comedy *One Touch of Venus* (1948, directed by William Seiter), she had played a goddess come to life. . . . She was to perform this feat in reverse three years after *Pandora,* in *The Barefoot Contessa* (1954, directed by Joseph Mankiewicz), in which she played a Spanish dancer who becomes a Hollywood star and finally, after her tragic death, a grave monument. Perhaps, though, these three films are not so much a coincidence as a sort of trilogy. According to James Mason, Mankiewicz. . . had been "deeply impressed" by *Pandora*.[3]

And there is not only Mason's word to attest to Mankiewicz's conscious engagement with Lewin's film. *The Barefoot Contessa,* after its opening narration, cuts to a Spanish taverna in which there's an erotic flamenco dance under way, mirroring the transition from narrative present to narrated past in *Pandora,* in which archaeologist Geoffrey Fielding's (Harold Warrender) recollections begin at another taverna, on the Spanish Costa Brava, on a rootless, moonlit night. Mankiewicz not only invoked similarly ancient, sensuous Mediterranean atmosphere, but employed Jack Cardiff, the same cinematographer, to convey it. Marius Goring—who in *Pandora* had played the meaningful but unbilled role of Reggie Demerest, the unhappy poet who commits suicide out of his unrequited love for Pandora—has one of the major roles, that of Alberto Bravano, in *Contessa*. And lest his viewers think these other similarities mere matters of coincidence or convenience, Mankiewicz signals his homage to Lewin's film by having Harry Dawes (Bogart), in his opening narration, paraphrase the same verse of Omar Khayyam that is used twice, as bookends, in the framing narration of *Pandora and the Flying Dutchman:*

The moving finger writes. And having writ
Moves on: nor all thy Piety nor Wit
Shall lure it back to cancel half a line
Nor all thy Tears was out a Word of it.

"But nothing could have helped," Harry says, at the end of his graveside narration. "The moving finger had already writ and moved on and nothing I could do could cancel half a line, or with my tears wash out a word of it." Both stories begin with the inexorable fact of their protagonists' deaths, and are narrated with a knowing, fateful sense of tragic inevitability.

The trio of films *One Touch of Venus, Pandora and the Flying Dutchman,* and *The Barefoot Contessa* form a metanarrative involving their use of statues and Gardner's assumption to the status of movie goddess. The three-dimensional facet of the artwork incorporated here is significant. My prior chapters have considered the incorporation and figuration of two-dimensional arts—that is, pictures—in motion pictures. The relationship between the still and moving image has one complex set of metacinematic implications. That between sculpture and movies has another set that overlaps with (especially where magic and mimesis are concerned) but is by no means likely to be identical to the other. Four related points are particularly striking here: the way that the three-dimensional, spatial properties of sculpture mobilize the spatiotemporal properties of the cinema; the way that statues seem to emphasize the corporeal, even carnal, problematics around cinematic bodies; the overdetermined valences of the statuary's signification, from fetish to cultural status symbol; and the relationship between *classical* statuary and a particular star of the *classical* Hollywood cinema: Ava Gardner.

It should be noted that while the artwork is a necessary element of *One Touch of Venus,* a film in which a statue comes to life, and of *The Barefoot Contessa,* in which the statue as grave monument is conceived as a pivotal framing and structuring motif, statuary was part of the conceptual design, the originary impetus for *Pandora and the Flying Dutchman,* a film in which it might otherwise be construed as incidental. Lewin later insisted upon the surrealist intentions of a particular image in the film, one of numerous scenes including sculpture: "the scene of the racing car on the beach—a modern machine being driven at great speed past the statue of a Greek goddess standing on the sands. As a matter of fact," Lewin continued, "it was this image which was the original thought that prompted me to develop the entire story and film of 'Pandora.'"[4]

And in addition to this generative image, Lewin littered his film with artworks: the quasi-surrealist portrait of Pandora that the Dutchman is painting when she meets him, other pictures, and, especially sculpture. When Pandora is suddenly inspired to disrobe and swim out to the yacht in the harbor where she

Pandora and the Flying Dutchman (Albert Lewin, 1951; photo courtesy of the Museum of Modern Art Film Stills Archive).

will find the Dutchman, for instance, she is standing just below a monumental female head that appears to watch her solemnly as she flings off her clothes and runs down to the shore. One of the most memorable scenes—another Lewin characterized as intentionally surrealist—is of a party on the beach, at which a jazz combo plays ("You're Driving Me Crazy") among fragments of antiquities (including *The Sleeping Hermaphrodite*) in the sand, as women in bathing suits and men in formal dress dance among them. Farther down the beach, where Pandora and Hendrick (the Dutchman) have wandered together, she drapes her bright yellow chiffon scarf over the shoulder of an ancient bronze dancing figure standing on tiptoes by the shore, and Hendrick's gaze turns mournfully out to sea. One senses that the director intended to evoke the immanence of the gods of the ancient world, or at least the loss of that immanence. But Lewin also clearly placed his star among antiquities, for among other possible reasons, to enhance her already statuesque aspect, to imbue her with mythic aura, and to underscore the temporal transcendence of his story and his medium. The other two films frame these intentions, each with a literal sculptural re-presentation. Ava is not merely statuesque; nor found among statues; she *is* a statue, born from one in the earlier film, memorialized as one in the latter.

Both the 1948 romantic comedy and the 1954 drama commissioned fairly prominent academic sculptors to create pseudo-classical statuary for which Gardner posed. Joseph Nicolosi (1893–1961), an Italian-born American sculptor, executed the figure for *One Touch of Venus*. The statue, which bears a passable but not remarkable resemblance to Gardner, is thoroughly indigestible as a veritable antiquity, recently excavated from the Anatolian earth. In Nicolosi's defense, however, certain conditions mitigated strongly against the figure acquiring the aura or patina of "authenticity." Materials are one. It would have been foolhardy, never mind improbable in terms of budgets and schedules, for a motion picture studio to invite an artist—even an academically trained one, like Nicolosi, accustomed to doing so—to work in the sort of materials that were used in antiquity and might survive many of hundreds of years intact, that is, bronze, or, more likely, hard stone, such as marble. The processes involved are too elaborate and the materials too expensive for the manufacture of what is, ultimately, a mere prop. Even so, one might expect more in terms of style from a neoclassical sculptor like Nicolosi. An anecdote from Gardner's memoir explains how the statue used in the film had to be made under considerable time pressures, due to a rather amusing and telling misunderstanding:

> Most Venuses I'd seen in art books were nude or had a magically clinging drape low on the hips, and Mr. Nicolosi clearly had the same idea. Because when I took off my clothes behind a screen and appeared modestly clothed in a two piece bathing suit, he looked at me rather severely and gave a sigh that could have been heard as far away as the Acropolis. . . .
>
> Nude? Me? Not even MGM had *that* in their contract. Bare my breasts? What would Mama have thought? . . . The artist, however, prevailed. . . . "Your body is beautiful. It will make all the difference." And do you know what? He was right. Immodest as it may sound, I have to say that the final statue looked very nice indeed. It was carted off to the studio with filming scheduled to begin in a little more than a week.
>
> Then came the explosion. A *nude* statue! Who said anything about nudity? Tits! Didn't anyone tell you that tits aren't allowed in a Hollywood film? It doesn't matter how beautiful they are, it's immoral and indecent. Plus, the goddamn statue has to come to life on screen. Do you want us to be accused of corrupting the whole of America?
>
> As the owner of the offending objects, I sat back and did not say a word. After all, I'd done my bit for the arts. But the poor sculptor, who'd poured his soul into this clay, was shattered. No one had told him they'd wanted a Venus dressed up like Queen Victoria. Finally, another statue was made, this one with me wearing the belted-at-the-waist off-the shoulder gown that Orry Kelly had designed for Venus, and America's morals survived to fight another day.[5]

Another factor, of course, although one with which one might not expect Nicolosi, who studied with Solon Borglum and was a fellow of the National Sculpture Society with numerous public commissions, to be particularly sympathetic, is that the film is a comedy. The aesthetic distance between the Venus de Milo and Savory's "Anatolian Venus" ultimately affords another possible source of amusement in a rather sweet and frothy amusement.

Although he, too, worked under time and budget constraints, in impermanent materials, Bulgarian-born Italian sculptor Assen Peikov (1908–1973) achieved much more convincing results in the two sculptures of Ava Gardner that he made for *The Barefoot Contessa*.[6] Of course, it should be noted that his statuary was supposed to represent the work, not of an ancient Hellenistic master, but of someone exactly like himself: a contemporary portrait sculptor, active among the Italian elite.[7]

One Touch of Venus

There was a Spanish Bonifacius
Who wrote of mortals loving statues;
But an Italian changed the plan,
And made a statue love a man.
CHARLES GODFREY LELAND[8]

One Touch of Venus was an adaptation of a successful Broadway musical (book by S. J. Perelman and Ogden Nash, music by Kurt Weill; directed for the Broadway stage by Elia Kazan), that itself was loosely based on a turn-of-the-century comic novel, Anstey's *The Tinted Venus*. The film had two directors, Gregory La Cava and William Seiter, only the second of whom is credited. The musical element of the film is much reduced—only a couple of Weill's songs remain. Robert Walker plays Eddie Hatch, a department store window trimmer, who, as the movie opens, is not even married, but is already henpecked by his plucky, domineering fiancée, Gloria. Whitfield Savory, the department store magnate, is an art collector and self-styled purveyor of culture and has acquired a priceless antiquity—the so-called Anatolian Venus—as the centerpiece to an art gallery in store. With the unveiling of the great statue mere moments away, Savory calls in Eddie to repair the curtain-raising mechanism. One cocktail under his belt and Eddie, left alone with her, is moved to kiss the alluring lips of the Anatolian Venus, who is magically animated by the kiss.

From this point, as Ava Gardner succinctly put it in her autobiography, "I climb down off the pedestal and make everyone's life a comedic hell by falling

Robert Walker, Joseph Nicolosi's statue of Venus, and Ava Gardner in a publicity photo for *One Touch of Venus* (William Seiter, 1948; photo courtesy of Jerry Ohlinger's Movie Material Store).

madly in love with him."[9] A noteworthy plot point is that the goddess of love incarnate spends the entire story lusting after poor Eddie, who is more concerned with concealing her from Gloria than he is moved by her considerable charms and sexual entreaties. In proper comedic fashion, it all gets sorted out by the end, of course: Gloria finds her more appropriate match in Eddie's friend Joe, Venus regretfully returns both to sculptural form and Olympian heights, and Eddie (his memory purged of the whole sordid mess) meets Savory's brand new floorwalker, Venus Jones, who naturally bears an uncanny resemblance to the goddess of love.

The Barefoot Contessa

It would be off the mark to reproach Mankiewicz for opening up a number of themes without grappling with any of them since his idea was not so much to make a satire about Hollywood (although it is the most vicious one ever made), or a film about impotence (which is, of course, symbolic), or a guide to the

Riviera and its denizens as to paint one of most beautiful portraits of woman ever filmed, in the person of Ava Gardner, Hollywood's most exquisitely beautiful actress.

FRANÇOIS TRUFFAUT[10]

The Barefoot Contessa, the film that seems to consciously construct a trilogy out of its dialectical relations to the previous two Gardner vehicles, was written and directed in 1954 by Joseph Mankiewicz, who, with Albert Lewin, was one of classic Hollywood's few genuinely intellectual residents. It tells retrospectively, indeed posthumously and nonlinearly, a fictional story that is said to have been based loosely on or inspired by the life of Rita Hayworth. Maria d'Amata (née Vargas) is discovered dancing in a Spanish taverna, experiences a meteoric rise in Hollywood movies, and retires prematurely, withdrawing to a life among the very rich—first the international jet set and then marriage to an Italian count, played by Rossano Brazzi. Narrated by three of the mourners at her funeral, including her husband and her mentor, director Harry Dawes (Bogart), the film begins at the foot of the statue of her that will mark the grave of the Countess Maria Torlato-Favrini. The opening scene is characterized by a mesmerizing, elegiac, but bitter lyricism. Jack Cardiff's camera tracks through the muted Mediterranean colors of a provincial Italian cemetery in the rain toward the statue's foot, accompanied by Mario Nascimbene's nostalgic theme and Bogart's mournful and ironic voice-over narration ("My name is Harry Dawes. I go way back—back to when the movies had two dimensions, and one dimension, and sometimes no dimension at all."). The reason for the demise of the contessa is all important for analysis of themes related to statuary, although we do not learn it until the very end of the film. She was murdered by her jealous husband, the count Torlato-Favrini (here again, as with Lewin's film, one thinks of *Othello*, or Browning's "My Last Duchess"), when he discovered her with their chauffeur. Earlier that very night Maria had visited her mentor, Harry Dawes, and confided to him that on her wedding night she had learned that her husband was incapable—due to a war injury—of carnal relations, that she had used the chauffeur to become pregnant, and was now going to meet him to break off the affair. It was her misguided conviction that her husband would gratefully accept the child as his heir, the only possibly continuation of the Torlato-Favrini line. Thus the statue is linked structurally to Maria's body—her sexual body and her dead body. The corporeal element is critical. Indeed, the entire narrative of *The Barefoot Contessa* revolves around problematics related to the corporeal fact (and beauty and desirability) of Maria's body, and what it embodies. As Maureen Turim has noted, the film's "narrative hinges on the disjuncture between genuine sexual expression and the representation of sexuality in images."[11]

The Barefoot Contessa (Joseph Mankiewicz, 1954).

Maria is established from the outset of the film as a rather anomalous figure in Hollywood terms. Like Pandora she is a ubiquitous object of desire. But she defies mere objectification. Her attentions cannot be bought and she seems determinedly uninterested in anyone who desires her. She regards with scorn Kirk Edwards (Warren Stevens), the Howard Hughes–like multimillionaire cum film producer who acts as though he owns her by virtue of having "discovered" her. And she regards with contempt Albert Bravano (Marius Goring), the Latin American playboy and jet-setter on whose yacht she escapes Edwards but who gets no closer to her than his predecessor. Bravano's yes-man, erstwhile movie publicist Oscar Muldoon (Edmond O'Brien), in his voice-over narration, says disparagingly of his employer, who also bought him away from Edwards, "if Bravano had to choose between really having Maria—in secret—and not having her, but with the whole world thinking he did, he'd want it just the way it was." As Cheryl Bray Lower puts it, "Maria despises the sterile falseness of the men in Hollywood, who . . . fawn over her beauty and use her as a trophy in order to perpetuate the myth of their virility."[12]

Rather than accepting her status as object, Maria is shown obliquely and repeatedly as the subject of what is implied to be a base, carnal desire for "uncomplicated" men—workers, servants, musicians—who make no demands other than sexual ones of her (some criticism of the film has described the character as a nymphomaniac). This baseness—which probably would not be framed as so remarkable in a male protagonist—is explicitly and metonymically represented by her titular bare feet. In dialogue that Mankiewicz must have labored to get past the censors, despite the general loosening of censorship in the mid-fifties, Maria herself uses the experience of being barefoot in the dirt as an instantiation of and analogy for her taste for what we can only infer is a kind of debased sexuality. (The erotic conflation of barefootedness and statuary is suggestive of one of cinema's most perverse and radical erotic images—Gaston Modot's toe-sucking lover in Buñuel's *L'Age d'or*).[13] But Maria's bare feet are mobilized in two evocative directions in *The Barefoot Contessa*, signifying at once her predilection for uncomplicated, carnal sex and her desire for and construction into a fairy-tale scenario. Harry equates her with Cinderella, the shoeless princess who emerged from the ash heap and who is a prototypical fantasy for all girls who would, like Maria D'Amata, or Rita Hayworth, or Ava Gardner herself, ascend from humble backgrounds to the Hollywood firmament and beyond. In short, Mankiewicz's film confronts some of Hollywood cinema's most sacred cows.

A Prisoner of Her Image

> Rita Hayworth once said the problem with her life was that the men in it fell in love with Gilda, her most glamorous role, and woke up the next morning with her. That's a sentiment I can fully identify with. I've always felt a prisoner of my image, felt that people preferred the myths and didn't want to hear about the real me at all.
> AVA GARDNER[14]

The focus on the corporeal aspect of Maria's existence and Ava Gardner's appeal underscores how paradoxically, indeed hypocritically, desire had come to be constructed and construed in classic Hollywood, where bodies, under the auspices of the Hays Office (post-1934)—the fetishizations of Dietrich by Sternberg and other exceptional phenomena notwithstanding—although objectified, tended also to become somehow de-eroticized. They were not treated as flesh, but rather as supports for almost inhumanly glamorous heads, as bodies to be dressed, not undressed. Well, that is, until Rita Hayworth, the WWII pinup whose postwar films—most notably *Gilda* (1946)—are one symptom of the disease that Mankiewicz is treating here. It is, at some level, no coincidence that the year before Gardner played the goddess of love incarnate in *One Touch of*

Venus, Hayworth appeared as the earthly incarnation of the muse Terpischore in another musical comedy, *Down to Earth* (Alexander Hall, 1947).[15] The eroticization of the body of the war period and postwar movie goddess is part of a larger set of problems—social and cinematic, that Mankiewicz seems concerned with. The postwar Hollywood cinema is fraught with contradictions that surface as a result of profound social and demographic changes. No doubt as part of a larger ideological imperative to relegate women to their "proper" sphere (domestic) and functions (sexual object/mother/domestic servant) in the aftermath of the necessary social reorganization of the war period, female characters are often simultaneously enhanced in terms of their aura as sexual objects, even as their agency is undermined, challenged, or diminished. By virtue of this ambivalent attitude, sexual desirability comes to seem an almost inhuman attribute.

In *The Barefoot Contessa,* the tension between objective and subjective desire is the very source of tragedy. Cheryl Bray Lower argues that

> Mankiewicz not only demythologizes Hollywood but also deconstructs the concept that a woman exists only to please a man. Here he gives life to another in his long line of strong female protagonists who fall victim to patriarchal strictures. Maria is the ultimate object of the gaze: a woman who is never allowed to merge her real self with the image that men perceive of her. She is a token of Kirk Edwards' success, an expensive good luck charm for the rich playboy, Bravano, and a beautiful museum piece for Torlato-Favrini. . . . Plagued by a 1950s conservative patriarchal culture that demanded acquiescence to a man's ideal of female perfection, an outgoing, transgressive woman was a mockery of one of its cardinal rules. A woman may adorn and serve a man but not act like one, and she most certainly cannot express the sexual side of her personality and expect to live life on her own terms. In *The Barefoot Contessa,* Mankiewicz, unwittingly and yet profoundly, addressed the constraints of these rigid postwar dictates that Hollywood espoused as gospel through the Production Code.[16]

It must be noted that with *The Barefoot Contessa,* Ava Gardner's own legend and star persona, which had acquired a certain assertive, difficult, nonconformist, and unladylike patina, came very close for many—insiders, fans, and critics—to merging with her role. Jean Domarchi, for instance, claims that Gardner actively sought roles in the 1950s in which she could "finally be herself" and that despite evidence that *The Barefoot Contessa* was both more about and meant for Rita Hayworth, it is a veritable "portrait" of Gardner.[17] Claude Gauteur coins the term "avagardnériens" to characterize the sort of "autobiographico-mythologique" roles into which he claims Gardner knowingly moved as she adapted to her fate as a kind of goddess-auteur. For him the path was paved by two roles that prefigure her divinity (*One Touch of Venus*) and her Hemingway-esque fatality (*The Snows of Kilimanjaro*), traits associated with the stature fully realized in the trilogy of *Pandora and the Flying Dutchman, The Barefoot Contessa,* and *The Sun Also Rises.*[18] This kind of slippage is ubiquitous and one must treat it with suspicion, and as evidence of Gardner's assumption to paramount (or MGM, as it were) star stature. Yet Lena Horne might have been describing the character Maria D'Amata when she said, of her friend Ava Gardner:

I think she drank because she was bored with people often. I think it upset her that men that she *did* like were not as strong as they *could* have been. And she liked the ones who were not too intimated by her. She didn't emasculate anyone, but she was an equal partner. And many men at that time didn't like that. . . . Both of us had to like who we went to bed with. And when it came to the power people who could have perhaps done tremendous favors for us, we thought they were ugly and unlovable. She was just a wild, good-looking girl that they wanted to harness, and dominate. . . . She was an unfeminine, very feminine woman. . . . She never believed that the image that they saw was what she really was. And she resented that her image made people expect something, when she wanted to be herself. . . . You want to be able to think for yourself, and Ava always did. She hated the fact that we were made to feel like we were being possessed by somebody, or that we were owned body and soul if we wanted to work.[19]

Horne's identification with Gardner seems to have been mutual, which raises a somewhat subliminal aspect of Gardner's appeal, as well as her reputation for nonconformity—a kind of unacknowledged racial nuance. Like Rita Hayworth, who was of Hispanic background, Gardner projected an image that seemed easily to slip from sensuality to outright exoticism, and thus to induce a sense of racial vertigo. As Molly Haskell observed, "Gardner's combination of sensuality and aesthetic appeal . . . made her into something larger than life, too exotic to be an American woman, and as a result she was always playing half-castes (*Bhowani Junction*), outcasts (*The Barefoot Contessa, The Killers*), and revenant redeemers (*Pandora and the Flying Dutchman*)."[20] Haskell almost, but not quite, captures the vaguely scandalous yet magical aura that Gardner lent to such parts. Her image did not quite conform in terms of either racial or gender types to the oversimplified templates available in popular culture. *The Barefoot Contessa* exposes this dissonance and makes literal the problematics that are allegorized in *One Touch of Venus* and *Pandora and the Flying Dutchman,* in both of which Gardner's characters—as goddess and femme fatale—insisted, although fatefully, on their own desire. It also thematizes some of the most uncomfortable social realities of Hollywood culture. And the classical statue in each instance seems to raise the problem of Hollywood classicism, a product of Hollywood culture, a problem having to do with representation and desire.

One pivotal scene in Mankiewicz's film well illustrates this, by means of both divergence from convention and repetition. It arrives first in the publicist Oscar Muldoon's narration, which describes Maria's life from her departure from Hollywood with the Latin American playboy Alberto Bravano to the last time he ever saw her, at a casino in Monaco. Muldoon savagely describes the vanity and vacuity of the life of the super rich and their parasites on the Riviera; then, as Cardiff's camera paints perhaps the film's most loving portrait of Ava Gardner, in a pale pink satin ball gown, Muldoon continues, "and in the middle of all this fantastic unreality was Maria, more unreal in a way than any of it. She moved among all these crazy people, through the casinos, and beaches, and ballrooms, from Marseilles to Monaco, as if she were loaded with novocaine. She showed no pain, no pleasure, no interest, no nothing. . . . You figure. . . . I can't." When Muldoon's retrospective voice-over yields to the scene's present, we witness a violent confrontation that brings Maria's relationship with Alberto Bravano to an end. Bravano storms out of the casino to the dining room, to the table where Maria, Muldoon, and their company are seated, and he denounces Maria, whom he blames for a bad turn of chance at the gaming tables: "You put a curse on me, not only for the night, but from the unhappy moment when I first knew of your existence, as you will put a curse always on everyone and everything near to you. . . . You are not a woman! I do not know what you are, but you are not a woman. You will not let yourself be loved. You cannot love. Once you had the look for me of an exquisite lady. Now, I do not see that look. I only see that you have the body of an animal . . . a dead animal!"

This scene is significant in manifold ways. First—in a rare sort of Hollywood cubism—it is shown (and heard) twice, first from the point of view of Muldoon, the film's second narrator, then again from the point of view of the count, Vincenzo Torlato-Favrini, the third narrator. I employ the term "cubism" guardedly to suggest the tension between volumetric objects and flat pictorial space that is generally suppressed by illusionistic pictures (still or moving) but has been explored fruitfully by modernism. The term also lends itself to Mankiewicz's nonlinear narrative; told from the often overlapping points of view of several narrators (like *Citizen Kane*, *Rashomon*, and *The Bad and the Beautiful,* among others), *The Barefoot Contessa* dares to show the same scene twice and thereby also shows it in the round—it "sculpts" the space around the action by showing it once from what is more or less Muldoon's vantage point and once from an opposite point of view that correlates to Vincenzo's. It doesn't collapse the space into one frame, like one of Picasso's cubist portraits, but it disrupts narrative continuity, the seamless forward flow of the movie story in a comparable manner. And, as with the conspicuous camera movement of the film's opening sequence, it also underscores the three-dimensionality of Maria (earlier, of her representation), demonstrating the way that movement is a temporal process, and the way sculptures—and bodies—instigate movement in space and time.

In this confrontation, the corporeality of Maria's body is Bravano's focus because it signifies. But it signifies falsely. Remember, he is the character of whom Muldoon said that if he had to choose between having Maria and having the world believe he did, he would choose the latter. So, the body that Bravano abhors is one that he has wanted to treat as a token, but has not "had." Nor can Vincenzo, the count, "have" it. His "manhood" was destroyed in the war. Mankiewicz actually wanted Vincenzo's problem to be constitutional, not the result of an accident, but was prevented by the Hays Office, an agency he held in very low esteem. "My Hollywood Cinderella of *The Barefoot Contessa* married her prince and found that he was either homosexual or impotent. I couldn't do either, so I manufactured some tale about his having been wounded somewhere below the belt in the War."[21] Remarkably, in all three films, men will not, do not, cannot take Ava Gardner as their lover: Hendrick in *Pandora and the Flying Dutchman;* Eddie in *One Touch of Venus,* and Vincenzo (among others) in *The Barefoot Contessa.* Isn't it strange that a movie goddess whose sensual appeal is foregrounded, whose body is presented, and represented, is coupled repeatedly (here and elsewhere—three years after *Contessa,* for instance, she played Lady Brett Ashley in *The Sun Also Rises*) with men who, for various reasons, cannot "have" her? Gilles Deleuze has commented on this peculiarity. "Another type of originary woman, imperial and athletic, is often portrayed by Ava Gardner: three times impulse draws her irresistibly to marry the dead or impotent man."[22]

Does this theme not in fact underscore some paradoxical realities of the experience of Hollywood filmgoing? In fact, although their beauty seduces their viewers, those viewers obviously cannot "have" movie stars. Stars are physically inaccessible. They are constructs: phantasms. Nor, because of the Production Code, could carnal relations be shown or insinuated in the Hollywood phantasmagoria. Robert Walker, James Mason, Marius Goring, Rossano Brazzi cannot "have" Ava Gardner either, at least not on screen. Hollywood's obsessive reworking of romantic love and construction of ideal love objects under the aegis of the Hays Office comes to seem like a dream (sometimes a nightmare). The fascination of this dreamworld is achieved through a kind of magic, not unlike that of dreamwork itself. Atavistic and unconscious forces are engaged here. That's why it is critical to note the magical scenario of the film that initiates this trilogy.

Beauty So Eloquent

> The beautiful image stood bathed in the radiant flood and shining with a purity
> which made her most persuasively divine. If by day her mellow complexion
> suggested faded gold, her substance now might have passed for polished silver.
> The effect was almost terrible; beauty so eloquent could hardly be inanimate.
> HENRY JAMES, *THE LAST OF THE VALERII*[23]

The story of *One Touch of Venus* has been observed in many cultures, as myth,
legend, or folklore. In some creation myths, the first people were images of clay,
brought to life by the gods. This particular theme—of the animation of a female
statue—haunts Western culture, certainly from as far back as Pygmalion and
Galatea, but according to the literary iconology explored by Theodore Ziolkowski, has had a series of very particular revivals and transformations in the modern
period. He isolates the turn of the eighteenth to the nineteenth century as a
critical turning point in Western culture's attitude toward animistic magic. Referring to Emma Lady Hamilton's famous attitudes, in which she "act[ed] all the
antique statues in an Indian shawl," Ziolkowski notes that "this bizarre conceit
of representing 'living statues' is simply another example of the late eighteenth-
century obsession with statues: with statues *per se*, with statues that come to life,
with people who turn into statues, and with the ambiguous relationship between
people and statues."[24]

The particular theme of a statue of Venus, the goddess of love, coming to
life and pursuing a mortal man has its own particular iconology dating back
to medieval times. In his book *Disenchanted Images: A Literary Iconology*, Ziolkowski tracks this and two other magical motifs (actually three images that he
found in Jean Cocteau's film *The Blood of a Poet*) according to what he calls the
"generations of disenchantment." He begins at a moment around 1800, during which there is considerable "acceptance of magic images—either credulous or by convention," then turns to the period of the 1830s and 1840s, when
Romantic writers such as Prosper Mérimée, in his story "The Venus of Ille,"
"exploited the effects of the supernatural while leaving room in every case for
a rational explanation." Later in the century, around 1870, come "the skeptical historicists who deny the possibility of miracle while attempting to comprehend the consciousness of those who believe"—Henry James, for instance, who
in his story "The Last of the Valerii" "investigate[s] the psychology of credulous iconomaniacs without suggesting for an instant that anything supernatural
really takes place."[25]

According to Ziolkowski, the last and "fourth stage in the process of disenchantment . . . often involves a reanimation of the disenchanted images by
transposition into a literary form where the marvelous can still be taken literally:

parody, horror fiction, or fantasy." As an example of the parodic transposition, he offers F. Anstey's *The Tinted Venus*, the very novel from which *One Touch of Venus* was adapted.[26] It is somewhat ironic that Ziolkowski finds the images whose literary ancestry he traces—the animated statue of Venus, the haunted portrait, and the magic mirror—in a film. What Jean Cocteau discovered upon taking up the camera in 1931 is something that all moviegoers know: the medium lends itself to myth and magic. If we reexamine this trilogy of films from the one that begins with Ava Gardner born utterly magically as a goddess from stone (*Venus*), to the one in which a supernatural aura surrounds her uncanny resemblance to a long-dead bride and a mythic portrait (*Pandora*), to the one in which the mythic is metaphorical and internalized (*Contessa*), perhaps ironically, since we are supposedly already disenchanted, we see a cinematic transformation comparable to the literary trajectory Ziolkowski noted, from the marvelous, to the fantastic, to the naturalized. As he reminds us, "Ancient beliefs do not always disappear when people stop accepting them: they transform themselves."[27]

Here the transformation is swift. In the course of less than a decade—very much as a function of the themes explored in these films, I would argue—Ava Gardner went from attractive bit player in Hollywood to movie goddess of the highest order. The first film in this trilogy playfully celebrated the magical properties of the medium that could revivify the myth that the statue stood for. The second invoked these allegorically. The third brought the story down to earth; it is a parable, though, that shows how art objects and love objects function in the collector's and the viewer's imagination. Mankiewicz's dialogue is deeply insightful in this respect:

"We have come to the end of the line . . . literally to the end of the line. It is time for the Torlato-Favrinis to get off the world," the impotent Vincenzo says to Eleanora, his widowed, childless, and barren sister, as they sit together on a balcony while his fiancée swims on the beach below. Eleanora has asked him how he can be so cruel as to marry Maria given his inability to make love to her. "We can not have come this far and this long to leave nothing behind but some undistinguished, unidentifiable portraits to be hung on the back walls of curiosity shops, to gather the dust of the future." "The last Contessa," he continues, watching Maria emerge from the sea, "the world will some day see paintings of her, and of her and me, and then think, what a pity they have gone and left nothing behind. . . . We will be remembered." "Because the last Contessa was a movie star?" replies Eleanora, shocked. "Vincenzo, you cannot marry a woman as if you were putting on a play, because she's the type you have in mind, because she is perfectly cast as a portrait of the last Contessa Torlato-Favrini!" "Perhaps I have become, as you put it, obsessed by our name and our past and the absence of our future, by our paintings," Vincenzo admits to his sister. "As if in some magical way our long line of paintings will accomplish what we cannot."

Of course, classically beautiful Ava Gardner *was* perfectly cast as a portrait. She is literally portrayed in each of these films, and others. Portraits, in two dimensions or three, defy death and invoke it simultaneously: they are commemorative, memorial. Here, these portraits in the round are that—statues are always and never dead—but they are not only that. These statues are emphatically overdetermined. As reified, aestheticized images of ideal femininity they certainly also function as fetishes. They can be kept and they do not "lack." They also contain and silence the threatening image of powerful female agency. This is literalized in the plot of *One Touch of Venus*, in which the male protagonist, Eddie, is shown as thoroughly unhinged by the bold, assertive, unembarrassed, sexually forward goddess of love; and the world is righted only when she has resumed her inert, silent, marmoreal form. This containment is evident, too, in *The Barefoot Contessa*. The silent, magisterial statue of Maria is precisely what Vincenzo wanted: not the real, earthy woman with desires, wants, and impulses, but the beautiful, inarticulate icon that can speak to the ages of his familial rank and stature.

Here the signification of the statue, for Hollywood, merges into the movies' perennial concern with class and status (etymologically and morphologically, statue and status are virtually the same word). As an undisputed emblem of Western culture, the (neo)classical statue signifies both Hollywood's claim to culture and, paradoxically, its association of classicism with suspect, effete qualities of the "old world." Even for a "highbrow" like Joseph Mankiewicz, the statue seems to simultaneously speak to that which is beautiful in the Mediterranean world his film captures so vividly and to the sterility, the decadence, and the obsolescence of European society. And then there is the common "classicism" of such statues and of the classical Hollywood films that they stand for and in: legible, legitimate, made with regular proportions and smooth, seamless contours, according to long-established canons. Overdetermined—magical idol, fetish object, memorial portrait, status symbol, bearer of cultural patrimony, classical canon—the statue somehow embodies many of the conflicts and contradictions effortfully suppressed by the classical Hollywood film. The unacceptable, repressed nakedness of the one statue (*One Touch of Venus*) returns metonymically in the focal bare feet of another (*The Barefoot Contessa*), as both condense, or displace, the surplus of contradictory meaning around issues of gender, class, sexuality, and desire in cinema and society.

The statue represents, in short, the return of the repressed, much as, according to Sigmund Freud in *Delusion and Dream*, does a classical Roman bas relief of a barefooted woman in Wilhelm Jensen's novel *Gradiva: A Pompeiian Fancy*. This is the story of a man—a classicist—who falls in love with a woman he believes to be dead two thousand years, a woman whom he magically associates with the antique sculpture.[28] Freud persuasively demonstrates how the

Ció Abellí, Ava Gardner statue at Tossa de Mar, 1998 (photo courtesy of Ció Abellí).

novel illustrates the way repressed and unacknowledged conflicts and desires are displaced and condensed in the archaeologist's almost fetishistic overestimation of the sculpture. But as Ziolkowski's iconology demonstrates, Norbert Hanold's bizarre love affair with a sculptural woman is anything but unprecedented. Shortly before his death, Heinrich Heine is said to have remarked to a friend that he had really never loved anything but dead women and statues, a perverse but somehow eloquent articulation of the paradox I see operating across this trilogy of films.[29] It's not hard to imagine a melancholy cinephile saying the same thing of dead women and movie stars. Lest it seem a problem or an omission that the portrait of Ava Gardner as Pandora is a painting, rather than a sculpture (despite that film's profusion of statuary), or that the statues of her as Venus and the Contessa Torlato-Favrini have gone the way of most movie props (into oblivion), note that if you visit Tossa de Mar, the ancient Catalonian village where Lewin's film was shot, and where the memory of Ava Gardner's presence is cherished still, you'll find high up on one of the cliff-top promontories there, overlooking the sea, a bronze statue by sculptor Ció Abellí of Ava Gardner, over life-sized and barefoot, as Pandora, commissioned after Gardner's death and dedicated in 1998.

CHAPTER 4

Survivors of the Shipwreck of Modernity

Maria Vargas thus rejoins Pandora; only the Flying Dutchman is missing. This character from another time who will never live again. For the days of myth are gone . . . Hollywood, which no longer knows what love is, can no longer propose its ideal representation. The story is over.
JACQUES SICLIER, *LE MYTHE DE LA FEMME DANS LE CINÉMA AMÉRICAIN*

Maria morte commence, statufiée, à vivre éternellement.
CLAUDE GAUTEUR, "PORTRAIT D'AVA GARDNER"

At the end of *The Barefoot Contessa* we are left standing at the graveside of Maria d'Amata and, according to some of the film's and its star's ardent admirers of the period, the apotheosis of Ava Gardner and the death of the classical Hollywood cinema of which it arises are imminent. Let us imagine, then, that among the mourners—offscreen—at that cinematic graveyard are not only Claude Gauteur and Jacques Siclier, but also their contemporary and fellow cineaste Jean-Luc Godard. Godard's *Le Mépris/Contempt* (1963) has been described as a eulogy for the classical cinema, so perhaps this image is not too extravagant a conceit.[1] Made a decade beyond *Pandora* and *The Barefoot Contessa*, Godard's eulogy expresses a kind of longing for those predecessors through integration that is rather different from the sort of homage paid by its many other citations and nods (of and to *Some Came Running*, *Rio Bravo*, and *Hatari!*, among others).

In "Mourning and Melancholia," Freud asks, "Now in what consists the work which mourning performs?" His answer explicates the difficulty the psyche has in comprehending the loss of a beloved object:

> The testing of reality, having shown that the loved object no longer exists, requires forthwith that all the libido shall be withdrawn from its attachments to this object. Against this demand a struggle of course arises—it may be univer-

sally observed that man never willingly abandons a libido position, not even when a substitute is already beckoning to him. This struggle can be so intense that a turning away from reality ensues, the object being clung to through the medium of a hallucinatory wish-psychosis. The normal outcome is that deference for reality gains the day. Nevertheless its behest cannot be at once obeyed. *The task is now carried through bit by bit, under great expense of time and cathectic energy, while all the time the existence of the lost object is continued in the mind. Each single one of the memories and hopes which bound the libido to the object is brought up and hyper-cathected,* and the detachment of the libido from it accomplished. Why this process of carrying out the behest of reality bit by bit, which is in the nature of a compromise, should be so extraordinarily painful is not at all easy to explain in terms of mental economics. It is worth noting that this pain seems natural to us.[2] (my emphasis)

If one looks at *Contempt* as a bit of the work of mourning—for a type of movie that the mourner at the same time knows to be gone, or obsolescent, but wishes to preserve—in psychoanalytic terms, some of its contradictions and paradoxes begin to make sense. For, while the film shares many characteristics with earlier Godard films, it is infused to a remarkable degree with an atmosphere of sadness that is at odds with its own construction, dependent as that is on pastiche, intertextuality, stylistic reflexivity, and even parody. And unlike the more generally flip and casual references to Hollywood movies in Godard's earlier films, *Contempt* exhibits a deeper, less ironic—although by no means unambivalent—connection to the cinematic objects whose loss it attempts to work through.

"The characters are like shipwrecked survivors of modern civilization who land on a mysterious island that turns out to be the world of Homer," Godard said of *Contempt,* continuing, "I have tried to contrast Homeric serenity with our universe of television sets and flashy cars."[3] This juxtaposition of an ancient deific Mediterranean landscape with godless modern spectacle must ring a bell for those familiar with Albert Lewin's *Pandora and the Flying Dutchman.* Lewin focused on just such a juxtaposition in his film and claimed that "the scene of the racing car on the beach—a modern machine being driven at great speed past the statue of a Greek goddess standing on the sands" was the "image which was the original thought that prompted me to develop the entire story and film of 'Pandora.'"[4] Mankiewicz reiterated Lewin's strategies, not only through use of the classicizing statue, but by transporting Maria Vargas backward in historical time—not supernaturally but via milieu—from Hollywood, to Monte Carlo, to the Renaissance palazzo at Rapallo (in a roadster, no less). While Lewin had a surrealist aesthetic in mind, neither he nor the other two directors engaged this juxtaposition for strictly surrealist effect, but rather, it seems, to weigh the film down, to make it timeless and reflective, to anchor it inexorably to history and the oblivion of time.

In casting Brigitte Bardot, the reigning goddess of French film, in *Contempt*, Godard must have remembered Ava Gardner in the roles that commenced with *One Touch of Venus* and her precedent, in which there was calculated slippage between movie goddess and authentic deity.[5] Obvious narrative echoes of *The Barefoot Contessa* and *Pandora* reinforce this intertextual connection. Mankiewicz's story began with a small Hollywood scouting party in Europe and established the tense relationship between a near legendary, near has-been of a director and a young, rich, crude, powerful bully of a producer—Harry Dawes and Kirk Edwards (Humphrey Bogart and Warren Stevens)—that is pretty neatly mirrored in the relationship between Fritz Lang (himself) and Jeremy Prokosch (Jack Palance) in *Contempt*. The scene of Maria's screen test in Rome, probably at Cinecittà itself, too, is an obvious precedent for the Cinecittà scenes in Godard's film. As for *Pandora*, the narrative connection is literary and mythic; the film being made in *Contempt* is an adaptation of *The Odyssey*, whose protagonist is, like Lewin's, an ancient mariner. Indeed, Lewin's Flying Dutchman, the "eternal Jew of the sea,"[6] is also the Ulysses of the North.[7] There are many other narrative elements that connect *Contempt* to *The Barefoot Contessa* and *Pandora and the Flying Dutchman*, as well as iconographic details. In addition to sports cars, the films share the rather fetishistic interest in beautifully bare feet, for example. But it is much more than mere mechanics or detail that Godard finds to admire in these two morbid, beautiful, almost perverse movies, which simultaneously exemplify and deconstruct the classic Hollywood cinema.

Indeed, Godard would seem to have been thinking of *Pandora* when he wrote, "through the most splendid of paradoxes . . . the immortals seek to die. To be sure of living, one must be sure of loving; and to be sure of loving, one must be sure of dying." But, in fact, this quote is taken from Godard's review of a film by Jean Renoir: *Elena et les hommes*.[8] Interestingly, it was Renoir himself, who in tribute to his American friend at the Cinémathèque Française in 1958 (just one year before *Breathless* and the other firsts of the New Wave), said, "There are unconscious artists and others who are perfectly conscious," and anticipated the influence of Lewin's heady, vertiginous, top-heavy films on the coming generation of auteurs. He continued, "The former are neither inferior nor superior to the latter. But the latter are indispensable in periods of transition. Albert Lewin is indispensable to our epoch."[9]

Renoir was prescient about Lewin's influence. What Catherine Russell observes about *Contempt*'s "narrative mortality" is to be found also in *Pandora*, which like Godard's film "articulates a fall of the cinema from myth to allegory, from image to language, from the unquestioned mimeticism of Hollywood and neorealism to . . . discursive self-consciousness." "Narrative mortality," Russell elaborates from Walter Benjamin's writings on aesthetics and allegory, "emerges as an allegorical means of glimpsing an immediacy of representation within the ruins of classicism."[10] Russell also writes eloquently about the final shot of *Contempt*—one strongly reminiscent of *Pandora*—which begins with Godard himself, as Lang's assistant, shouting, "Silence!" as the Odyssey crew shoots the solitary actor/Odysseus confronting the vast expanse of sea and sky, and then pans out to sea: "an image of endless space and time and the 'eternally the same.'"[11] As Jean Collet has observed of this ultimate image, "it seems that all earthly joy and all plenitude are fused in the actor's long silent gaze, the filmmaker's long look at the vast world."[12] And elsewhere, Collet adds,

> The silence of *Contempt* . . . is the same silence that suffuses the last scene of the 1965 *Pierrot le fou;* . . . the same immense sky blending into the blue of the sea across the scope of the screen. But though Marianne and Pierrot whisper the poem of Rimbaud: "Elle est retrouvée, quoi l'éternité . . ." we know that these two voices at last reconciled are voices from beyond the tomb . . . Godard the pessimist discovers that one must pay for this contemplation and this harmony with the world by forfeiting one's life . . . a great circle is closed, that of nostalgia for the couple, for a love beyond time and space.[13]

This nostalgia, explicit in *Pierrot,* implicit by means of negation in *Contempt,* for a love beyond time and space, is a residue of Godard's intense engagement—in a Bloomian, that is *Oedipal* sense—with Lewin's film (among others). For a rhapsodic, mystical, Surrealist achievement of love beyond time and space (and what, after all, *is* sur-reality, if not this 'beyond'?) is precisely what *Pandora* aspires to. "It's as though we are under a spell, outside of time, unending," Pandora marvels as she and her Flying Dutchman hover in a suspended ecstasy on the verge of a death for which he has longed for centuries and that her love has enabled. "Unending," he echoes before their craft founders and sinks in a sudden squall. One knows this is the type of pure, mystical love Maria D'Amata dreamt of as she spurned her craven suitors in *The Barefoot Contessa* and that she thought she had found with Vincenzo, when he so miraculously removed her from the sordid milieu of Monte Carlo.

Lewin's lovers are embarrassing, though. So are Mankiewicz's. They tend to talk like this when we want them to be silent—sublimely silent—in that sublime sort of silence Collet observes at the end of *Contempt.* But so, it must be admitted, do Godard's! If they're not as corny as Lewin's lovers, or quite so heady as Mankiewicz's, they're certainly as windy. This is a paradox common to all three oeuvres. Lewin, Godard, and, to a certain extent, Mankiewicz, each constructs his films with an excess of noise, music, and, *especially,* speech: what Collet calls, adopting a Bakhtinian term, "polyphony," and what Richard Combs, one of

Albert Lewin's more astute reviewers—in a discussion of *The Picture of Dorian Gray*—has called a "pile up of dialogue," that "itself begins to suggest another dimension . . . a formal puzzle of appearances and reality, form and essence, body and soul . . . figured . . . in the interplay of vision and sound."[14]

In Lewin's work, this paradoxical and not always easy confrontation of vision and sound is a function of the director's commitment to recovering something of the aesthetics of the silent cinema, to which he remained deeply and studiously attached, as well as of his native propensity toward rather layered, academic, allusive structures. Mankiewicz shares this latter predisposition; with his tendency to employ multiple narrators, voice-over, and flashback, he complicates narration in ways that also uncouple image and sound. In Godard's work—in *Contempt* especially—the interplay seems, while also indebted to Lewin and Mankiewicz, among others, a function of a kind of embittered romanticism, a vestigial classicism. The polyphony scrapes away at the fulsome beauty of the Bay of Naples, Brigitte Bardot, and Georges Delerue's elegiac score.

Lewin, also a skeptic, also ironic, was yet full of awe. So, on occasion (think of *The Ghost and Mrs. Muir*), was Mankiewicz. The Hollywood skepticism is agnostic, while Godard's is atheistic. As he put it, "*Contempt* is man cut off from the gods and from the world . . . as though there were no one left on earth. These are the survivors and this is what they do. Cinema replaces the watchfulness of the gods."[15] But the gods exhibit a certain ambiguity. Their sculptural vestiges seem vigilant, as in the scene in *Pandora* Lewin himself remarked upon, in which a disarmed goddess seizes the moving camera's point of view, or another, in which a monumental gaze from on high regards Pandora's impulsive dash down to the sea. The statuary in "Lang's" *Odyssey* in *Contempt* (images that are unlike anything in the Lang oeuvre; they are more like Cocteau)[16] seems to echo Lewin's, as well as the statue of Mankiewicz's *Contessa,* and the ancient statues that Ingrid Bergman's Catherine encountered with such perturbation at the National Museum of Naples in Rossellini's *Viaggio in Italia.*[17] Godard adopts from Lewin, Mankiewicz, and Rossellini a kind of camera movement that orbits the static statuary in a manner that makes it seem almost alive, or observant. Cinema, then, *induces* the watchfulness of the gods, or, as Catherine Russell suggests, "mortifies" it. In *Contempt,* she says, relative to its intertextual reference to *Viaggio in Italia,* "two myths are mortified—destroyed under the auspices of melancholy. The first is that of marriage [Bardot] . . . The second is that of . . . the myth of the auteur [Lang]."[18]

As statuary gives rise to a dialectical tension about modernity and antiquity, as well as life and death, architecture and setting are used poignantly in Godard's film and its sources, two American movies that partook quite spectacularly of the possibilities offered by "runaway" productions of their era. *Pandora,* as discussed, is set sublimely among the ruins and ramparts of Tossa de Mar, an

Michel Piccoli as Paul ascends the roof of the Casa Malaparte, Capri, in *Contempt* (Jean-Luc Godard, 1963).

ancient Phoenician town on the Costa Brava. There are many scenic locations in *The Barefoot Contessa*, which was shot entirely on location in Italy (although set in Spain and Hollywood, as well). An exceedingly painterly shot introduces the grounds and architecture of the Renaissance palazzo that is Vincenzo's ancestral home in Rapallo. Shot with a diffusion filter, it shimmers with an impressionist mist that underscores the fairy-tale atmosphere of Maria's arrival (in his beautiful convertible) at her Prince Charming's palace.

Godard's film has a number of contrasting settings, including the modernist interior of Paul's and Camille's Roman flat, the decaying exteriors of Cinecittà, and the film's most eloquent setting: the Casa Malaparte at Cap Massallo on the island of Capri, where the conclusion of the film is enacted. This house, "simple, elemental, at once ancient and modern, monastic yet sensual . . . both beautiful and daunting,"[19] was built for the Italian fascist writer and war correspondent Curzio Malaparte, by the modern Italian architect Adalberto Libera. Placed on a precipitous outcropping of Caprian shoreline, the house simultaneously evokes the eternal immobility of a ziggurat (with its monumental exterior stairway to the roof dominating the approach) and the incipient flight of a ship setting sail (it points out to sea and its rooftop solarium has a curved, sail-like screen atop it). "It is the image of my nostalgia," Malaparte said on its completion in 1942.[20] The house and its attendant mysteries not only set the mood for but also help clarify the film's central conflicts. "The mystery of the house," according to architects Francesco Garofalo and Luca Veresani, "lies in its appearance as a calculated object, organically closed in the relationship between its parts and, at the same time, directly placed on the jagged profile of the rock, within a system connecting it to the elements of the landscape."[21]

The house is thus both organic, or "primitive"—part of the landscape—and, paradoxically, modernist, or "civilized." This dialectic, internal to and resolved within the Casa Malaparte, seems to reflect and even reify a number of the film's themes, including its dialectic of gender (see below) and the question, debated by producer, director, and screenwriter in and around the house, on location, about how to go about adapting *The Odyssey*. While Prokosch sees the film as epic, monumental, spectacular, and awesome, Lang believes "the world of Homer is a real world," and that it "belongs to a civilization which has developed in accord with and not in opposition to nature," and Paul advocates a more modern, psychological interpretation. The house itself manages to be all these things—spectacular, monumental, organic, in accord with nature, modern, and even psychological (the ship-like forms suggest identification with or a drive toward the sea). The characters, and perhaps the director, too, however, remain blind to the possibility that their film could resolve, rather than choosing between, these approaches.

Certainly, one of the most striking characteristics of the house itself and of Godard's engagement with it is the stunning elevation of the site. The resulting exalted point of view is another key structural feature that *Contempt* echoes from *Pandora* and *The Barefoot Contessa*. In *Pandora*, after a rather remarkable prologue set on a fishing boat in untranslated Catalan, the camera ascends to a vantage point high above the events it portrays, a conceit that has drawn some notice: it is shot through the aperture of a bell tower in which a bell is tolling—for the drowned lovers, as it turns out. The bell, it may be noted (at least on the big screen), is inscribed with the Spanish for the director's given name, "Alberto." Farther back, then, the camera tracks, adopting a higher vantage point of the scene far below, as people flock to the beach like ants (cf. Buñuel and Dalí).[22] It seems like an objective point of view, as Gilles Deleuze has observed: "The beach is seen from a distance and from a height, through a telescope on the promontory of a house. But very quickly we learn that the house is inhabited, the telescope used, by people who are very much a part of the set under consideration: the beach, the point which attracts the groups, the event taking place there, the people mixed up in it. . . . Has the image not become subjective?"[23]

Mankiewicz seems to echo this vantage point in *The Barefoot Contessa*, in the scene with the film's most meaningful dialogue, between Vincenzo Torlato-Favrini and Elena, his sister, as they sit on a patio of their estate above the Ligurian coast, watch Maria swim in the Riviera below, and discuss the inevitable extinction of their class and themselves. Godard has discussed the narrative impact of such lofty situations in his own film: "In *Contempt*, I maintain a normal remove from my characters; very close to them and at the same time quite far away. It's a film seen from above. Hence the title, 'contempt,' looking down upon."[24] When he says, then, that "cinema replaces the watchfulness of the gods" in the context of a film about film that itself represents the gods parenthetically—as icons of Lang's production—it is almost as though Godard means to remake *Pandora* without its metaphysical heart: to substitute the camera's irrational eye for the meaningful if ineffable causation that Lewin left implied but unexplicated, floating on the wine dark sea at the conclusion of *Pandora*, or to remake *The Barefoot Contessa* without its moral.

Death is nothing if not meaningful in *Pandora and the Flying Dutchman* and *The Barefoot Contessa;* indeed, in the one it is salutary, in the other it is genuinely tragic. In *Contempt*, on the other hand, death seems arbitrary and cruel, although perhaps not entirely unmotivated. As Gregg Horowitz has written of the car accident that kills Prokosch and Camille, it is "an accident twice over. First, it is an accident in the common sense that it was an event intended by no one. Second, however, it is also a narrative accident. Godard presents Camille's death as a narrative *coup*, an event both denarrativized—it is caused by and causes nothing—and denarrativizing—it moves the causality of the plot toward the plane of fate."[25] In early Godard generally, though, death often does seem motivated, albeit ironically, by the narrative's need for an ending. Killing off a protagonist summarily not only solves the problem of how to conclude the story, such that it is; it also literalizes the presentiment of death that all narrative endings induce.[26] Camille and Jeremy die a cruel, meaningless death, so opposite Pandora's and Hendrick's joyous, meaningful one, and Maria's tragic, violent one. But all three films end at what Godard would call "a normal remove" from the events that unfold within them. What is "normal," though, about a remove that enables and is enabled by distanciating, auteurist conceits like Lewin's signature bell, Mankiewicz's signature voice-over ("My name is Harry Dawes. I go way back—back to when the movies had two dimensions, and one dimension, and sometimes no dimension at all"), and Godard's signature "silence"?

The Civilized Man . . . The Primitive Woman

> The asymmetry of the categories—male and female—is made manifest in the unilateral form of sexual myths. We sometimes say "the sex" to designate woman; she is the flesh, its delights and dangers. The truth that for woman man is sex and carnality has never been proclaimed because there is no one to proclaim it. Representation of the world, like the world itself, is the work of men; they describe it from their own point of view, which they confuse with absolute truth.
>
> SIMONE DE BEAUVOIR[27]

In their equivocal posture, engendered by concurrent aesthetic thrall and intellectual remove, it must be noted, Lewin, Mankiewicz, and Godard all remain deeply preoccupied with mythologies of the feminine. It is a problematic, and problematized, foregrounded figure of woman—mysterious, mystifying, impulsive, narcissistic, mercurial, and painfully beautiful to behold—that is the strongest common attribute of these three films. Indeed, you might say the classical cinema's consummate figure of the feminine, epitomized by Ava Gardner in the 1950s, is one of the primary "memories and hopes" that binds Godard's films to its predecessors as it pursues its work of mourning. "Brought up and hyper-cathected" by means of the casting of Brigitte Bardot, she is the basic source of *Contempt*'s libido attachment. Or, to use a slightly different diagnosis, it is this figure of woman that is held in contempt. For in psychoanalytic terms contempt is not really a looking down upon from above; it is a defense against overpowering desire, a turning away from what one wants but fears cannot be had, or may be lost, by demeaning it.[28]

This is why the character of Camille, embodied by Bardot, is so "mesmerizing."[29] She is really less a character than a vivid cipher for the contradictions of the film's attitude toward sex and gender. Geneviève Sellier has observed the same, and, relying on Andreas Huyssen, linked gender relationships in *Contempt* and Louis Malle's 1962 film, *Vie Privée (A Very Private Affair)* to the French auteur's ambivalence about art and culture, high and low:

> In *Vie Privée* and *Le Mépris*, the characters played by Bardot, ciphers both of "the feminine", are excluded from the world of male creativity. Both films distance and marginalize the popular, as manifested in forms that were most threatening to the auteurist as a vehicle of high, elite culture: forms incarnated in the figures of the French female star and the American producer. As Andreas Huyssen has noted, modernism conceals its envy of the popularity of mass culture under the guise of condescension and contempt.[30]

But if Godard's conflicts about high art and mass culture infect his perception of gender, and no doubt they do (the prostitution theme of *Contempt* has been sufficiently analyzed elsewhere), there is a much more primary problem in *Contempt*'s delineation of the feminine. As Sellier notes, Camille is represented as ignorant of and more or less uninterested in Paul's work and the larger artistic issues around it. She does not care what film they see or indeed whether they go to the movies at all. She is shown reading a book about Lang in the bathtub and looking at a book of images from Pompeii at Prokosch's villa, but in each context, she may be doing so defensively, to avoid discourse, and unlike the men around her, she never comments on art, literature, or film. Camille has no career (she had been a typist before her marriage), no evident ambitions or interests. Paul, on the other hand, has much to say about art, even if only to himself. From the vicissitudes of the echoes made by knocking on the breast and pubis of the hollow modern statue of a female figure in their Roman flat, to Dean Martin's sartorial style in *Some Came Running*,[31] to the proper inter-

Contempt: "The civilized man . . . the primitive woman."

pretation of Homer, art and culture are his active frame of reference. Camille's actions and interactions relative to art, in contrast, are gestural, bodily, and inarticulate. She doesn't explain that she is identifying with Ava Gardner or Anna Karina by putting on a dark wig, the way Paul explains donning a hat. She *is* a movie star. She doesn't pose as a goddess. She *is* a goddess. There is a stunning sense of immanence in her portrayal. As Sellier notes, "Bardot's mythical aura automatically links her to the film's other 'gods' . . . Godard, as ever, is both critic and advocate in *Le Mépris* of dominant modes of female representation. He analyses Bardot's iconic dimension, but always returns to her body, her sexuality."[32] Bardot's stature as goddess so thoroughly inhabits her body, is so exclusively linked to her sexuality, that she can only ever be, paradoxically, both icon and cipher of the eternal feminine.

This basic schema of masculine and feminine is, of course, rather routine. As Simone de Beauvoir thoroughly exposed, it governs representations of woman in Western culture generally. It is a facet of *Contempt* that Godard inherits, relatively unchanged, from the Alberto Moravia novel that he adapted. Godard, ironically, distanced himself from his source by holding it in contempt: "Moravia's novel is a nice, vulgar one for a train journey, full of classical, old fashioned sentiments in spite of the modernity of the situations. But it is with this kind of novel that one can often make the best films."[33] And certainly, whether or not this is a fair characterization of *Il Disprezzo* (I think it is not), Godard's adaptation is at some remove from the claustrophobic, unsettling interiority of Moravia's novel, which is narrated from within the confines of a writer's obsessive, almost delusional retrospection. Godard turns a fictional German movie director who is explicitly "not in the same class as the Pabsts and the Langs"[34] into Lang himself, and he switches the interpretive positions of director and writer:

in the novel Rheingold, the director, advocates the Freudian point of view, while Molteni, the writer, passionately adheres to an idealized view of Homeric simplicity. Marsha Kinder has considered *Contempt*'s levels of adaptation and the way Godard "chooses a story from a psychological novel and boldly strips it of its introspective analysis and focuses instead on the dramatic gestures and exterior signs."[35] But neither Kinder nor Godard himself seems quite cognizant that in the movement from interior to exterior, from psychological novel to art film, the mythology of the feminine is only reified.

"Like a Plant . . . She Never Wonders about Herself"

Emilia of Moravia's novel is a different physical "type" than Bardot's Camille — Sophia Loren would be better casting: she is dark and voluptuous, with large brown eyes, a severe, prominent nose, and a luminous smile. Riccardo Molteni, her husband and the novel's narrator, describes her with a kind of euphoric mystification. She is not "a woman who could understand and share my ideas, tastes and ambitions," he says, but rather beautiful, uncomplicated, simple, passionately domestic.[36] Molteni admits that she is in fact of normal or even small stature but that he perceives Emilia as "majestic," "massive," "powerful" in her beauty. "She had the most beautiful shoulders, the most beautiful arms, the most beautiful neck I had ever seen . . . an air of grace and of placid, unconscious, spontaneous majesty such as comes from nature alone and which, on that account, appears all the more mysterious and indefinable."[37] Emilia's sensual physical immanence and intellectual ineffability are the soul of Moravia's novel. Her husband's obsessive quest to understand the reason that she has stopped loving him can become the stuff of an entire novel because, his unreliability as a narrator notwithstanding, she is represented as so *essentially* mysterious. And she is not merely mysterious or unknowable in the existential way that all people could be said to be unknowable, ultimately, even, or especially, to those who love them; she is mysterious because of the mythic manner in which she is drawn.

The reasons for Emilia's contempt are obscure because she will not, or cannot, state them. Emilia is silent and withholding in a manner that in fact reflects expectations imposed upon her sex by her culture generally, and the topos of the novel in which she finds herself specifically. She is a construct of masculine obfuscation. What Sarah Kofman says of woman in Freud's writings is just as true in Moravia's (whose modernism was deeply influenced by psychoanalysis): "Because woman does not have the *right* to speak, she stops being *capable or desirous of speaking*; she 'keeps' everything to herself, and creates an excess of mystery and obscurity as if to avenge herself, as if striving for mastery. Woman lacks *sin-*

cerity: she dissimulates, transforms each word into an enigma, an indecipherable *riddle.*"[38] Riccardo Molteni's relentless investigation into his wife's "reasoning" is predicated on a notion of her nature as sexist as the analytic investigation, of which Kofman writes:

> Because the patient's "insincerity" not only is unconscious but also involves willfully holding back things she is perfectly well aware of, the analytic treatment cannot be seen as a simple restitution of women's right to speech; it is also an attempt to "tear" from them their secret, to make them "admit" or "confess"—in short, an attempt not to give them speech but to extort speech from them.[39]

Whether Kofman's narrative fairly describes the Freudian undertaking or not, it well characterizes *Il Disprezzo*'s myth of the feminine. Moravia and his narrator come close to recognizing that this feminine cipher is a fantasy. Near the end of the novel, Molteni realizes, with an epiphany, that Rheingold's psychological interpretation of Homer, for which the writer has had nothing but contempt (he has, in fact, held almost every character in the novel in contempt), in fact perfectly describes his relation to Emilia: "Ulysses is the civilized man, Penelope the primitive woman."[40] He suddenly recalls Emilia's accusation, "You're not a man" (significantly, Godard preserves this line) and jumps on it—contemptuously—as evidence of her conventional, even primitive, worldview. "The phrase itself, so sweeping, so slovenly in character, suggested that this ideal image had not arisen in Emilia's mind from a conscious experience of human values, but rather from the conventions of the world in which she had found herself living." "In fact," he continues, "Emilia despised me and wished to despise me because, in spite of her genuineness and simplicity, or rather just because of them, she was completely ensnared in the commonplaces of Battista's [Prokosch of the film] world."[41] Molteni proceeds to dwell on the contrast between the ideal, simple, concrete values of an ancient world that he believes his wife's natural disposition mirrors, and the complex, corrupt modern world:

> And, in order to have the Emilia I loved and to bring it about that she judged me for what I was, I should have to carry her away from the world in which she lived and introduce her into a world as simple as herself, as genuine as herself, a world in which money did not count and in which language had retained its integrity, a world—as Rheingold had pointed out to me—after which I could aspire, certainly, but which did not in fact exist.[42]

In recalling this last clause, attributed to Rheingold, Molteni seems almost to grasp that the Emilia of his perception is as unreal as the Homeric universe of his literary imagination, "which did not in fact exist." But trapped within the prison house of his narrator's neurosis, Moravia cannot offer even a hint of a less chimerical creature behind the misperception. According to Janice M. Kozma, who has studied Moravia's representation of women, this is not unique to *Il Disprezzo*. She details the ubiquity in Moravia's prose of metaphoric representations of women as plant, animal, and food, and the equation of femininity with the inexorability of death, the bestial rapaciousness of wild animals, and the pleasurable use value of fruit. "For Moravia it is only the man who lives, who is engaged by life and the quality of existence. Women are indeed the 'Other,' the contrast to living, breathing, functioning men." And, "for Moravia there is never the attribution of an intellectual life to his female characters; there is never a normal rapport that puts women on an equal basis with men . . . This provides the male characters with a convenient excuse simply to dismiss women as individuals, thus freeing themselves to go about the business of contemplating their own problems of existence."[43]

Godard, of course, does not and indeed cannot create so abstracted and unreal a figure of the feminine as this. The metaphors and mental images that are so prominent in Moravia's novel have little place in the film. With the exception of very limited voice-over, and some ambiguous flashbacks and flashforwards, no cinematic device is employed that might establish this extreme degree of subjectivity.[44] And the film's dependence on real bodies only permits so much unreality in a character (of course, Luis Buñuel found one way around this self-evident truth—precisely in order to throw into doubt the reality of the feminine object—by casting two women in one role in *That Obscure Object of Desire*). The use of Bardot, however, whose very body brings so much mythic and metaphoric baggage to the part, goes some way toward compensating for the cinema's concreteness. Godard need not find cinematic ways to engage metaphors of plant, animal, or food: they're part of the whole sex kitten package with Bardot, whose face alone for one contemporary of Godard's "simultaneously expresses the infantile and the feline" and whose "tiny roguish nose accentuates both her *gaminerie* and her animality; her fleshy lower lip is pursed into a baby's pout as often as into a provocation to be kissed."[45]

In fact, even prior to finding concrete expression in the form of Bardot, the quintessential *femme-enfant*, Godard's conception of Camille is every bit as Other, as immanent, and as metaphorical as Moravia's of Emilia, as his screenplay's written sketch of her reveals:

Calm as a sea of oil most of the time, even absentminded, Camille suddenly becomes stormy, by turns nervous, inexplicable.

Throughout the film we wonder what Camille is thinking about and, when she suddenly abandons her peculiar passive torpor and acts, this action is always as unpredictable and inexplicable as that of an automobile which, rolling along a fine straight road, suddenly jumps the curb and crashes into a tree. . . . in contrast to her husband, who always acts on the strength of a complicated series of rationalizations, Camille acts nonpsychologically, so to speak, by instinct — a sort of life instinct, like that of a plant that needs water in order to continue living. . . . Though one might wonder about her, as Paul does, she never wonders about herself. She lives full and simple sentiments, and cannot imagine being able to analyze them.[46]

Conceived in terms of metaphors — a sea of oil, a storm, a car wreck, a plant — from the outset of *Contempt*, Camille/Bardot is additionally subjected to another sort of trope that is as enduring, and in a sense even more impenetrable: she is removed from discourse, reduced to image under the aegis of art. As Harun Farocki notes of the famous opening bedroom scene, "Camille's body connotes 'art' more than 'sexuality'; the camera transforms it into a reclining sculpture."[47] In numerous other scenes Camille seems more icon or objet d'art than personage. Art objects placed in the scene (the female statuary in the Roman apartment and villa) signal this. Other artworks are invoked. In the set of flashbacks that are intercut with the long apartment scene, for instance, as Kaja Silverman has noted, there are a number of images in which Camille "offers herself to the look . . . in several of them Camille looks into a mirror. Here we have a very classical heterosexual tableau: the man loves the woman, and the woman loves herself through the man's love for her."[48] Whether such shots conjure Fragonard, Ingres, Manet, Picasso, or Matisse, they use the female body to insert the film into a larger narrative, that of the dominant tradition of Western image making — French painting in particular, which is something that Godard had been wont to do in his movies from the outset, perhaps with more irony, by means of more blatant signs, such as the reproductions of Renoir or Picasso that appear on apartment walls in *Breathless* or *Pierrot*. This art historical Godard, of course, returns with a vengeance in the 1980s with *Passion*, in which a film is being made from well-known art historical tableaus, including some of the female nude, such as Ingres's *The Bathers*. "Now the female body begins to be reconstituted as the prop of cinema," writes Laura Mulvey of *Passion*, which, it should be noted, is the only Godard film after *Contempt* to star Michel Piccoli, and which Godard explicitly contrasted with *Contempt*, claiming that the filmmaking in *Passion* should not be interpreted as anything "more than a metaphor, more than a representative for work on a piece of art . . . I am not making a film about filmmaking."[49]

Mulvey is the rare admirer of Godard who has permitted herself to undertake a rigorous feminist examination of his oeuvre. This author of one of feminist film theory's foundational essays ("Visual Pleasure and Narrative Cinema"), who described the reduction of woman to fetish in classical cinema so decisively, revealed the paradoxes of Godard's representations of women and sexuality in her 1980 discussion with Colin MacCabe. The wish to claim Godard for feminism, and the concomitant difficulty, is palpable:

> It is possible to argue that Godard's use of the image of the body is resolutely unexploitative. The length of the shots and the fact that the image of the body is not presented as spectacle makes us uneasy in our position of the voyeur. If we look at this woman's body then we are aware of our own look, which is not hidden in the folds of the narrative and the movement of the camera. . . . But although these arguments are valid they do not resolve the problem . . . the potency of that image is such that it is doubtful that any simple demystification is possible. To use that image is immediately to run the risk of introducing the discourse in which the enigma of woman will offer the truth of the male situation; to reveal the truth of the image is to risk the inevitable demand for a true voice to complete it.[50]

And of the problem of female subjectivity that arises from this analysis, Mulvey and MacCabe described Godard's film work in a way that paid due attention to what was radical in his work but also made the legacy of sexism that it inherits and preserves very clear:

> Godard makes an important attempt to depict woman from "inside," but this positioning always implies an "outside," an alternative, masculine point of view from which woman's threatening qualities predominate. Her image does not relate to women but is a phantasm of the male unconscious, familiar as the Romantic image of *La Belle dame sans merci* or as the heroine of the *film noir*. In *Pierrot le fou*, Marianne is the origin of violence. It is here that Godard views woman from outside in a fantasy based on fear and desire. She is mysterious, ultimately elusive, fascinating and destructive.[51]

Returning in the 1990s, still ambivalent, always again fascinated by Godard's representation of sex and gender, which had perhaps been affected by Godard's collaboration since the mid-1970s with Anne-Marie Miéville, Mulvey persisted in "trying to decode a deep-seated but interesting misogyny." She "came to think that Godard's cinema knows its own entrapment, and that it is still probing, struggling to give sounds and images to mythologies that haunt our culture. For feminist curiosity, it is still a gold mine."[52]

At the same time that Mulvey magnanimously gave Godard the benefit of a bit of feminist doubt, Godard in fact admitted his own "entrapment" and implicitly acknowledged the profound sexist biases of the cinematic tradition that he mourned and incorporated in *Contempt*—and also the importance of the image of Ava Gardner—when he described one of his *Histoire(s) du cinéma* episodes: "There's one I called '*Fatale Beauté*,' in remembrance of a film by Siodmak with Ava Gardner, called *The Great Sinner*, an adaptation of Dostoyevsky's *The Gambler*. The idea is that, for the most part, it's been men that have filmed women, and that's proved equally fatal to this [hi]story."[53]

Godard's reflections on Ava Gardner and the unilateral sexing of cinema bring us back to Maria D'Amata, the idol at whose graveside we began. This paradoxical character embodies so many of the contradictions of the feminine in classical cinema. As Cheryl Bray Lower correctly maintains, Mankiewicz was prescient in his lucid picture of the social and sexual hypocrisies of Hollywood, the jet set, the obsolescent nobility, and 1950s society in general. His was an almost subversive and proto-feminist critique. At the same time, though, his feminism is articulated through a narrative structure in which the female subject is dead before the story has begun. The only character who can say nothing about Maria D'Amata's tragic curriculum vitae is Maria herself. Her silence is even more inexorable than the enigmatic reticence of Camille Javal. We are left to understand Maria according to the subjective retrospection of the men who discovered, constructed, represented, and murdered her.

The Body of a Dead Animal

Among the first-rate, man's life is fame, woman's life is love. Woman is man's equal only when she makes her life a perpetual offering, as that of man's is perpetual action.

HONORÉ DE BALZAC[54]

Once you had the look for me of an exquisite lady. Now, I do not see that look. I only see that you have the body of an animal . . . a dead animal!

ALBERTO BRAVANO TO MARIA D'AMATA, *THE BAREFOOT CONTESSA*

About twenty minutes into Jacques Rivette's 1991 *La Belle Noiseuse*, a contemporary tale inspired by Balzac's *Le Chef-d'oeuvre inconnu*—and winner of the Grand Prix at Cannes—the renowned painter Edouard Frenhofer finally arrives, belatedly, in the garden of his chateau, where a small party of visitors awaits him. In that Frenhofer is played by Michel Piccoli, this moment induces a strange sort of recognition—a déjà vu, conjuring, as it does, the scene about twenty minutes into *Contempt* in which Paul Javal, also played by Piccoli, arrives late at Prokosch's villa, after the meeting at Cinecittà. Nearly thirty years later, Piccoli now plays the Lang part—the role of the old master—in a story that resonates with echoes of *Contempt*. Actually, one might say that *Contempt* is to *La Belle Noiseuse* what *Pandora and the Flying Dutchman* and *The Barefoot Contessa* were to *Contempt:* it is a profoundly cathected, vaguely ambivalent, anxious but cherished object of memory and influence—integrated, echoed, rewritten. But we shall return to that larger frame; we left Frenhofer's visitors in the garden: an art collector friend, Balthazar Porbus (Gilles Arbona); an ambitious young painter and fervent admirer of Frenhofer's, Nicolas (David Bursztein); and Nicolas's beautiful, capricious girlfriend, Marianne (Emmanuelle Béart). Waiting with them, apologetically, is Frenhofer's wife, Liz (Jane Birkin).

Piccoli is late this time, it soon becomes clear, because his character, Frenhofer, lives in a strange sort of timeless world, or at least one in which time is less structured than most.[55] He arrives carrying a trussed box and a dead hare, and discovering his visitors, asks, rather perplexed, what day it is and then apologizes for having forgotten them. After introductions and a brief rest, he rises to lead the visitors to his studio, which he has promised to show them. Marianne holds Nicolas back for a moment and expresses foreboding: "Something strange is going on," she insists.

The dead animal is one of a number of seemingly naturalistic, unexplained details in this long, absorbing, estimable, and very problematic film that retrospectively becomes meaningful. Marianne is right to be unsettled. The dead hare can be understood, in light of what unfolds in *La Belle Noiseuse,* as an image of the female object of desire, or rather what becomes of this object when she becomes the object of art. The dead animal is an image of the relationship between the painter and his model/muse: between Frenhofer and Liz. Liz's avocation is taxidermy (her avowed vocation is living with Frenhofer). She lovingly restores and preserves the bodies of dead animals. Taxidermy is an obvious analogy for painting—trying to "fix" the living image using inanimate material—but as metaphor it also imputes a kind of magic to the mimetic act, which by capturing the subject kills it.[56]

Liz, then, as the primary model for Frenhofer's unknown masterpiece, identifies with the dead animals she preserves. Late in the film she tells her husband that she sneaked into his studio at night and saw him asleep. "I thought you were dead," she confesses, adding obscurely, "and me, too." Frenhofer has killed her, it is implied, in trying to fix her in his painting, *La Belle Noiseuse.* This animal metaphor is certainly enlivened by what we see of his preliminary efforts on the painting. One canvas that Frenhofer brings out to paint over was obviously an early version, or a false start. It is a large sketch of Liz's serpentine figure. Only the face and the hands have been worked out. The face is recognizable, intense, and relatively naturalistic. The hands are executed in a more expressionist vernacular; they are attenuated and blood red—more like talons or claws than human hands. Frenhofer, meanwhile, speaks of the violence of the artistic process. He warns about love's jealousy of art and vice versa. He says of his unfinished "masterpiece," which almost destroyed his relationship with Liz, "you see blood."

Marianne is offered to Frenhofer as a surrogate. Nicolas, in what he comes to fear was a kind of Faustian bargain, volunteers her without consulting her. She is a sacrifice, given so the master can revive work on his dormant masterpiece, which Nicolas desperately wishes to see and which has been put away, untouched and unseen for ten years as Frenhofer and Liz have aged (the actors' ages are about sixty-five and forty-five, respectively, to Béart's twenty-five). The couple seems to have been recovering from the havoc the painting wreaked in their relationship; it is suggested that they barely survived it, emerging scarred into their current limbo—an uneasy calm. Now again, Frenhofer will have a living animal, Marianne, in his studio. Liz envies her but also fears for her. She too may "die" in offering herself up as a sacrifice to art. When Frenhofer poses Marianne he is, as she says, like a cat stalking a bird; he speaks of "crushing" her, as if she were a bug, and "breaking" her, as if she were a wild animal. And she is like a wild animal—with her long mane, her bright eyes, and her bare feet (she arrives at the Chateau carrying her shoes in her hand): fiery, beautiful, and unpredictable. Liz, too, is animal like, if now somewhat tame. She is lean, sinewy, and high strung, also generally barefooted (an attribute of femininity that recalls the imagery of barefootedness in *Contempt* and its progenitors, *Pandora* and *The Barefoot Contessa*); her long hair is unkempt, her expression rather like that of a frightened doe. Frenho (as Liz calls him), Nicolas, and Porbus, it should be noted, are always seen neatly and presentably dressed and shod. The master may have a slumbering Minotaur inside him, but his tail is always neatly tucked in.[57] These are civilized men . . . and primitive women. The analogy between woman and animal is drawn in manifold ways.

Marianne is furious when Nicolas tells her that she has been offered as a model. Although she hung back during the studio visit, showing disinterest in the master's work, she has seen enough to know that Frenhofer paints nudes. "You sold my ass!" she charges, quite correctly. "Deliberately, and bluntly," as Thomas Elsaesser puts it, "*La Belle Noiseuse* parades a world of men who enter into a kind of bargain or exchange whose object is a woman: not only is the young painter's girlfriend offered as a bait or gift, she is also intended to substitute for Frenhofer's wife."[58] The parallel to *Contempt* is very clear. Indeed, Marianne's visage displays an expression of betrayal and dismay that is a poignant echo of Camille's. So, too, is the contempt that arises in her from this betrayal. But while Camille's wound was always inarticulate—it was left to the film narration to signal the moment of exchange as significant—Marianne's is not only articulate ("you sold my ass!"), it is fierce. If Camille as embodied by Bardot was a *femme-enfant*, a sort of domestic animal (a baby animal, a sex kitten), Marianne, as embodied by Béart is a *beau-monstre*, a wild animal. Perhaps there are strains of *Pierrot le fou* in this agon, too. Substitute Rivette—or Frenhofer—for Godard in this sentence, and you'd have no problem believing it was written about Béart's "character" in *La Belle Noiseuse:* "Marianne is the origin of violence. It is here that Godard views woman from outside in a fantasy based on fear and desire. She is mysterious, ultimately elusive, fascinating and destructive."[59]

This mysterious, elusive, fascinating, and destructive creature inexplicably honors the bargain. She expresses a suspicion and distaste for the old painter but then seems to charge into a naked emotional and physical prostration as his model as though it were fated, and perhaps also to spite Nicolas—to force him to regret the agreement he made at her expense and, she believes, at the expense of their love. Again, here are echoes of *Contempt,* in which Camille seemed to stage the kiss with Prokosch so that Paul would witness it and see the results of his casual proffering of her company—the destruction of their marriage, the loss of her love and her fidelity. On her second day of modeling, after hours of posing, Marianne begins to reject being forced by Frenhofer into painfully unnatural, rather expressionist poses (in plainly sadomasochistic passages, he bends, pushes and strains her naked body into postures reminiscent of Rodin) and begins to adopt poses "instinctively." She speaks, angrily and in a rather stream-of-consciousness mode, about painful memories and flings herself moodily about on the floor. As she *exposes* herself—emotionally and physically—she becomes even more feral. She sees Frenhofer's mounting excitement and imputes predatory, sexual designs. You're like a cat with a bird, she says—glowering. She scorns Nicolas, too, who she says knowingly "blew it" when he volunteered her services. She folds her knees under her and puts her head and arms down (very Rodinesque); thrusting her formidable rear end toward Frenhofer, who is manifestly inspired by this exposure. "Continue!" he commands. "Continue what?" she asks. "I'm telling you my life's coming to a stop. Everything is over between Nicolas and me . . . He's the only man I could live with. Others . . . I spit in their faces . . . including you!" "What violence!" Frenhofer comments, disconcerted, yet intrigued.

Rivette's film—like a Gothic tale in realist garb—elegantly smoothes over the striking anachronisms of such nakedly gendered myth, as well as concomitant artistic ones. In the contemporary art world, the struggle portrayed to find Truth (transcendent or base) in art (mimetic, abstract, or conceptual), especially through the rendering of the female nude, would seem retrogressive or quaint. Sidney Peterson, who in the late 1940s made *Mr. Frenhofer and the Minotaur*—his own avant-garde and very tongue-in-cheek film version of *Chef d'oeuvre inconnu*—mocked Balzac's romantic pretensions and "the mixed triviality and even mawkish sentimentality of [his] somewhat Hollywoodian approach to the subject of a quest for the absolute."[60] But *La Belle Noiseuse* conjures these romantic notions with little irony and considerable sympathy, offering them up on the prostrate female form. It is nonetheless a compelling, paradoxically realist dramatic film, with classical camerawork and mise-en-scène; a remarkably intelligent script, written with Pascal Bonitzer and Christine Laurent; subtle, convincing performances; a musical, contemplative rhythm; absorbingly textural image and sound, with drawings and paintings emerging in almost real time to the sound of rustling paper, scratching pens, and the oceanic murmur of distant cicadas in a setting both beautiful and timeless.[61] A quarter of a century beyond *Pierrot*, almost thirty years after *Contempt*, and more than forty years after Peterson's rather parodic experimental film, *La Belle Noiseuse* turns back the clock even further: to a time long before "television sets and flashy cars." For although it is set in the present, little other than the wardrobe and fleeting shots of the arrival of Porbus's red sports car at Nicolas's and Marianne's hotel at the beginning of the film and Julienne's blue jeep at the Chateau near the end signal its contemporaneity. The story unfolds as if in a parallel universe—one that is wholly consistent with its nineteenth-century source.

While Godard used the contrast between ancient and modern dialectically as a thematic trope in *Contempt*, Rivette resolves the difference, or perhaps denies it, by setting his story in a place that is antique-modern, a slightly dilapidated eighteenth-century provincial estate, the Chateau d'Assas, just north of Montpellier in southern France. This edifice, attributed to Jean-Antoine Giral, the Languedoc's most prominent architect of the period, was built on the ruins of, and to an extent incorporates, earlier structures, going back to the Middle Ages, but it also, clearly, has been used and adapted in the twentieth century and makes an atmospheric and believable setting for Rivette's film. One knows that eminent modern artists, such as Picasso and Balthus—of the type and stature we must imagine the fictional Frenhofer to be—occupied comparable estates in their later years. Rivette, then, displaces or avoids the "world of television sets and flashy cars" that Godard confronted with Lang's "gods in exile" (to borrow from Heine), though there is explicit mention in *La Belle Noiseuse* of Porbus's red sports car. Liz asks him if it's true that drivers of red cars pay higher insurance—another detail that seems to invoke *Contempt*, in which, of course, red is the color of Prokosch's fatal roadster.

As with *Contempt*, *La Belle Noiseuse* is "almost an essay on portraiture, roleplaying, acting."[62] But in both films the male performers are clothed—literally and figuratively—in layers of performativity. In *Contempt* Piccoli plays Paul Javal, but he also plays Odysseus analogically, plays at playing Dean Martin in *Some Came Running*, and plays Jean-Luc Godard; apparently Piccoli was asked by the director to wear his (Godard's) tie, hat, and shoes.[63] Similarly in *La Belle Noiseuse*, Piccoli plays Edouard Frenhofer, but he also plays Picasso, as well as Bernard Dufour, the artist who actually executed the works for the film, and, of course, he plays Jacques Rivette. Anne-Marie Faux has described these levels of portrayal as *emboitement* and contemplated the metacinematic implications of portrayal in *La Belle Noiseuse*. She also raises the question of what happens to the project of portrayal when the acting body is stripped bare, as Béart's is for much of the film. Nakedness conflates performer and character. The bitter memories and inchoate fears exposed in the modeling scenes may not, in fact, be Emmanuelle Béart's, but those certainly are her breasts and buttocks. The body ceases to be a rhetorical device and collapses into itself. The ineluctable flesh simultaneously reregisters the figure from that fictional character to this corporeal entity and, paradoxically, reconjures the specter of myth.

For the role of the model/muse has always already been written and Rivette inherits along with her body a history, a mythology, and a rhetoric. Just as Godard's ironic distancing of his film from its literary source only obscured the extent to which it shared Moravia's profound sexism, Rivette's (and Bonitzer's and Laurent's) rather considerable modifications of Balzac's narrative do not obviate the legacy that comes down to us through Dufour from Picasso (and Rodin, Manet, Courbet, and Ingres . . .) from the culture in which *Le Chef-d'oeuvre inconnu* was conceived.

"There's a Woman under There!"

It's ten years now, young man, that I've been struggling with this problem. But what are ten short years when you're contending with nature? How long did Lord Pygmalion take to create the only statue that ever walked!
FRENHOFER TO POUSSIN IN *LE CHEF-D'OEUVRE INCONNU*[64]

As Dore Ashton has observed, "Balzac's fable, or his inspiring myth, remains alive for modern art because, as Valéry intoned, 'In the beginning was the Fable!' He concurred with Balzac's view of a world without laws of time and space, the world invented by eccentric geniuses such as Frenhofer, abstract to the verge of mystery. . . . Frenhofer is the archetypal modern artist, existing in a constant state of anxiety, plagued by metaphysical doubt."[65] Ashton thoroughly grasps the ego ideal that a figure like Frenhofer constitutes for a modern (male) artist. She does not acknowledge, however, the extent to which the anxiety and doubt that attend him are attached to that inevitable object of his desire, contempt, and art: the female body, especially, the model. As Alexandra K. Wettlaufer has summarized in an excellent study of the thematization of art in postrevolutionary French literature, Balzac's narrative was one of a number that articulated the tensions and vicissitudes of art, sex, and commerce against a shifting cultural, industrial, and socioeconomic field.

The model's body represented the confluence of sex, desire, art and money, and as such became a loaded symbol for the myriad anxieties surrounding art and representation for both creators and consumers in nineteenth-century France. The metaphor of prostitution, so closely tied to the iconic figure of the model, was also increasingly applied to the artist's own activity, as he sold his body of work to the highest bidder. The bourgeoisie's ambivalence toward artists and their world—one part fascination, one part repulsion—was echoed by the artists' own hostility toward the audience upon whom they relied, as the laws of the marketplace asserted their forces upon creative production. The commodification of art and the commodification of sex . . . generated parallel dislocations and malaise as the once elevated spheres of love and art became equated with money.[66]

Rivette's scenario preserves Balzac's anxiety about art and commerce. These problems did not end with the nineteenth century. Just as there is a convoluted and barely suppressed discourse on art, commerce, integrity, and prostitution in *Contempt,* so is there, then, in *La Belle Noiseuse.* As with Camille's inarticulate response to Paul's acceptance of the $10,000 script job, which is structurally connected to her reaction to being pushed into Prokosch's car, Marianne seems to fear that her husband's first solo exhibition and chance for commercial success is potentially corrupting and links it to his proffering of her services. This adds another valence of signification to the overdetermined image of the model. Even, or especially, when it shouts "art," it also quietly whispers "prostitution," and this is as true of the twentieth-century nude as the nineteenth.[67]

Certainly what Wettlaufer observes of Balzac's assumptions—that the "metaphysics of art and the formulations of genius during this period embraced the ideological associations of woman-nature-body and man-culture-mind"— is equally true of these classic, esteemed art films.[68] Not only at the height of the Nouvelle Vague, at a time when many films adhered to an unexamined sexism, but still, at the "postfeminist" end of the twentieth century, they reiterate a mythic representation of femininity—of woman as muse—linking her to art history and place. The beauteous Bardot and Béart embody a pernicious notion of the feminine that is enigmatic, narcissistic, immanent, and explicitly linked to nature, verging on bestial. Their bodies are art: glorified and exalted, but at the same time, as flesh, despised as corrupt.

Such notions of femininity find their most concrete expression in *La Belle Noiseuse*'s paintings. This is somewhat ironic because a key conceit of the film is that the finished work is not shown. Of Frenhofer's supposed oeuvre in the film, we see the following: older paintings and drawings scattered about the house and studio; the unfinished canvas that dates to the artist's original work on *La Belle Noiseuse* some ten years earlier and, painted over it, the beginnings of a new version, also abandoned (Frenhofer makes a slashing red "X" across it); numerous sketches and studies made from Béart's actual poses; and a "faked" masterpiece. The unknown masterpiece remains unknown. As Thomas Elsaesser puts it, "Frenhofer, coolly and methodically, fakes himself by hiding his *La Belle Noiseuse* forever, while passing off a painting quickly daubed during one late-night session as the fruit of ten years' creative agony."[69] We only see enough of the "authentic" masterpiece—a vivid red corner ("you see blood") peeking out from a drop cloth as Frenhofer bricks it up in a wall (à la Poe)—to be sure when we see the blue nude that Frenhofer presents to his eager audience the next day that it is, in fact, nothing like *La Belle Noiseuse.*

Rivette's ending is one of his film's most dramatic divergences from Balzac's novella, in which the revelation of Frenhofer's unknown masterpiece is probably its most influential passage:

> "The old fraud's pulling our leg," Poussin murmured, returning to face the so-called painting. "All I see are colors daubed one on top of the other and contained by a mass of strange lines forming a wall of paint."
>
> "We must be missing something," Porbus insisted.
>
> Coming closer, they discerned, in one corner of the canvas, the tip of a bare foot emerging from the chaos of colors, shapes, and vague shadings, a kind of incoherent mist; but a delightful foot, a living foot! They stood stock-still with admiration before this fragment which had escaped from an incredible, slow, and advancing destruction. That foot appeared there like the torso of some Parian marble Venus rising out of the ruins of a city burned to ashes.
>
> "There's a woman under there!" Porbus cried.[70]

The "incredible, slow, and advancing destruction" is, in Balzac's moral, the accretion of years and years of obsessive endeavor and doubt, a congenital disease of the artist who will perfectly capture nature, the supposed aspiration of the Renaissance and Baroque painters whose milieu Balzac conjured. But for modern artists, this passage is thrilling for the way it anticipates a modernist canvas (one can't dismiss the possibility that the image evoked of a woman buried in paint held a certain erotic charge, too). For Picasso, or Wassily Kandinsky, André Masson, or Jackson Pollock, a "mass of strange lines," a "wall of paint," a "chaos of colors, shapes and vague shadings," or the "ruins of a city burned to ashes" are words that suggest sublime modern paintings. Paul Cézanne—as close to the "ideal" of a real Frenhofer as such modern painters knew—himself identified proudly and painfully with Balzac's legendary master precisely, one suspects, because of the deforming effect grandiose ambition and profound doubt had on the project of transforming the spatial and tangible world into flat images.[71]

But Rivette's moral is wholly other. The "truth" his Frenhofer will reveal through his mastery of the medium is not the perfect mimetic reflection of nature that Balzac's protagonist sought. It seems to be some "truth" of character, a baring, or reflection of the subject's very soul. We know this from the dialogue—it is implied that Frenhofer's sadistic "breaking" of the body is in order to expose what is within (like cracking an egg?); moreover, we know it from Marianne's reaction to Frenhofer's painting. For, although the viewer never sees the finished *Noiseuse,* three characters in addition to Frenhofer do, all women: Marianne, Liz, and Magali, the cook's teenaged daughter, who secretly assists the painter in its ultimate interment. Marianne is stunned and speechless upon viewing it, and flees the studio. Then she is shown locked in the bathroom looking half hysterically at her reflection, tormented. Later, she confesses that she saw something terrible about herself in the painting, something "hard and cold." Liz, too, sees something frightening; she sneaks into the studio and looks at the work, marking its verso with a black cross before slipping away.

The viewer need not see the horrifying image, though, to know more or less what it is. We were shown the new pose that Frenhofer settled upon before executing it. Marianne stood back to the painter, turning to look over her shoulder at him, fiercely, one hand raised, turned toward us and tensed (as per his manipulation), claw-like, as if to scratch. If we add to this image what we earlier saw of the incipient Liz version of *La Belle Noiseuse*—in which her hands were like bloody talons, and the evidence of the blood-red corner of the finished masterpiece of which we caught a fleeting glimpse—it is not too difficult to imagine the voluptuous bloody animal that Frenhofer made of his model.

The "faked" masterwork that he passes off on Nicolas and Porbus the next day—to the evident surprise and relief of both Liz and Marianne—makes an interesting comparison to the unseen painting. It is based on sketches of the rather self-abasing pose that Frenhofer had earlier pursued—in which Marianne knelt on the floor, her legs folded under her, her head lower than her resplendent rump. In the painting, which, in contrast to the bloody entombed *Noiseuse,* is of an overall blue, the figure is rather minimally rendered with vigorous contour. Its most striking features are the prominence of the buttocks and the absence of a head. The acephalic figure becomes ambiguous. Indeed, this "partial figure" looks very much like a phallus and testicles (an effect achieved in a number of surrealist images and objects, including photographs by Man Ray and Brassaï, as well as in Louise Bourgeois's audacious fetish sculpture, *Fillette*).[72] There is perhaps no more eloquent expression of fetishism. The female body, viewed from the very angle that points to her lack, is dehumanized and turned into the phallus itself.

Bernard Dufour (b. 1922), the painter who executed the Frenhofer works for the film, is a specialist in the female nude. If not a household name, he has been

It's my first posthumous work.

La Belle Noiseuse (Jacques Rivette, 1991): Michel Piccoli as Frenhofer presents the image of woman as fetish (painted by Bernard Dufour) that stands in for the absent "unknown masterpiece," as a fetish stands in for the absent phallus in psychosexual terms.

a prolific and esteemed figure in French contemporary art for over forty years, and is a prominent illustrator of books. He achieved his greatest exposure and attention in the very years Rivette and the French New Wave did, exhibiting frequently in late 1950s and early 1960s. His work was featured in major international exhibitions, such as Documenta II (Kassel 1959) and in the French pavilion at the Venice Biennale of 1964. His recent work in graphic art, painting, and photography concentrates on the graphic rendering of the female genitalia, often in compositions that minimize or exclude the head and face.[73] So, the nudes in the film are more or less typical of his oeuvre, although the portrait-like element of Liz's face is unusual, distracting as it does from the emphasis on the sexual function of the female body.

Together, the two works that are completed at film's end—visible and invisible—bespeak the truth that Frenhofer seeks in painting. But Marianne is wrong, of course, to see *La Belle Noiseuse*, or for that matter its beheaded surrogate, as having anything to do with her "self." The truth of *La Belle Noiseuse* is what it reveals about the eternal feminine object of the master's artistic imagination, a fantasized object of vicious beauty, castrating tenderness and mortal animal flesh . . . the body of a dead animal. What is "cold and hard" is not Marianne's soul but the surrogate painting, which — reducing woman to her sexual parts — reveals the hard, cold comfort of a fetish, inspired by angst. The unknown masterpiece and its contents, then, had been foreshadowed in the scene that introduced Frenhofer, in which he arrived belatedly in the garden, bearing a trussed box (the unknown) and a dead hare (the masterpiece). Near the end of *La Belle Noiseuse*, lying together in bed, Frenhofer and Liz speak of death — the figurative death that is their life together and the literal death to which they can look ahead. "I'd like to know," the old man wonders, "what remains dead and cannot be restored." "Everything," answers Liz. What she means is everything, except that which was always already dead and yet can never die, the ambivalent image of the eternal feminine, "the wound of the world."[74]

CHAPTER 5

Out of Her Element

"Talk about beauty and the beast . . . she's both."
RYAN TO DECKARD, *BLADE RUNNER*

The image of woman that emerged symptomatically on the incomplete and unseen canvases of Jacques Rivette's *La Belle Noiseuse* was that of what Barbara Creed has called the monstrous-feminine, of "what about woman that is shocking, terrifying, horrific, abject."[1] Rivette's classic art film, with its nineteenth-century literary source, its contemplative durée, its impressionist scenes of plein air meals in the placid summer landscape of the Languedoc, and its long hard look at artistic facture, does not look like a horror film of the sort that interests Creed. Such films rarely win the Grand Prix at Cannes. But just below its civilized façade, *La Belle Noiseuse* is both Gothic and horror, invoking a dark world of barely suppressed angst worthy of Poe, Tourneur, or Cronenberg. So do the films that are the subject of this chapter defy generic expectations to reveal a very similar mythology of the feminine as Other. These two commercial narrative films of the 1980s, *Splash* (Ron Howard, 1984) and *Children of a Lesser God* (Randa Haines, 1986), are both centered upon romance, but *Splash* is a romantic comedy and a fantasy (or fable) and *Children of a Lesser God* is a "message picture," a contemporary melodrama.

The monstrous-feminine that emerges from these films is the mermaid, literal (*Splash*) and figural (*Children of a Lesser God*). The mermaid, unlike the specters of horror in Creed's analysis, is one of Western culture's most enduring and ambivalent images. Beautiful and monstrous, seductive and deadly, she stands at once for woman's indissoluble association with nature and for the supernatural forces of myth. Hybrid sea figures are elements of myth and visual culture throughout recorded history and around the world. In Western culture, representations associating woman with water date back to antiquity and include the birth of Venus; watery mythological hybrids such as sirens, naiads, and nymphs; Rhine maidens, the legendary Mélusine; and the Lorelei. In modern culture the mermaid's prominence seems to ebb and wane, and to be linked to shifting ideas about femininity. Her longest vogue (or *vague?*) was in the last quarter of the nineteenth century and into the first years of the twentieth. Certainly, the publication of modernity's best-loved mermaid tale, Hans Christian Andersen's *Little Mermaid,* in 1837 set the stage for myriad nineteenth-century mermaid images.

But the visual fascination around the mermaid derived from rather more decadent sources than Andersen. Countless fin-de-siècle images—by Pre-Raphaelites, symbolists, and others (including Edward Burne-Jones, Arnold Böcklin, Edvard Munch, Gustav Klimt)—gave form to this seductive icon of decadence, perversion, irrationality, and fatality. The surrealists, especially the Belgian among them—René Magritte, and Paul Delvaux—occasionally pursued the symbolist fascination with the psychosexually loaded image, but from World War I to World War II, the mermaid image faded somewhat, reemerging with a splash after the end of World War II. In 1948, two mermaid movies appeared more or less simultaneously: in Britain, *Miranda* (directed by Ken Annakin, with Glynis Johns), and in the United States, *Mr. Peabody and the Mermaid* (directed by Irving Pichel, with William Powell and Ann Blyth).[2]

It is tempting to see the periodic reemergence of mermaids—symbolizing as they must cultural anxieties about nature and femininity—as symptomatic of cultural flux. Certainly each wave is characterized by its era's own spirit and troubles. The 1948 movie mermaid is not nearly so perverse or fatal as the fin-de-siècle creature, but she clearly expresses a desire to see women back in their "natural" element. Susan White has described *Mr. Peabody* in just such symptomatic terms, as one of "numerous post–World War II Hollywood products that express anxiety about the possibility of male fallibility and female independence."[3]

The 1980s produced not only the literal and figural mermaids of *Splash* and *Children of a Lesser God,* but also, by decade's end, Disney's phenomenally successful *The Little Mermaid* (1989), the subject of considerable scholarly focus, including excellent psychoanalytically oriented investigations by Susan White, Lauren Dundes, and Alan Dundes.[4] It was in that same decade that Teresa de Lauretis noted significant flux in both culture at large and popular cinema, suggesting that "it is not by chance that all the nature-culture thresholds are being thematized and transgressed in recent movies: incest, life/death (vampires, zombies, and other living dead), human/non-human (aliens, clones, demon seeds, pods, fogs, etc.), and sexual difference (androgyns, transsexuals, transvestites, or transylvanians). Boundaries are very much in question, and the old rites of passage no longer avail."[5] Like Creed, de Lauretis referred to the genres of extremity, that is, horror and science fiction. But in the two mainstream films of more neutral generic pedigree that I am concerned with—essentially comedy and drama—nature-culture thresholds are thematized and transgressed no less vividly. Instead of vampires, zombies, aliens, clones, transsexuals, or transylvanians, *Splash* and *Children of a Lesser God* offer mermaids. In each case a kind of subgeneric twist permits this: *Splash* is a comedy and a fantasy (veritable mermaid), while *Children of a Lesser God* is a drama and a message picture (figurative mermaid).

Both films employ obscurely anachronistic devices related to their subgenres (fantasy and message picture). And these devices serve both to reveal (*Splash*) and disguise (*Children*) the meanings that inhere in the films' narrative and iconography. So, while superficially *Splash* seems to revel in puerile humor and sexual objectification, and the rather more serious *Children of a Lesser God*, adapted from a successful stage play by Mark Medoff, appears to plead for recognition of female subjectivity, close analysis of each film's structure reveals that *Splash* raises more questions about the representation of woman as Other than does *Children of a Lesser God*, which never escapes from its own phallocentric terms.

Immersion and Immanence: The Watery World of Woman

> Over and over again: the women-in-the-water; woman as water, as a stormy, cavorting, cooling ocean, a raging stream, a waterfall; as a limitless body of water that ships pass through, with tributaries, pools, surfs and deltas; woman as the enticing (or perilous) deep, as a cup of bubbling body fluids; the vagina as wave, as foam, as a dark place ringed with Pacific ridges; love as the collision of two waves, as a sea voyage, a slow ebbing, a fish-catch, a storm.
> KLAUS THEWELEIT, *MALE FANTASIES*[6]

As Klaus Theweleit effectively invokes in this compendium of metaphors, conventions that link femininity to fluid are as familiar as background noise. The watery woman and the underwater woman are expressions of an idea of femininity as immanent, as part of nature and nature's processes, as organically fluid and sensually immersed (and immersing). Female fluidity is associated with all aspects of her mystique, from her presumed sensuality to her narcissism, moodiness, and fatality. *Splash*'s Madison (Daryl Hannah), a certifiable mermaid, and *Children of a Lesser God*'s Sarah (Marlee Matlin), not a mermaid, but a deaf woman who is most truly "herself" when "sensually lost in her own silent world as she swims,"[7] then, have a common genealogy. But what is the epistemological source of these metaphors and these images?

The Fall: Man's Secret Desire

> Nor shall I ever forget the instance of the young homosexual with an indis-
> soluble fixation upon his mother, who in adolescence lay on the bottom of a
> bathtub filled with warm water and in order to be able to maintain this archaic
> aquatic status or foetal situation breathed through a long tube protruding from
> the water which he held in his mouth.
>
> SANDOR FERENCZI, *THALASSA*[8]

As Sandor Ferenczi's vivid recollection suggests, psychoanalysis offers one answer to the question of the meaning of the mermaid (and other female figures
associated with water): she represents the Mother in the most primitive sense,
and water represents the embracing amniotic fluid of the womb. Thus, Freud
finds that

> birth is regularly expressed in dreams by some connection with water: one falls
> into the water or one comes out of the water—one gives birth or one is born.
> . . . In myths a person who rescues a baby from the water is admitting that she
> is the baby's true mother. There is a well-known comic anecdote according to
> which an intelligent Jewish boy was asked who the mother of Moses was. He
> replied without hesitation: "The Princess." "No," he was told, "she only took
> him out of the water." "That's what she says," he replied, and so proved that he
> had found the correct interpretation of the myth.[9]

This interpretation, proposed by Freud and expanded into an ambitious phylogenetic theory by Ferenczi in his *Thalassa*, casts light on both *Splash* and *Children
of a Lesser God*. In each the male protagonist's romance is initiated by his falling
into the water and into the arms of the woman. In neither instance, however, is
the fall strictly speaking accidental.

In the first scene of *Splash*, Allen Bauer, an eight-year-old child, enigmati-
cally but quite deliberately throws himself off a pleasure boat into the ocean near
Cape Cod and is rescued by little Madison, the mermaid. Time seems suspended
as the two touch; Allen suddenly need not struggle for breath and an almost
mystical bliss surrounds him. The entire narrative of *Splash* unfolds from this
event; after he is rescued, the story jumps ahead twenty years and reveals that
as an adult, Allen (Tom Hanks) suffers from romantic dysfunction, a pervasive
nostalgia, and uncanny reminiscences clearly related to the "primal scene" of
twenty years earlier.

In *Children of a Lesser God*, a less fabulous scenario is introduced by James's
(William Hurt) fall into water. Pursuing "the most mysterious, beautiful, an-
gry" Sarah to the edge of a pool where she is swimming, he falls in the water

while attempting, in sign language, to tell her that he is falling in love with her. The obvious metaphorical analogy between falling in water and falling in love is reinforced in the scene by James's and Sarah's ensuing underwater lovemaking, which seems to be facilitated, rather than impeded, by their subaqueous environment (don't they have to breathe?).

Whereas Freud recognizes the prenatal fluid of the mother's womb as the predominant source of such symbolism,[10] Ferenczi, in *Thalassa*, explores the more esoteric possibility alluded to by Freud: that man, as evolved from a once aquatic creature, retains a phylogenetic memory of water-bound existence and that our experiences and notions of birth, death, and coitus are all linked to the traumatic rupture necessitated by the recession of waters and subsequent adaptation to dry land:

> The interpretation of being rescued from water or of swimming in water as a representation of birth and as representation of coitus . . . which is current in psychoanalysis, demands therefore a phylogenetic interpretation in addition; falling into the water would again be the more archaic symbol, that of the return to the uterus, while in rescue from water the birth *motif* or that of exile to a land existence seems to be emphasized.[11]

The merits of Ferenczi's theory are less the issue here than the telling association he observes between birth and coitus imagery, particularly as these are involved with water, and the concomitant relationship to notions of motherhood.[12] It is perhaps this association that infuses the underwater scenes with a magical sort of eroticism and poignancy.

Splash is almost explicit in its suggestion that Allen's romantic ennui is symptomatic of a repressed pre-Oedipal fantasy and that his romance with a mermaid is an enactment of that fantasy. The underwater scenes are tender, mellifluous, amniotic idylls, sensitively photographed and scored. The mermaid, with a monolithic tail instead of two legs, is of course a thinly veiled symbol of the phallic mother. Such an interpretation is kept barely subliminal in *Splash* through a clinically manifold set of male characters, each of whom has his own solution to the problem raised by "lack." Whereas Allen's solution is theoretically (but not textually or cinematically) impossible—that is, the actual acquisition of the phallic mother in the form of a fetishized woman who, at least in her primary form, does not lack, and an almost literal return to the womb—the more clinically plausible scenarios are offered by the film's comedic sidekicks, the characters of Freddie (John Candy), Allen's brother, and Dr. Kornbluth (Eugene Levy), the obsessed scientist.

Freddie, already a voyeur at ten, in adulthood is an avid consumer of porn magazines and skin flicks. This and his constant attempts to look up women's skirts suggest a scopophilic perversion and hint at fetishism, too (in that what one sees, presumably, when looking up a woman's skirt, is not her genitals but her underwear). Dr. Kornbluth, were he not a bumbling incompetent, would be a case study in sublimation, his infantile fantasy having been transformed into scientific curiosity. In that his unrelenting search for evidence of mermaids is seen as ridiculous, too, there is a degree of delusional neurosis represented in his character, not unlike that of Dr. Norbert Hanold, the deluded archaeologist of Wilhelm Jensen's *Gradiva*, the subject of Freud's *Delusion and Dream*.[13] That Kornbluth turns out to be right, after all, is of little consequence if one recognizes Madison not as a reality, but rather as a reification of collective fantasy. This rather graphic mapping of male desire and dysfunction is a function of comedy. Freddie and Dr. Kornbluth are the comic relief, while the central narrative concerns Allen's and Madison's love affair.

The negation of parents reinforces this symptomatic schema. Allen's and Freddie's father, we learn at one point, is long dead. There is no mention of their mother (the implication is that she, too, is dead). The only "mature" female character in *Splash* is Mrs. Stimmler (Dody Goodman), Allen's secretary, who is hilariously mixed up, silly, and confused for the duration of the story as the result of a recent accident (she was struck by lightning). In one scene, Mrs. Stimmler inexplicably wears a shower cap; in another, she wears her bra on the outside of her blouse. She, too, appears to figure strictly as a comedic sideline, but her dizziness and dislocated sensibilities suggest the inadequate, disenchanting "reality" of the post-Oedipal mother (substitute).

In *Children of a Lesser God* similar dynamics work obscurely. It is neither in the pathology of the protagonists nor in the narrative itself that Sarah is revealed as a male fantasy, but in the film's very structuring of word and image. The figural elision of falling in love/water discussed above is one such example. Many others are concerned with sets of oppositions wherein James's masculinity is defined in terms of what Sarah is not and has not. Language and speech, as will be discussed shortly, are key. Sarah cannot be readily deconstructed as a sign of male desire for the mother, as such. James, her lover, lacks the dysfunctional disturbances and sidekicks that make Allen's case transparent in *Splash*. This protagonist lacks neurotic traits. In fact he epitomizes masculine strength, prerogative, and transcendent will. The task of sorting through *Children of a Lesser God*'s hermeneutic system, then, is less a task of reading just below the surface of its narrative and more one of examining its terms.

The fantasy of returning to an imaginary, perhaps prenatal, existence in fluid, harmonious symbiosis that is suggested by the beauty of James's and Allen's underwater romances is then a major undercurrent (as it were) in both narratives. Other currents of the sexual dramas of both films elaborate this underlying fantasy—which does, of course, represent a kind of death drive—revealing the ambivalence and anxiety that are inspired by the mythic female object of male desire.

Bacchic Abandon: Woman's Sexual Appetite

A curious feature of both Madison and Sarah is their overt sexual appetite and aggression. In *Splash* it is the mermaid who initiates every sexual encounter, from the first kiss to the first intercourse. So voracious is Madison's sexual desire that she cannot wait until she and Allen are in the privacy of his apartment, but rather seizes him on the elevator when he brings her home. Indeed, Madison's immodesty is understood (by the viewer, unlike Allen, privileged with knowledge of Madison's nonhumanity) as entirely natural; she *has* no sense of modesty, and thus she is not in the least self-conscious about her nakedness when she emerges from the water at New York's Liberty Island. Allen responds to Madison's innate sexual initiative with simultaneous delight and disbelief. He manifests some suspicion and doubt, particularly when he is not with Madison, but never overt fear or anxiety.

Such is not the case in *Children of a Lesser God*. Sarah, too, is sexually ravenous, but her appetite is associated in several scenes with threatening (i.e., castrating) characteristics. In a scene before the one in which James falls into the water (discussed above) and Sarah's immense anger suddenly floats away as she and James fall into sexual rapture, she bitterly describes to James, who evidently imagined her sexually ignorant, her sexual history. Revealing that she had virtually prostituted herself at a rather young age to numerous teenaged boys, acquaintances of her sister's, Sarah signs, "Sex was always something I could do as well as hearing girls . . . better!" When, after describing this sordid past to James, she accuses him of wanting to deflower the "poor, little, deaf virgin," he reacts with tell-tale violence: "Do you think I'm threatened by that? You think that I give a god damn that you fucked every pimply-faced teenager . . . ? I don't. I don't give a shit!" Sarah has clearly touched a raw nerve.

This nerve suffers quite a lot of irritation in the course of the film. Sarah's sexuality is presented as excessive and potentially hostile. After having seen the movie *Some Like It Hot*—notably the featured scene is one of female sexual aggression (Tony Curtis's Jerry is pretending to be an impotent tycoon and Marilyn Monroe's Sugar is trying to "cure" him)—Sarah is so hot that she and James are barely home when she is undressing and the two are "doing it" on the floor. In another scene, her lust is directly linked to anger when she interrupts an argument with James to propose sex. In the film's most explicit sex scene, the position is female superior and Sarah curtails their lovemaking out of anger, launching herself up and off the supine James. During *Children of a Lesser God*'s climactic fight scene, James demonstrates that he believes Sarah's sexuality to be part of her problem when he challenges her to "use that little mouth of yours for something besides showing me that you're better than hearing girls in bed!"

This unusual representation of aggressive feminine sexuality, charming as it appears to be in *Splash* and frightening as it borders on being in *Children of a Lesser God*, suggests an uneasy and precarious construction of woman, the beauty of her natural immanence always too close to the horror of animal excess. That Madison's nonhuman genealogy evidently does not include the enculturated feminine virtues of passivity and modesty and Sarah's mouth is used as a sexual, and not an oratorical apparatus—that both display a rather Dionysian sexual vigor—suggests that both characters derive from a common conception of unbridled feminine nature, of what woman may be secretly, way down inside.

Silence: Speech, Subjectivity, and Desire

> There is no crime worse than silence, for it covers women's sex with its "thick veil," renders it inaccessible, indomitable, implacable: terrifying. . . . it is this self-sufficiency that is unbearable: because he "envies" her unassailable libidinal position, man projects his own insufficiency, his own "envy," onto woman. If woman is silent, if she keeps a "thick veil" drawn over herself and her sex, she must have her reasons, and good reasons, for wishing to remain enigmatic: she has to hide that "cavity filled with pus," she has to hide the fact that she has "nothing to hide. By seeking to make herself enigmatic, woman is only continuing the work begun by nature."[14]

Aside from their common aquatic predispositions and assertive sexuality, Sarah's and Madison's most notable shared feature is their lack of speech. Madison, the mermaid, is entirely mute until, inspired by a television advertisement, she utters her first word: "Bloomingdale's." Within six hours of this first utterance, Madison has acquired a full working vocabulary in the same manner—before the television display in the appliance department at Bloomingdale's. Initially, her speech is characterized by the platitudes and idioms of commercial soft-sell. Finally, it is entirely naturalistic, if a little "California," but it is always entirely received—never her own (although, it could be argued, so is all speech).

Sarah's lack of speech is, of course, considerably more intractable and central to *Children of a Lesser God*'s plot. She is profoundly deaf. James, her lover, is a speech teacher whose operative pedagogic assumption is that deaf people ought to (want to) speak. So essential is speech to James's character that he talks to himself when alone, in lapses of consciousness he talks to people who cannot hear him, and, most importantly, Sarah's insistent disdain for speech fills him with disbelief and contempt.

Language, which Sarah does have, in the form of sign language, is divorced from speech in *Children of a Lesser God*. James is not assuaged by the fact that Sarah can communicate. He is distressed by her inability (what he believes is unwillingness) to *enunciate*. Leading up to the climactic argument in which he accuses her, among other things, of willfully withholding her voice as a form of control, are numerous displays of James's privileging of sonant expression. These suggest that male envy of the perceived secret of feminine self-sufficiency which Sarah Kofman detects in psychoanalytic discourse and elsewhere, as well as the reaction to it: the extortion of speech.[15]

One recurrent motif has James offering to teach Sarah to speak. On each occasion she rebuffs the offer:

1. Their first meeting: "If you let me, I bet I could teach you how to speak."
2. Their second meeting: "Listen, how would you like to fake out Franklin and make me look real good?"
3. Their first date: "You know, I am a really good teacher, though. You *should* let me help you."
4. After having visited Sarah's mother: "Let me help you, damn it!"
5. After they have become lovers, in bed: "God, I can't ever get close enough (pushes her away and signs), say my name. Just once—say my name (she shakes her head). I'm sorry, I need it, I'm so . . . (she withdraws, signing reproachfully). I know I promised, I'm sorry, I forgot . . . I don't want you to speak. . . . It just came out!"

The obvious allusion to ejaculation in James's "it just came out" points to one source of James's anxiety. Whereas his enunciation operates as phenomenological evidence of his thought, as his ejaculation does of his orgasm, Sarah's thoughts, like her orgasm, are secret, obscure, and enigmatic, cause for his epistemological doubts about Sarah's love, Sarah's pleasure, and ultimately, perhaps, Sarah's humanity. In each of these "exchanges," Sarah angrily (in sign language) insists that she does not want to speak, that she has more than enough communication skills, that it is others who lack them.

The profound irony of this is that Sarah's insistence is always articulated by James. *Children of a Lesser God*'s method for constructing dialogue between the speaking man and the signing woman so that it can be understood by the hearing audience, is monologic and unilateral. James "translates" Sarah's signs into speech: "It went from your hands into my brain and out my mouth!" All William Hurt's lined are delivered verbally, while only some are in sign language, too. Marlee Matlin's lines, though delivered in sign language, are all incorporated into Hurt's. When Hurt is translating Matlin's lines, he is not always signing them. The film's dialogue, then, is not fully represented to the deaf viewer, who is further handicapped, presumably, by Hurt's amateur signing and by Matlin's, which although probably quite fluent, is not always shown in full, as she is often cut away from in order to show Hurt's responses. This disregard for the deaf viewer underscores the fact that the difference represented in *Children of a*

Lesser God is only nominally one to do with speech and hearing. The film's solution to the problem of translating sign is certainly not the only possible one; its employment reflects *Children*'s symptomatization of sexual difference.[16]

The most significant effect of putting Sarah's signs into James's mouth is the film's solution to the inevitable problem of the shifting personal pronouns: "you" and "I." Up until a certain point in the film, James substitutes "you" for Sarah's signed "I" and "I" for her signed "you": "If you let me, I bet that I could teach you how to speak . . . [she signs] . . . *and you could teach me* . . . , but I don't want to mop the floor!" The intention may well be to naturalize the incorporation of two "voices" (what do you call a nonvocal linguistic expression?) into one, but the semiotic result is the denial of Sarah's subjectivity: "The sense of uniqueness, identity, and unity which we tend to associate with subjectivity are the effects of the ability to say 'I' and to thereby appropriate language as one's own. But the dependence is reciprocal. Language is only possible because it is infused with subjectivity. The personal pronouns 'I' and 'you' enable the 'conversion of language into discourse.'"[17] It is not until Sarah's first lengthy discourse that the shifters begin shifting.[18] Thereafter, James reverts to generally substituting "you" for Sarah's signed "I" until the film's climax, when this very problem is raised by Sarah (but uttered by James): "Everyone's always told me who I am. And I let them. She wants. She thinks. And most of the time they were wrong. They had no idea what I'd said, wanted, thought . . . you think for me—think for Sarah—as if there were no I . . . Until you let me be an I the way you are, you can never come inside my silence and know me."

The eloquence of this "speech" is contradicted by the film's election of James (as opposed to, for instance, subtitles) to "speak" it. For even, indeed especially, when he stops converting her "I" to a "you," he ends up appropriating her "I." It's a no-win situation for Sarah's subjectivity. Moreover, James's reaction to Sarah is hostile: he stops signing and says bitterly:

"Well, that's all very moving, but how are you going to manage? You can lock yourself back inside your precious silent castle. . . . [Sarah signs something, evidently that James hasn't "heard" what she's been saying] I heard! I heard every word goddamn it. I translated for myself. It went from your hands in my brain and out of my mouth. And you know what? I think you're lying. I don't think that you think that being deaf is so goddamned wonderful! I think that you're scared to death to try. I think that it's nothing but stupid pride that's keeping you from speaking. Right? You want to be on your own. Then you'll learn to read my lips and use that little mouth of yours for something besides showing me that you're better than hearing girls in bed. [James stops signing and continues, yelling] Read my lips! What am I saying? You want to talk to me? Then learn my language! Did you understand that? Of course you did. You've probably been reading lips for years, but that's the great control game, isn't it? I'm the controller. What a fucking joke! Now, come on! Speak to me! Speak! Speak to me!"

James's impassioned devaluation of sign language, one that is shared by the film in its refusal to acknowledge sign language *as* a language like any other (suitable for subtitling, like any foreign language), suggests that Sarah's signing is something else. Indeed, the film itself emphasizes the physical (immanent) nature of signing in contradistinction to the disembodied (transcendent) character of speech. *Children of a Lesser God*'s very first dialogue illustrates this. Dr. Franklin, with his back turned to James and to the camera, speaks lines that cannot be "heard" (that is, seen) by Sarah, even were they signed, clearly inaugurating a distinction between speech, which is here divorced from vision and the body, and signing, not introduced until later, which depends upon vision and the body. Sarah's "language" is so inextricably bound up in her body, so mimetic in its expression, that it collapses the semiotic distance between sign and referent, much as does the hieroglyphic, as Mary Ann Doane has described:

> The hieroglyphic, like the woman, harbours a mystery, an inaccessible though desirable otherness. On the one hand, the hieroglyphic is the most readable of languages. Its immediacy, its accessibility are functions of its status as a *pictorial* language, a writing in images. For the image is theorized in terms of a certain *closeness*, the lack of a distance or gap between sign and referent . . . it is the absence of this crucial distance or gap which also, simultaneously, specifies both the hieroglyphic and the female. . . . Too close to herself, entangled in her own enigma, she could not step back, could not achieve the necessary distance of a second look.[19]

That the hieroglyphic nature of sign language is collapsed within the figure of Sarah with the hieroglyphic nature of woman is evidenced by the treatment of the marginal figure of Johnny, James's absolutely intractable student, who not only resists all attempts to make him speak, but also never is shown using sign language, either. He, profoundly deaf and male, has access neither to language (the symbolic) nor to the hieroglyphic body. But Sarah is a hieroglyph, sign and referent, trapped in too close, too narcissistic a relationship between self and world. Meaning inheres in but cannot transcend or escape her body.

Reflection and Projection: Woman's Self-Image

Thus Sarah's body functions in *Children of a Lesser God* as the vehicle of her expression. Her language, such as it is, is bound to her body, and so, it is suggested,

Marlee Matlin as Sarah, showing "what waves sound like," in *Children of a Lesser God* (Randa Haines, 1986).

are her very thoughts, her cognition. Out for a walk by the shore one evening, Sarah "tells" James what waves "sound like" by staging a beautiful, auto-erotic performance, caressing her own body, rhythmically exalting and pressing her breasts and releasing them. Like her solitary swims and other instances where she is shown peacefully and gracefully alone, and in contrast to her bitter and difficult social interactions, this incident illustrates the primary narcissism conceived as the core of Sarah's character.

Such a conception of the female narcissist is precisely that described by Freud as "probably the purest and truest feminine type." This type is characterized by a "certain self-sufficiency" and

> the importance of this type of woman for the erotic life of mankind must be recognized as very great. Such women have the greatest fascination for men. . . . the charm of a child lies to a great extent in his narcissism, his self-sufficiency and inaccessibility, just as does the charm of certain animals which seem not to concern themselves about us. . . . It is as if we envied them their power of retaining a blissful state of mind—an unassailable libido-position which we ourselves have since abandoned. The great charm of the narcissistic woman has, however, its reverse side; a large part of the dissatisfaction of the lover, of his doubts of the woman's love, of his complaints of her enigmatic nature, have their root in this incongruity.[20]

Here Freud himself participates, as Sarah Kofman has observed, in the my-thology of the eternal feminine. Whereas male narcissism is seen as pathological, inevitably a perversion, female narcissism, specifically the narcissism of "beau-tiful" women, is practically normative and the "truest feminine type." Sarah is a textbook instance of this truest type. Thus we find her (like Rivette's Marianne) before a mirror in moments of introspective crisis (it should not be forgotten that for Western civilization the mirror has been the enduring attribute of the mermaid for centuries). Perhaps reflecting upon James's desire that she speak, Sarah in one scene stands privately before a mirror and studies the reflection of her mouth as she mimics the shapes of speech. In another scene, she has attached a book of poker rules to her mirror frame and studies it as she makes herself up for the poker party she and James are to attend. Sarah's most dramatic private crisis, too, is enacted in front of a mirror that seems to take her by surprise as it throws her reflection back at herself while she's cleaning. Her violent reaction—she throws something at the mirror, smashing it—is not satisfactorily explained. Is it an attempt to break out of her narcissistic prison?

This brings us back to *Splash* and to Madison, whose facile acquisition (in-corporation) of language complicates her status as an embodiment of the Other, that is, as a function of the imaginary. In Hans Christian Andersen's *The Little Mermaid,* the popular fairy tale that looms in the background of *Splash,* the little mermaid sacrifices her voice, as well as her tail, in order to court the love of a mortal man and his immortal soul:

> "But remember," said the witch, "once you have taken human form, you can never become a mermaid again! . . . And if you do not win the prince's love so that he will forget father and mother for your sake, cling to you with all his mind and let the priest place your hands in one another's so that you be-come man and wife, you will not get an immortal soul! The very first morning after he weds another, your heart will break, and you will become foam upon the water. . . . But you must pay me. . . . And it is no small thing I am asking for. You have the loveliest voice of all down here upon the bottom of the sea, and no doubt you think you will be able to bewitch him with it, but that voice you must give to me. The best thing you possess will I have in return for my precious drink! For I must give you my own blood in it."[21]

The little mermaid, for the prospect of love and transcendence, accepts the witch's horrifying proposition and her tongue is cut off. The obvious analogy to castration in the mermaid's double loss—of tail and of tongue, as well as the dis-placement of the mother onto the figure of the witch,[22] whose own blood allows the mermaid's metamorphosis, unmistakably betray the story's implicit allegory of feminine sexuality and sexualization.

In *Splash,* significant liberties are taken with this story, that is, assuming it can be considered in some sense an adaptation.[23] Madison is initially mute, but acquires language, magically, through the medium of television. She also becomes self-conscious through television, which functions as her tree of knowledge. Indeed, Madison is very different from the little mermaid. Whereas Andersen's heroine relinquishes her underwater world forever in order to aspire to human love and immortality, Madison has "six fun-filled days" leave on earth, the duration of the full moon, before she must either return to the sea or stay forever. She, like the little mermaid, comes out of the sea for the love of a man, but while every step the little mermaid takes on her human legs, though graceful and elegant, is "like treading on pointed tools and sharp knives,"[24] Madison's earthly visitation entails neither agony nor speechlessness.

If we examine the characteristics of Madison as a character, however, we find that in a sense she really has no character. Whereas Andersen's mermaid story can be seen as an allegory of puberty, when a girl (particularly in the Victorian world) must subordinate herself and her powerful instincts to a repressive, patriarchal, Christian construction of womanhood, *Splash* gives us a mermaid who is finally a mere projection of a culturally constructed ideal of femininity. This is why it is in response to representations—the television set, certainly, but also the mermaid fountain that she gives Allen—and not before the mirror, that Madison's self-image is formed.

Like Freud's narcissistic woman, child, wild animal—like Sarah—Madison displays an innate self-sufficiency in her underwater form. And Allen, like James, is drawn to this enigmatic beauty. But whereas Sarah is conceived as a "real" narcissistic character and *Children of a Lesser God* constructs a melodrama around the fiction of her otherness and the disturbance it constitutes for James, *Splash* never affords Madison enough of her own character to relocate her otherness from the realm of the imaginary to that of the real. Thus the dissatisfaction, doubt, anxiety, and envy that accompany James's desire for Sarah are in Allen's case absent, or deferred. It is not until he learns that Madison is "a fish" that his confidence in his object choice is shaken, in part because, in a sense, Madison is not real.

The Horror, The Horror: Woman's Voice and Man's Dread

> Men have never tired of fashioning expressions for the violent force by which man feels himself drawn to woman, and side by side with his longing, the dread that through her he might die and be undone.
> KAREN HORNEY, "THE DREAD OF WOMAN"[25]

When Allen finds Madison in the appliance department at Bloomingdale's and discovers that all of a sudden she can communicate in impeccable English, the first question he asks her is her name. "It's hard to say it in English," she replies.

"Well just say it in your language," he urges. "All right," she says, "my name is . . ." and lets out a sonic screech of so high a pitch that the screens and picture tubes of all the TVs on display shatter. Allen's reaction, in *Splash*'s typically understated comedic manner, is more one of embarrassment than horror: "How 'bout those Knicks?" he remarks to the stunned salesmen.

If Allen finds Madison's idiosyncrasies somewhat odd, his utter enchantment prevents his doubts from becoming profound. In *Children of a Lesser God,* on the other hand, a similar moment yields a radically different effect. At the end of the scene described above, in which James accuses Sarah of willfully and selfishly withholding speech, Sarah finally, in a moment of intense emotional anguish and frustration, with an uncontrollably distorted voice, explodes, screaming a string of desperate, unintelligible sentences accompanied by wretched gesticulations. James, aghast and disgusted, turns his head away from this terrifying display.

The natural voices of Madison and Sarah, the menacing volume and pitch of their unintelligible "speech," suggest the dread of which Karen Horney writes.[26] These voices betray the suspicion that beneath the beautiful and silent surface of the enigma exists a creature "whose extraordinary and dangerous being might at any moment return through violence."[27] The dread evident in James's response, as well as the deferred dread that Allen experiences later, when the cumulative signs of Madison's alien behavior are explained by the revelation of her watery origins, reflects the underbelly of man's desire for the Other—his unconscious fear of being subsumed, of losing the autonomy of his ego.

As Horney elaborates, "What he fears in women is something uncanny, unfamiliar, and mysterious. If the grown man continues to regard woman as the great mystery, in whom is a secret he cannot divine, this feeling can only relate ultimately to one thing in her: the mystery of motherhood."[28] In the last analysis, it is the fact of motherhood, the epistemological intersection of life and death in her womb, that generates this anxiety—this dread. Both films underscore the issue of motherhood by asking the question, "what kind of children?" In *Children of a Lesser God,* when James asks Sarah what she "wants," her answer is deaf children. James responds that he doesn't "want" deaf children, but that he wouldn't mind if they were. In *Splash,* after Madison agrees to marry Allen, and just before she is exposed as a mermaid, Allen exclaims that he wants children, one of each: a boy and a girl. Madison's cryptic response is "Which kind?" In each case, the real issue—male or female—is displaced onto the film's textual ersatz categories of difference, respectively hearing/deaf and human/nonhuman. This is precisely the form of displacement that Constance Penley has noted in science fiction films:

In these films the question of sexual difference—a question whose answer is no longer "self-evident"—is displaced onto the more remarkable difference between the human and the other. That this questioning of the difference between human and other is sexual in nature, can also be seen in the way these films reactivate infantile sexual investigation. One of the big questions for the viewer in *Blade Runner,* for example, is "How do replicants *do it?*" Or, of *The Man Who Fell to Earth,* "What is the sex of this alien who possesses nothing that resembles human genitals?"[29]

The same question can be asked of Madison, about whose primary form one must wonder (her reproductive system is about to be tackled by the team of scientists investigating her when she makes her last-minute escape from their lab toward the end of the film). And how, one must wonder at the end of *Splash,* are Allen and Madison (phallic again) going to "do it"?

The Music Box: Woman's Positioning in the Cultural Apparatus

Where Sarah comes from, and where Madison comes from, there is no music. When Madison hears music for the first time, she likes it, so Allen gives her a music box with little dancers inside. Sarah, of course, has never heard and will never hear music. James loves music. The first thing he does upon moving into his new home is to set up his stereo and play a Bach recording. Some time after Sarah has moved in with him, he one day realizes that he hasn't listened to music since she came and lies down on the couch to listen to Bach, while Sarah sits obliviously, but not unhappily, in a corner, doing nothing, in front of a poster of musical instruments. Shortly, James gets up and removes the record. When Sarah looks at him inquiringly, he signs, "I can't enjoy it. I can't because you can't." Later, Sarah asks him to show her what Bach sounds like (just as she had shown him what waves sound like) and he attempts, miserably, to do so. He looks ridiculous; Sarah looks mystified. Later, after her dreadful fight with James, Sarah goes home to her mother. In an intimate and reconciliatory scene between the two women, Mrs. Norman (Piper Laurie), in a motherly gesture, recovers a music box, which evidently had belonged to the little deaf Sarah, and hands it to her daughter, who gazes fondly at the pirouetting ballerina within.

The music box, seemingly a minor detail in each of the films, is in fact a suggestive icon: an image of the mechanism by which cinema in general, as a function of culture, organizes the representation of woman—how the desire and the dread attached to her otherness are contained. Music is culture and "she" doesn't have it. The music box relocates the "organic" nature of feminine beauty into the system of culture, anchoring her to the cylinder from which the music is turned out. It is the prototypical cultural object that allows woman's beauty to be displayed, while circumscribing, indeed eliminating, her powerful threat. While both Sarah and Madison (like the little mermaid) display ineffable grace—Sarah as she swims and even dances, and Madison when she swims and when she skates—they do not depend upon any musical fluency. Their grace is organic; their bodies respond to an internal flux or rhythm that man can only marvel at.

When Sarah and James, for instance, go on their first date to a restaurant for dinner, Sarah proposes they dance. James agrees after expressing surprise that Sarah "can" dance. She explains that she feels the vibrations of the music. On the dance floor, she demonstrates a remarkably fluid and sensual sense of movement as she dances to "I'll Take You There," a Motown song by the Staple Singers. Sarah seems transported as she dances, essentially alone, in that she closes her eyes and dances quite expressively (and narcissistically), pretty much oblivious to James, who somewhat sheepishly withdraws to the margins of the dance floor and simply stares at the seemingly self-sufficient Sarah as she attracts a certain amount of attention, swaying, eyes closed, slowly (in comparison to the song's rhythm and the other dancers on the floor). The mise-en-scène in the scene is telling. The restaurant, which has an aquatic theme, includes a sort of tank, recessed into a wall and surrounded at the wall's surface with a string of pearly lights. Inside the tank, behind the almost cinematic plane of glass, there is a mannequin—a nude female figure in the pose of the Capitoline Venus—submerged in the water. This sculpture echoes the film's construction of Sarah as a liminally subaqueous creature and reifies the topos of the music box: woman's beauty is displayed but contained.

Madison's skating is not unlike Sarah's dancing. Despite having never seen

Children of a Lesser God.

Splash (Ron Howard, 1984; photo courtesy of Jerry Ohlinger's Movie Material Store).

ice before, she's a natural, and as she spins and turns gracefully, Allen with-draws somewhat to watch her. And here, too, the scene is structurally linked to the music box metaphor: it adjoins the scene in which the mermaid foun-tain is introduced. While the submerged Venus remained a realist, if odd, back-ground detail in *Children of a Lesser God,* the mermaid fountain stands for the repressed—returned with a vengeance—in *Splash.* At its "appropriate" urban site—where it, too, is associated with music—it is almost the catalyst for Allen to reveal to Madison his haunting memory of their childhood encounter. Sensing this, she somehow manages—as only a mermaid in a romantic comedy can—to both purchase the formidable fountain and have it moved into Allen's rather small apartment as a gift. As with many of the big laughs in *Splash,* this one comes very close to exposing the deep ambivalence around which the story is organized. The mermaid statue, with her fluid beauty and grace, is here surrounded by a basin of water, structurally circumscribed—her underlying threat contained—as are the subaqueous Venus and the pirouetting dancers in the music boxes, but the huge displaced object is a bewildering, shocking intrusion into the banal order of Allen's domestic sphere.

The sound tracks of the two films, particularly in *Children of a Lesser God,* underscore the sexually unilateral meaning of music. As in most Hollywood productions, music here functions as an indicator of mood. Both films use very "watery" music to accompany the images of Sarah and Madison swimming. And in both, such music is directly contrasted to the diegetic use of "cultural" music. The eerie, nondiegetic mood music that describes the atmosphere that emanates from the realm of the Other lacks the structure, the complex harmonies, the insistent rhythms that signify "music." This is particularly striking in *Children of a Lesser God,* which is virtually without silence, that very quality which is supposed to define Sarah. But Sarah's silence cannot be represented and must be invoked through nonmusical music—pseudo-ambient sound. This must be in part because "silence in a cinema is embarrassing" and music serves "to conceal the furtive pleasure of indulging in private fantasies in public places,"[30] but also because silence itself is defined as inaccessible.

The Horror, The Beauty: Man's Transgression

"I am not a fish!" screams Allen, submerged up to his chin, naked, awkward, humiliated, his hands covering his genitals, in *Splash,* after Madison has been found out. She and Allen both have been interred at the Museum of Natural History for observation. Before they are convinced that Allen is "only a man," the scientists try one more experiment. They hoist Madison into Allen's tank to observe their interaction. Allen now displays the horror and revulsion that had been deferred previously. "I guess they thought you might be one," says Madison apologetically. Allen cannot bear to look at her and violently rebuffs her physical advances. He is released. No amount of scrutiny shall expose Allen as a hybrid. The contrast between not only her anatomy, but also Madison's very prettiness and grace underwater, and the ridiculous sight of Allen, water up to his chin, utterly *out of his element,* underlines the seemingly intraversable threshold between nature and culture.

After Sarah leaves him, in *Children of a Lesser God,* James appears to become

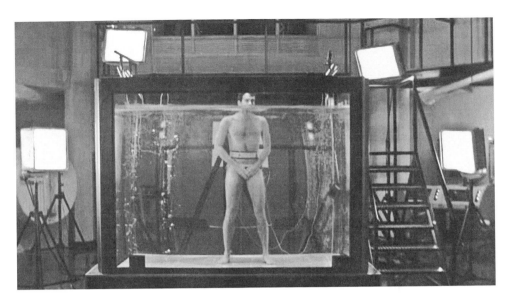

Splash: "I am not a fish!"

depressed. While Sarah is at home making amends with her mother, perhaps reconciling herself to the implications of the music box, James wanders—solitary, forlorn, confused—through his day-to-day routine. Sitting at a noisy coffee shop, he plugs his ears with his fingers, a curious expression on his face. He walks by the shore. Finally, he immerses himself one night in the pool; naked, he closes his eyes and is shown, in slow motion, suspended in what he imagines to be Sarah's world.

In both films the man is shown transposed into the immanent, cultureless, feminine domain. The contrast is illuminating. Allen's reaction, and the ridiculous sight of his body, shown full-length in a long shot, suggest the impossibility, at least in the "real" world, of this transposition. Allen does not become a fish; he does not identify with Madison. James, on the other hand, believes in the possibility of empathy, of understanding Sarah's element. *Children of a Lesser God* contrives this scene of identification by using the ambient music associated with Sarah to invoke her "silence," by avoiding the visibility of James's genitals, showing him only from the waist up, fragmenting his body, as it had Sarah's in the film's precredit sequence, in which Sarah slept in a dark room, sea winds blowing through the windows. The rife sounds of the wind, banging shutters, and tinkling glass, appended by an elegiac, eerie musical score, resounded as the camera in close-up fragmented Sarah's body and the deep blue moonlit darkness of her room. James's identification is achieved through art (and artifice)—through cinematic framing, editing, lighting, score, and sound.

Beauty and the Beast: Love and Transcendence

Both *Splash* and *Children of a Lesser God* end with resolution and reconciliation. After escaping her imprisonment, Madison no longer has any choice; she must return, forever, to the sea. At the last moment before she is to leave him, Allen, who has come to accept Madison's difference, learns that he may go with her:

MADISON: I was ready to stay with you forever.
ALLEN: I know, but now that they know who you are they're never going to leave you alone.
MADISON: I can't ever come back to you.
ALLEN: I wish I could come with you.
MADISON: You can.
ALLEN: How?
MADISON: It can be done.
ALLEN: How?!
MADISON: Remember when you were eight years old and you fell off the ship? You were safe under the water, weren't you?
ALLEN: Yeah . . . ?
MADISON: You were with me.
ALLEN: You mean that was real? You mean that was you?! This is great! I can go with you and still come back and see Freddie at Christmas!
MADISON: (sadly) You can't ever come back.
ALLEN: (despairingly, after a long pause) Madison . . .
MADISON: I understand.

As Madison swims away, Allen suddenly changes his mind. Culture, which has been often represented as ridiculous and oppressive in *Splash*, particularly those figures of male authority—the police, the union, the scientific establishment, the museum—is here represented by the National Guard, who, as they close in on Madison, compel Allen to make that happy and horrible choice between nature and culture, to relinquish this world forever, for eternal love and death. For this event can really only be understood as the actualization of the fantasy represented in *Splash*'s opening (primal) scene, the child's return to the imagined symbiosis and inertia of the phallic mother's womb. And *Splash*'s "happy ending" is a murky one. At the very end of the film, as the credits roll, we see the glimmer of Madison's and Allen's dark underwater destination, a place of which one can know nothing. Is this place not death? The ending is ambivalent, expressing the paradox that Simone de Beauvoir so well captured: "Man would fain affirm his individual existence and rest with pride on his 'essential difference,' but he wishes also to break through the barriers of the ego, to mingle with the water, the night, with Nothingness, with the Whole. Woman condemns man to finitude, but she also enables him to exceed his own limits; and hence comes the equivocal magic with which she is endued."[31] The ultimate meaning of Allen's desire is a myth—an impossibility, as Beauvoir suggests and Lacan elaborates:

> Aristophanes' myth pictures the pursuit of the complement for us in a moving, and misleading, way, by articulating that it is the other, one's sexual other half, that the living being seeks in love. To this mythical representation of the mystery of love, analytic experience substitutes the search by the subject, not of the sexual complement, but of the part of himself, lost forever, that is constituted by the fact that he is only a sexed living being, and that he is no longer immortal.[32]

Annihilation is the meaning of Allen's love for Madison. The transcendence of *Splash*'s ending is the fantasized transcendence of the realities of life: gendered sexuality and death, in which the idealized mother stands "at the source and fading-point of all subjectivity and language—a point which . . . threatens the subject with collapse."[33]

Children of a Lesser God avoids this knowledge in its happy ending. James's supposed transgression of symbolic boundaries allows him to ask Sarah, when she returns to see him at the film's end, "Do you think we could find a place where we can meet—not in silence and not in sound?" It has been necessary, up until this point, for all of James's lines to be both signed and spoken, and hers to be translated by James. Sarah's response to James's question, now, however, is allowed to obscure the problem of representing such a compromise. She signs, "I love you," which by this point in the film, does not need to be translated. He signs the same in response, without "saying" it. Together, they make the sign for "connect," as previously demonstrated by Sarah. The camera pans away from the two as they embrace and then moves out to sea and sky as the music swells.

Children of a Lesser God's solution to James's and Sarah's communication gap is a pseudo-solution. If Sarah's silence did not have to be made somehow representable as such—if her signs did not have to be treated as hieroglyphic instead of semiotic—it would have been unnecessary for James to have sounded them for her. So the solution of the two characters' problems is, in fact, only a solution to the film's problem. And at that level, too, it is spurious. Any discourse more complicated than "I love you" could not be rendered. The spirit of compromise and self-knowledge aroused by James's and Sarah's profound love is supposed to forge a "place where we can meet—not in silence and not in sound." But such a place is an illusion, one made of clichés that allow the myth upon which the film is predicated to remain unexamined.

Finally, then, rather like *Contempt*, *Children of a Lesser God* supports a myth of the feminine as Other—as silent, immanent, mysterious—a myth of woman as nature, but in this version of the myth conjugal love is not "mortified." It is represented as the bridge across that perilous chasm between nature and culture. *Splash*, one might say, is a travesty of this very construction, enabled by the mechanisms of comedy to expose the unconscious sources of the myth.

CHAPTER 6

Playing with Fire

Now at that time the men had no fire and did not know how to make it, but the women did. While the men were away hunting . . . the women cooked their food and ate it by themselves. Just as they were finishing their meal they saw the men returning, away in the distance. As they did not wish the men to know about the fire, they hastily gathered up the ashes, which were still alight, and thrust them up their vulvas, so that the men should not see them. When the men came close up, they said, "Where is the fire?" but the women replied, "There is no fire."

KAKADU MYTH, FROM FRASER, *MYTHS OF THE ORIGIN OF FIRE*

Martin Scorsese's contribution to the 1989 anthology film *New York Stories* cleverly acknowledged its director's digression from the kind of wise guy theme for which he was, fairly or not, becoming known. The credit sequence of *Life Lessons*, his story of the relationship between two painters set in the somewhat rarefied New York City art world of the 1980s, runs over the image of "splattered" paint. This splatter simultaneously references the kind of visceral process-painting (à la Jackson Pollock) executed by the film's protagonist, painter Lionel Dobie (Nick Nolte), and the kind of viscera associated with "execution" of a different sort, more commonly seen in other films, such as Scorsese's own *Good-fellas*, which would be released the following year. This pun suggests Scorsese's self-consciousness about both the violence with which his auteurism is marked and the mounting of a scenario (written by Richard Prince and based on Dostoyevsky's *The Gambler*) that can so plainly be seen as autobiographical. And *Life Lessons* does feature its share of violence, though mainly of the sort expressed through artistic sublimation of powerful sexual impulses, and only occasionally of the more predictable sort associated with a virile temperament.

 Life Lessons is but one of several American films released during the 1980s that mixes themes of art, sexual desire, and violence. But its picture of the New York art world is somewhat retrograde, focusing on an increasingly obsolescent—or at least atypical—master/muse theme, and featuring a kind of muscular, male, modernist painting practice that was experiencing a rather histrionic last gasp by the late '80s with the overexposed careers of neo-expressionist artists like Julian Schnabel, Sandro Chia, and Anselm Kiefer. The film does note, with some cynicism, the emergence of another art phenomenon: "performance art," one of several relatively new and high-profile modes of artistic practice in that period that are by no means incidental to the disturbances that ripple through a number of films, as they did through the art world. As the film opens, Dobie's studio assistant-*cum*-mistress, Paulette (Rosanna Arquette), has been spurned by her choice of lovers, Gregory Stark (Steve Buscemi), a performance artist rather in the mold of Eric Bogosian. An unreconstructed latter-day New York School type, Dobie is skeptical, to say the least, of this appellation. "Who is this guy?" he asks Paulette; "I know him, right?" "Gregory Stark," she replies. "That kid?" he responds incredulously; "the comedian?" "A performance artist," Paulette corrects. "*Performance artist,*" sneers Dobie. "What the hell is a performance artist? The person's an actor, a singer, a dancer . . . I mean, do you call the guy who picks up your garbage a sanitary engineer? A *performance* artist!"

Dobie later accompanies Paulette to a Stark show, one really only distinguishable from stand-up comedy by its trappings. Set in an abandoned subway tunnel, Stark's performance ends with a monologue that voices stereotypical male preoccupation with issues of anger, conflict, and confrontation, and concludes with the sudden explosion of a bare, jury-rigged light fixture over his head. The film itself supports Dobie's suspicion of Stark and the very notion of a "performance" art by cutting away repeatedly during the scene in question to low-angle shots of Dobie's stony, imposing, judgmental visage. Later, in the film's most violent outburst beyond the action of the canvas, Dobie—in righteous, chivalrous indignation, supposedly in defense of Paulette (who is mortified)—assaults Stark in a coffee shop, giving large, histrionic form to the clichés disclosed in the stand-up performance. While Stark plays with exposing, but does not deconstruct, the ways in which masculinity itself is a performance, Dobie performs the big burly myth itself, replete with all its concomitant imagery: beard, bourbon, cigarettes, penetrating insight, and sexuality.

The heroic, macho typology bodied forth by Lionel Dobie in *Life Lessons,* which is discussed at much greater length in the next chapter, may seem somewhat outmoded in terms of the art world of the 1980s. Indeed, when this narrative is seen in terms of the others I shall discuss, it seems positively quaint in its view of the gendered nature of art and inspiration (not unlike Rivette's *La Belle Noiseuse,* discussed in chapter 4). This model, however, does not seem so obsolescent in terms of the sexual politics of New Hollywood feature filmmaking, a practice very much dominated in the 1980s (as before and after), in theory (auteurism) and in practice (the biz), by white men and their anxieties. Certainly, as a thinly veiled autobiographical confession, Scorsese's film exposes some undeniable generalities regarding gender and power in the film industry, if not in the world of art.

The other films I'm concerned with here, including an earlier one by Scorsese, indeed reflect more centrally certain significant economic, demographic, and artistic changes in the 1980s art world, which included a boom, comparable to that on Wall Street, that was felt from the elite auction houses and blue-chip galleries uptown, down to the profusion of little upstart galleries and alternative venues in the East Village. Indeed, one key cinematic representation of both Wall Street and contemporary art is that offered by Oliver Stone's *Wall Street* (1987), to which half a dozen elite galleries—as well as a number of prominent artists and collectors (including Julian Schnabel)—lent artworks, used in the film mainly as décor for the home and office of millionaire corporate raider and junk-bond specialist Gordon Gekko (Michael Douglas).

Wall Street represented the most materialistic, venal, and—obviously—capitalistic extreme in movies figuring art and featured the kind of monumental artworks that not only dominated the high end of the art market at that time, but also, not coincidentally, in their cinematic scale constituted the perfect backdrop to Stone's story of monumental egos, power, and corruption. Interestingly, Daryl Hannah, whose presence seems always symptomatic of something in films of the 1980s, including one that is central to this discussion, plays a significant role in *Wall Street,* too. As Darien Taylor, she is an interior decorator who acquires art, rugs, and other furnishings for Gekko but whose sexual availability, it is implied, is part of the package. Art as a high-priced commodity and setting for commerce was central to the mise-en-scène of *Wall Street,* but the artists who made it were of negligible narrative interest (although a number of name artists played as extras in the film).

In three other films of the 1980s, artists—specifically female artists—were central. Scorsese's *After Hours* (1985), Ivan Reitman's *Legal Eagles* (1986), and Dennis Hopper's *Backtrack* (a.k.a. *Catchfire,* 1989) conflate representations of women and contemporary art, and of women artists particularly, with danger: ranging from explosive passion to kidnapping, fire, sadomasochistic acts of aggression, stalking, paralysis, murder, and annihilation. In all instances, the themes of art, femininity, and danger are imbricated and co-implicated. This chapter seeks to identify why and how the women and the art, separately and together, seem to become sources of anxiety and loathing, and why, combined, they are wont to create an incendiary provocation. Problematic questions like "Is it art?" and "What does a woman want?" appear to entangle one another in the cinematic-cultural unconscious. I think the answers to these questions may be found in a peculiar nexus of psychological and sociohistorical conditions.

Kiki, Paul, and her papier-mâché sculpture, which serves as both augury and index of his dawning terror in *After Hours* (Martin Scorsese, 1985).

Driving Mr. Softie: *After Hours'* Downtown Odyssey

If Hopper's *Backtrack*, to which I shall return, is the most hallucinatory of these films, Scorsese's black comedy *After Hours* is the most fertile, especially in the psychoanalytic possibilities afforded by its many symptomatic moments. Written by Joseph Minion, *After Hours* actually plays like a combination of Homer's *Odyssey* and MGM's *The Wizard of Oz* (1939), adapted by Kafka and directed by Freud. Its protagonist, Paul Hackett (Griffin Dunne), a word processor for a generic, midtown-Manhattan corporation, is lured late one night downtown to SoHo by a chance encounter in a coffee shop and eventually finds himself trapped in a nightmarish half-world of unpredictable events and volatile characters, unable to get home. Arriving at a loft to which Marcy (Rosanna Arquette), object of his interest, has invited him, Paul finds her absent—gone on a mysterious errand to the "all-night drugstore"—according to her roommate Kiki Bridges (Linda Fiorentino), a "sculptress" whom Paul finds at work. The sultry Kiki persuades Paul to help dip papier-mâché for her work in progress, a rather derivative, expressionist screaming figure that functions in the film as both an augury and index of Paul's dawning terror.[1] Kiki also induces Paul to offer her a massage, in the course of which the conversation turns ominously to the theme of burns, a major leitmotif of the narrative:

> PAUL: You have a great body.
> KIKI: Yes, not a lot of scars . . .
> PAUL: It's true. It never occurred to me . . .

KIKI: I mean, some women I know are covered with them—head to toe—
   not me.

PAUL: Scars?

KIKI: Uh-huh . . . horrible, ugly scars . . . I'm just telling you, now.

PAUL: I don't know . . . I know when I was a kid I had to have my tonsils taken
   out. And after the operation, they didn't have enough room in pediatrics, so
   they had to put me in the burn ward. Well, before they wheeled me in, the
   nurse gave me this blindfold to put on and she told me never to take it off.
   If I did, they'd have to do the operation all over again. I didn't understand
   what my tonsils had to with my eyes, either. But, anyway, that night—at
   least I think it was night—I reached up to untie the blindfold and I saw . . .
   [Kiki suddenly slumps back against Paul; then snorts. She is asleep.]

Kiki's enigmatic intimations about scarred women and Marcy's strange behavior upon her return compound Paul's discomfort. His discovery in Marcy's bag
of burn ointment and a medical text with gruesome images of burn victims,
along with her volatile personality, touch an obvious psychic nerve, inducing an
increasingly anxious Paul to conclude that Marcy has been disfigured by burns
and (along with us, the viewers) to actually perceive telltale scars with a quick
glimpse of her thigh. Only later, after Paul's erratic behavior and sudden re-
jection have contributed to Marcy's unstable state of mind and probably to her
suicide, do we find that the film has imposed Paul's delusion on us! When he ex-
amines her naked corpse, Paul discovers with simultaneous relief and horror that
Marcy is "disfigured" only by a tattoo (albeit a tattoo of a skull). That Paul and
we are led to conclude that a disfiguring wound is hidden from view, and hidden,
more to the point, in the vicinity of her genitals, points to the underlying source
of Paul's angst: a primary dread of the female genitalia. This is, of course, an
essential aspect of the psychic content of Paul's tonsillectomy memory, which is
very like a screen memory, the term adopted by Freud to describe how the af-
fect and power attached to repressed ideas (in this case a thinly veiled castration
scenario) are hidden behind suitable "screens" derived from actual experience,
enhancing them with their characteristic uncanny vividness. The death's head
iconography, another of the film's leitmotifs, reinforces the ontological connection between the feminine and death.

A psychoanalytic reading of this first episode of Paul's nightmare is more
than justified by the imagery connected with the subsequent episodes, each one
associated with a female figure of Medusal horror.[2] Indeed, as Steve Reinke has
pointed out, castration anxiety is the explicit foundation of the film's scenario.[3]
Scorsese foreshadows Paul's subsequent after-hours odyssey with an image
whose significance could not be *less* ambiguous. As Paul is resigning himself to

charm Julie (Teri Garr), a cocktail waitress who has her eye on him, in hopes she might help him get home, he visits the men's room to pull himself together. There, next to the mirror, a graffito attracts his attention: a crude drawing of a man whose erect penis is in the jaws of a shark. And as it turns out, Julie— also a portrait artist and photocopy shop clerk, with a 1960s style and a circuit of mousetraps around her bed—does soon threaten to trap Paul with her guilt trips and her beehive hairdo and, of course, her mousetraps (real and figural). Shortly after Paul has extracted his finger from her hairdo, where it had become stuck, he observes a mouse, caught by the spring of a trap. There's no mistaking the expression of empathy on his face as he struggles to get away from Julie, who is loathe to release him.

Gail (Catherine O'Hara), the next potentially fatal female Paul encounters, in fact wounds him with a taxicab door. She drives a "Mr. Softie" ice-cream truck—the phallic insult here has not been lost on all critics[4]—and represents a more menacing kind of castration threat. She not only is shown as rather butch (she drives a Mr. Softie truck and wears a studded belt) and therefore castrating, but also as sadistic. She torments Paul by repeatedly making him forget a phone number he's obtained from directory assistance, demands she be permitted to dress the wound she gave him and then discovers, and reads from, a fragment of newsprint stuck as papier-mâché to his arm: "a man was torn limb from limb by an irate mob last night in the fashionable SoHo area of Manhattan. Police are having difficulty identifying the man because no form of ID was found on his shredded clothing and his entire face was pummeled completely beyond recognition." "Wow!" she exclaims, seemingly aroused, "What does a guy have to do to get his face pummeled!?" Gail then tries to pull off the bit of papier-mâché.

GAIL: Let me get it off for you.

PAUL: Ow! Just stop touching it.

GAIL: I want to get it off for you!

PAUL: Stop touching it!

GAIL: I know, I'll burn it off.

PAUL: No, you're not going to burn it off.

GAIL: Matches. I just need matches.

PAUL: No. No matches!

GAIL: I'm going to ask a neighbor.

PAUL: No, lady, no!

GAIL: My name is Gail.

PAUL: Lady, NO!

Just as Paul's "perception" of her wounds was later cast into doubt over Marcy's dead body, so are these scenes with Julie and Gail, although handled matter-of-factly, ambiguously open to being viewed as evidence of Paul's delusional dementia. Their incipient violence suggests that the repressed has returned, and is knocking at the door. The newspaper account of the man stalked by a vigilante mob presages plot turns yet to come in *After Hours*, when, through a series of mishaps, Paul comes to be suspected of a series of burglaries. This is not the first foretelling of events in this black, black comedy, in which such circularity can be seen alternately as magical or paranoid. In the aftermath of his narrow escape from Gail, Paul climbs, appropriately enough, a *fire escape,* from which he witnesses (or does he?) a horrifying act of domestic violence: a woman (blonde, like most of the film's "sirens") shooting a man at close range.

The last act of *After Hours* begins with the appearance of another female figure, utterly grotesque and yet totally realistic in terms of 1980s New York bohemia: a woman with orange dyed and sculpted hair, black lipstick, a black ring painted around her right eye, and punk regalia—stockings, garters, and chains—who walks into a coffee shop and hands Paul an invitation to a "Club Berlin." She is a figure who reminds us that this nightmarish demimonde from which Paul cannot escape is (or at least overlaps with) the art world, a world Scorsese, manifesting some of his usual biases, draws as populated by gay men and Gorgons, although its borders and boundaries seem controlled by archetypically male authority figures: the cabby, token-booth clerk, cop, bouncer, bartenders, and so on. But this is not quite the art world of *Life Lessons:* it produces baffling, nontraditional, often immaterial art; the announcement handed Paul is for a "conceptual art party."

Here the film's problematics of art, danger, and the feminine coalesce. Paul finds the Club Berlin empty save for a bartender and June (Verna Bloom), a quiet, self-effacing, and seemingly benign older blonde, who, though bewildered by his interest in her, comforts him as they dance together to a song Paul selects from the juke box: Peggy Lee's "Is That All There Is?", an existential lament that begins with a spoken narration about a fire witnessed by a little girl. When the vigilante mob, led by Gail, closes in on him, June, who it turns out is an artist, steals away with the fugitive Paul to her underground atelier, attached to the club. Here in her cave—or womb-like lair—June, Calypso-like, "protects" Paul. Scorsese has said that a previous script ending had June "suddenly growing in size while people were banging on the door shouting, "We'll kill him," and then literally showed Paul climbing up into June's body to escape by "returning to the womb"![5] But in the final version, the seemingly normative and maternal June turns into the most terrorizing gorgon of all, as Paul literally becomes the paralyzed sculptural image of terror that had earlier augured his nightmare.

Paradoxically, it is as the subject-turned-object of art theft that Paul finally makes his escape, as Neil and Pepe (Cheech and Chong), the actual burglars, break into June's studio and remove him through the ceiling to their van above. Their discussion about the aesthetic merits of their loot reflects the film's consciousness of widespread public perplexity about postmodern art, as well as discourse about its value as a commodity in a changing marketplace:

> PEPE: Hey, man, is it worth taking this thing?
> NEIL: What, are you crazy, man? This is art.
> PEPE: Art sure is ugly, man.
> NEIL: That's how much you know, man, you know. The uglier the art, the more it's worth.
> PEPE: This must be worth a fortune, man.
> NEIL: That's right. It's by that famous guy, Segal.
> PEPE: It is?
> NEIL: Yeah, you seen him? He's on the Carson show, man, plays banjo all the time?
> PEPE: I never watch Carson.
> NEIL: Yeah, well, that's how much you know about art.
> PEPE: I don't know, man, I'd take a stereo any day.
> NEIL: What do you know, man? A stereo's a stereo. Art is forever.

These words—"Art is forever"—are the film's last. *After Hours'* disturbing, mystifying mix of art, sexuality, and violence is resolved with a joke that puts art in its place, so to speak.

"I Think I'm Uncomfortable": Performance Art,
Radical Narcissism, and *Legal Eagles*

The burgeoning market for art in the 1980s and the high-profile attention to art as a commodity are central thematic concerns of another symptomatic film of the period, *Legal Eagles,* a convoluted thriller involving murder, arson, art theft, and fraud. Here, too, a sexy blonde artist is a potentially fatal femme. In the film's pre-credit sequence, back story is conveyed via dramatic images of an eight-year-old Chelsea Deardon's birthday party and the fire afterward that shattered her world, killing her father, a well-known painter. The grown Chelsea (Daryl Hannah) is a performance artist who is arrested for theft in her attempt to reclaim a painting of her father's that was supposed to have been destroyed in the fire. But she is also rendered as a preternaturally, almost savagely alluring and mystifying woman. Robert Redford plays Tom Logan, an assistant district attorney who loses his job and becomes reluctantly involved in the case, thanks to Chelsea's spunky, resourceful lawyer, Laura Kelly (Debra Winger) and Chelsea's own dangerously seductive behavior. That the film, after unraveling a diabolical scheme on the part of the trustees of Deardon's estate to profit from arson, manslaughter, and fraud, doesn't manage to convince of Chelsea's "innocence," only underscores the mythic anxiety with which this character is drawn (the broadcast TV version of the film, in fact, has a completely different ending in which she is *not* entirely innocent).[6]

Chelsea is presented as distraction personified. When she walks into the hall where Logan—introduced by the district attorney as his probable successor—is giving a speech, her appearance unnerves everyone in the room, as shown in a series of reaction shots strangely reminiscent of those attending the entrance of Marilyn Monroe and Jane Russell into the dining hall scene in *Gentlemen Prefer Blondes* (1953) some thirty years earlier. But Hannah's Chelsea Deardon lacks that parodic self-consciousness so abundantly manifest by those object lessons of the 1950s, as well as the "radical narcissism" characteristic of the feminist body artists of her own era, of whom she seems a faint echo.[7] The embodied distraction of this characterization is the narrative thread that ties together *Legal Eagles'* episodic moments of chaos, violence, and explosion. Chelsea's provocative, childlike presence is linked structurally, if not logically, to a series of disturbances, from the reluctant sexual entanglement of Logan and ensuing implication of corruption, to murders, sabotage, and pyrotechnic destruction (the explosion of a warehouse and burning of an art gallery).

The mythic contours of this character are underscored throughout *Legal Eagles* by means of contrast. Debra Winger's role offers a constant, more earthly alternative and, inevitably, a less dangerous and more "appropriate love interest." Chelsea's narcissistic allure is countered by Laura's neurotic spunk; her arty obtuseness with the attorney's quick-witted intelligence. In her next film, Winger again played the down-to-earth, rather tomboyish alternative to a (blonde) woman of deadly allure, played by Theresa Russell as the titular *Black Widow* (1987). Winger's function echoes that of similarly drawn characters in films that create an overwhelming and ominous sense of excessive, almost bestial feminine threat. *Cat People* (1942) and *Vertigo* (1958) are two that come immediately to mind. It should be noted that the characters played by Jane Randolph, Barbara Bel Geddes, and Winger in these films are not only spunky and down-to-earth: they are professionals (architect, designer, attorney, Justice Department investigator)—and therefore "masculinized"—while those played by Simone Simon, Kim Novak, Russell, and Hannah are described more by their aura, a large part of which is magical and cannot entail anything so mundane or practical as work, another significant part of which is feral, and therefore unemployable.

But, in fact, in *Legal Eagles,* the mystification aroused by Chelsea Deardon flows as much from her chosen métier, performance art, as from the stunning, narcissistically seductive, statuesque yet childlike aura that Hannah lent to any number of roles in the 1980s (notably in *Blade Runner* [1982], *Splash*—as discussed in the previous chapter—and *Clan of the Cave Bear,* in all of which she plays *femmes* rather *enfant* and *fatale*). One of *Legal Eagles'* most memorable scenes is the supposedly spontaneous staging of a performance piece that could only happen in a movie. A multimedia extravaganza, it is all set up and ready to perform in Chelsea's loft when she is unexpectedly escorted home by Logan, this despite the fact that the piece involves carefully synchronized recorded and live sound, movement, projection, and the manipulation, ignition, and explosion of numerous props! "Hearts desire, hearts desire, never ever play with fire," echoes a childlike song. The performance proceeds, a kind of fugue on the theme of fire, one we know to have primary and traumatic meaning for Chelsea. A rather effective pastiche that borrows from a range of high-profile work of the period,[8] this performance makes evident how deeply imbricated are the film's understanding of art and femininity. It draws on manifold aspects of fire: its fascinating kinetic and formal properties, its erotic connotations, its consuming, destructive power—aspects contemplated by Gaston Bachelard in his *Psychoanalysis of Fire*[9]—and collapses all these properties of the performance into the performer, Chelsea herself, drawn as a fascinating, erotic, dangerous flame.

At the end of the performance, Chelsea steps behind a large screen on which is projected an image of herself, just as a fuse she has lit burns down and the screen bursts open in flame. As the explosion subsides one sees a life-size figure engulfed in flames, and for a beat the audience—with Logan, who has grabbed a fire extinguisher (placed strategically near his seat)—must imagine that Chelsea has self-ignited. But the figure is revealed to be a mannequin, a prop, as Chelsea herself appears calmly next to Logan. "Well, what did you think?" she asks

Incendiary performance art in *Legal Eagles* (Ivan Reitman, 1986).

the stunned lawyer. He is speechless and then stutteringly replies, "I . . . think . . . umm . . . fine." "*What did you think?*" Chelsea repeats insistently. Logan's reaction is halting and baffled. "I think, uh . . . I think I'm uncomfortable," he finally admits. "Good," Chelsea remarks.

Legal Eagles shares Logan's perplexity in the face of this spectacle. While it perfectly well understands, even if it does not sanction, the venal, material self-interest exhibited by the film's villains regarding traditional, material, saleable art objects,[10] it remains uncertain about a so-called art that can neither be sold nor exhibited in traditional ways, and one, moreover, that often derives its power from its very immediacy and immanence. As Carolee Schneemann, a pioneer of performance art, has stated, "There's something female about performance itself, I think, because of how it is ephemeral and close to the unconscious—involving display, use of the self."[11] These remarks underscore how close, too, performance is to cinema, also an ephemeral art of display that is "close to the unconscious," yet one that often claims not to be an art at all, or at least often seems unwilling to partake of that rubric, or to forego remuneration! Here we begin to see how the question, "But is it art?" as regards new and potentially subversive art forms is provocative and disruptive to cinema, another medium of which that question has historically been asked.

"Murder Has Its Sexual Side": *Backtrack*'s Hallucinatory Postmodernism

That these new and potentially subversive forms are often associated with women and femininity is part and parcel of the disruption they constitute within a male-dominated industry. "Too close for comfort" expresses something of the crazy scenario at the center of Hopper's "straight to video" labor of love, *Backtrack*, a film that in fact takes me back to where I began, at least chronologically.

Released in 1989, the same year as *Life Lessons*, Hopper's scenario is like Scorsese's *Goodfellas* on acid.[12] Its protagonist is Anne Benton (Jodie Foster), a conceptual artist whose work is not simply based on that of Jenny Holzer but is in fact made by Holzer, one of the most prominent artists associated with postmodernist art practices in the 1980s. The resemblance between Holzer—who already when *Backtrack* was produced had been chosen to become the first woman to represent the United States at the 1990 Venice Biennale—and Foster's Anne, however, ends with their work. Holzer's "truisms" and other aphoristic texts, which add to seemingly authoritative, neutral, or received ideas a sharp, critical, often paradoxical twist, were originally conceived to be "exhibited" in the streets, subways, parks, and other public places of Manhattan, not in museums and galleries (though by 1989 they had certainly appeared in such), and they evolved in their presentation from simple Brechtian placards to billboards, to urban furniture (benches, bus shelters), to the LED signs employed in *Backtrack*.[13] The work doesn't seem quite as pertinent in the atomized, sprawling Los Angeles that is the background to *Backtrack*, though it does constitute a repeated and ironic disturbance to the scenario. In fact, twenty of Holzer's phrases appear in the film, mostly in LED form, shown in full or occasionally in part, including several that seem almost to comment on the clichés invoked by the action:

SALVATION CAN'T BE BOUGHT AND SOLD

MURDER HAS ITS SEXUAL SIDE

I AM CRAZY BORED AND FAMILIAR WITH THE ENDING

LACK OF CHARISMA CAN BE FATAL

CLASS STRUCTURE IS AS ARTIFICIAL AS PLASTIC

GO ALL OUT IN ROMANCE AND LET [THE CHIPS FALL WHERE THEY MAY].

As a hybrid of a "real" conceptual artist and a fictional object of desire, Hopper's heroine is a paradoxical figure: tough, ambitious, skeptical but given (unlike Holzer) to wearing rather girlish, sexy short dresses and lingerie. Like *After Hours*' Kiki Bridges or *Legal Eagles*' Chelsea Deardon, Anne Benton suggests some popular fantasy of a woman artist: sexually provocative, mystifying, potentially dangerous; although as played by Foster, who is better suited to the sharp, spunky, tomboyish kind of alternative role, she lacks the preternatural narcissism of those others.

The film's plot is set in motion when Anne, victim of a blowout, stumbles upon a mob hit at a deserted petroleum plant near the freeway while looking for help. Having seen the face of the mobster who committed the crime, as well as

Jenny Holzer's LED work as Anne Benton's in *Backtrack* (Dennis Hopper, 1989).

his henchmen, she is soon the object of an all-out mob search that claims the life of a boyfriend, and from which she cannot be protected by police or FBI. These organizations have been infiltrated by the mob and the faux-legitimate business that is their boss's cover. Through her wiles, Anne eludes her pursuers, collects some money, and skips town incognito. She adopts a new identity and gets a job at an ad agency in Seattle. Meanwhile, the mob has hired the best hit man in the business, Milo (Hopper), to track her down.

Milo, a most improbable but inevitable movie figure, pursues his undertaking with the kind of passion, creativity, intelligence, and slightly lunatic insight that Hollywood generally ascribes to artists, very much in contrast to Anne, who is never shown working and whose actual practice is treated by the film with relative incomprehension and indifference. In order to hunt her down, Milo immerses himself in the study of Anne, much like a scholar, a lover, an artist, a connoisseur. He buys her work, surrounds himself with her aphorisms, contemplates her underwear and other effects, and locates her by recognizing ad copy that, although uncredited, bears her "signature" (it reads, "protect me from what i want"—one of her "truisms"). That Milo might be taken as the "real" artist in this story is strongly suggested not only by Hopper's rather hackneyed manic intensity but also by Milo's demonstrated affinity for the work of "real" artists: Charlie Parker and Hieronymous Bosch. In fact, the film effects a profoundly counterintuitive role reversal: Anne, an artist and a woman, is the cool, composed, calculating character, while Milo, a hired gun and a man, is the intense, emotional, passionate virtuoso.

Bob Dylan and Dennis Hopper as artist and hit man in *Backtrack*.

Anne just barely survives her first encounter with Milo but he eventually tracks her down in New Mexico after interviewing an artist friend whose work is plainly based on that of Frank Stella—with whom I doubt Jenny Holzer is close friends, and who is played by Bob Dylan (!)—and an encounter with an avatar of D. H. Lawrence (Alex Cox), seemingly conjured by Anne's imagination, at an annual pueblo church festival (!!). When Milo finally catches up to his prey, this murder artist is loath to "finish" his work.[14] "I know everything there is to know about you," he tells her, revealing to a terrified Anne, whom he has surprised in bed, something of the fascination he feels. "You know nothing about me. All you need to know about me is that I'm giving you a choice: either I finish you now, or I let you live. And if I let you live, your life is mine and you belong to me."

From this point, the story becomes an embarrassingly unconvincing and perverse love story. Anne, who at first bristles at her captivity and virtual rape, soon chooses to stay with and love Milo, and with him plots to disable the mafiosi who threaten their lives and happiness, by the end clearly taking pleasure in arming and defending herself with explosive fire power. Atmosphere associated with the visions of Georgia O'Keeffe and D. H. Lawrence (patron saints of the bohemian desert), her mystical discovery many miles apart of two shards of Indian pottery that fit together, and the rescue of a trapped lamb from a rocky crevice seem to signify Anne's deliverance from the cold, detached, cosmopolitan purgatory of life as a conceptual artist. The film ends with Anne and Milo blissfully sailing away from shore, presumably not long after having blown up a dozen armed mafiosi and, it seems, an entire oil refinery in the climactic confrontation of this crazy, mixed-up story of art, sex, crime, and punishment. Where they're going is not at all clear.

What *is* clear is that the 1980s were years in which the worlds of art and business were in a volatile, even violent state of flux, as was public discourse about gender, sex, and sexuality. Films such as these captured some of the vicissitudes of the moment. Novel—often mystifying or perplexing—art forms and practices, like the performance art featured in *Legal Eagles* and the LED aphorisms in *Backtrack,* emerge as symptomatic of larger cultural and social problems at the same time that they collapse into the insoluble riddle of femininity due to their otherness, immanence, irreverence, or mystery. An incipient flammability—an incendiary violence—rendered literal in the manifold explosions, flames, and fires seen in these films, is associated with this riddle.

After all, one enduring collective identity crisis of the commercial narrative film is played out in the conflict between art and business, two poles of simultaneous identification and anxiety for popular film, especially in the United States in the 1980s, a decade in which the era of the Hollywood Renaissance overlapped with the era of the blockbuster. Another source of enduring ambivalence and anxiety for culture generally, as well as Hollywood cinema particularly, is, of course, woman. Hollywood's most fervent devotion is to the depiction of feminine beauty as the cradle of heterosexual desire. But such devotion has always involved a suppression, a sublation of something horrifying in the ineffable sensuality of the feminine (*vagina dentata,* as illustrated in *After Hours,* or, as in the Kakadu myth about women and fire, what you might call *vulva flammea*). These films, and others, suggest a slippage between two alluring, enigmatic, sometimes threatening terms—art and femininity, a slippage that is both a persistent structural attribute of the classical film ethos and a symptom of the sociopolitical cultural flux of the 1980s.

The fictional woman artist will likely never cease to be a problem, but she takes on a range of other attitudes in movies of the subsequent decades. Three examples are illuminating. In Robert Altman's biting Hollywood satire *The Player* (1992), Greta Scacchi plays June Gudmundsdottir, an artist much more aligned elementally with ice than with fire. This cool, Icelandic beauty makes vague, luminous art, and is indifferent to movies. She is not the source of the film's violence but, as the rather frosty lover of the screenwriter-victim, David Kahane (Vincent D'Onofrio) and subsequently the love object of his assailant, Griffin Mill (Tim Robbins), she is obscurely implicated. The languid narcissism that Scacchi brings to this, as to many of her roles, ultimately makes art seem less like a métier than a kind of organic emanation, but Altman needs her at the same time to symbolize art (as opposed to commerce)—an obscure object of desire for Griffin Mill, David Kahane, and Hollywood in toto.

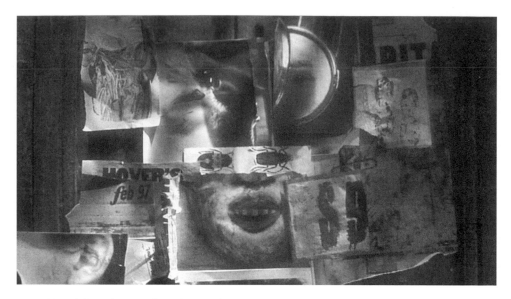

Maggie's vindictive collage (by David Carson) in *Addicted to Love* (Griffin Dunne, 1997).

In *Addicted to Love* (1997), his directorial debut, Griffin Dunne creates a black(ish) romantic comedy with disturbing echoes of *After Hours*. In a role of the innocent abroad (here again in SoHo), not unlike his own role in Scorsese's 1985 film, Dunne casts Matthew Broderick. And in a part that seems intended to prove that hell hath no fury like a woman artist scorned, Dunne casts—against type—Meg Ryan as Maggie, a character who manages to combine the mercurial and girlish instability (Marcy), artistic narcissism and savagery (Kiki), obsessive and castrating sexual fixation (Julie), sadism and mannish vindictiveness (Gail), and ultimately paralyzing possessiveness (June) that *After Hours* employed five actresses to embody.

In a screenplay that betrays every sign of its writer's (Robert Gordon) attentiveness to courses in film history and theory, Sam (Broderick) is a gentle, jilted, small-town astronomer and Maggie a fierce, cynical urban artist; they end up teaming and shacking up together in an abandoned warehouse across from the loft in which his ex-girlfriend Linda (Kelly Preston) has moved in with Maggie's erstwhile fiancé, Anton (Tchéky Karyo). Abject but resourceful, in one space Sam has rigged astronomical equipment to create a camera obscura that permits him to watch a real-time, screen-sized projection of the goings-on across the street, where he is convinced he will witness the deterioration of a misguided fling. When Maggie—who has been stalking Anton, it turns out—arrives and adds an electronic bug, the two can literally sit back on the couch and play *Rear Window* while they munch junk food and Chinese takeout, with much less need for speculation than Hitchcock's characters, and no need for binoculars.[15] In her spare time, Maggie works vindictively on an enormous collage that occupies one wall of their warehouse and stages extravagant spectacles of revenge on Anton, which she photo-documents. Eventually she discovers the mean bone in Sam's body and the two conspire to destroy Anton's and Linda's idyll, almost succeeding before acknowledging at last that they've fallen for each other. Interestingly, Maggie is never explicitly identified by the script as an artist, or as having any career at all. Evidently art is just the right ingredient for rendering this pathologically eccentric, castrating beauty believable.

In *The Shape of Things* (2003), Neil LaBute's nasty gender inversion of *Pygmalion* (a concept with delightful potential, here dashed), Rachel Weisz plays Evelyn, an MFA student, the nature of whose artistic praxis seems vague and irrelevant until the film's cruel denouement, when it is revealed that her thesis project has been the physical, emotional, and sartorial "sculpting" of Adam (Paul Rudd), the insecure, overweight (but quite literate) nerd who is transformed in the course of the film by his relationship with her into a more attractive, and possibly more shallow, specimen. Evelyn is even more unfeeling than her Shavian prototype, though, and certainly more duplicitous, as she uses sex to seduce her clay, who knows not that he is being molded. Given the overall misanthropy of LaBute's scenario—there's a male character who is arguably more reprehensible than her—it's hard to say whether Evelyn's amorality is meant to be a gendered trait. But plenty of its constituent parts depend on classic myths of the feminine and stereotypes of the woman artist, including her use of seduction as a form of deceit, her mercurial temperament, and the close association of her work with her self and her body.

Altman's, Dunne's, and LaBute's films suggest that against the ever shifting dynamics in the relationship between art, movies, and society, gender plays a protean and always rather mythic part. If she is not mere muse or object of art, but emerges as its supposed agent, the woman is an unnerving and problematic proposition. Be it through fire or ice, the woman artist constitutes an elemental threat to the cultural status quo. *The Shape of Things* illustrates this graphically: Rachel is introduced as an artist-vandal who transgresses the boundary around a neoclassical male nude statue in the university museum in order to use paint to (re)expose the phallus that has been long hidden by an added fig leaf. This exposure quite literally points to the threat that she constitutes to the symbolic order, or shape of things.

CHAPTER 7

Dirty Pictures, Mud Lust, and Abject Desire: Myths of Origin and the Cinematic Object

Couples. We tend to think in couples even when we try very hard not to; we revise the concept of the couple, we re-write it, we mediate it in new ways, but couples are very hard to get away from. It's just the way we think in the West, have been trained to think—based on the force of the copula, of copulation (cf. Derrida). . . . For there would appear to exist a seeming historical necessity for the heterosexual woman who wants to create, to write—and be read—to couple herself, in fact or fantasy, albeit if only temporarily, with a man who also writes or wrote, a famous man in her life or in her writing—if not the necessity, *then the* desire *to do so.*
ALICE JARDINE, "DEATH SENTENCES"

If it is interesting to contemplate the ways in which the representation of art in films tends to allegorize the medium as art, and the way in which the artist figure tends to constitute either a self-portrait or a kind of negative version thereof, then it might be doubly interesting to consider the representation of artist couples in film. The sexual relationship between two artists offers another permutation in cinematic self-reflection. In three contemporary films—*Artemisia* (1997), *Camille Claudel* (1988), and *Life Lessons* (1989)—not only are art and artistic process thematized, but cinema (the one art, according to André Breton, with the greatest "power to make concrete the forces of love") is shown, by extension, as the product of that love.[1] Art is the progeny of sexual passion in these films—the child of the artist-parents. In each film, the nature of the artistic relationship represented—its romantic, psychosocial, and sexual aspects—suggests something about larger issues relating to the experience of film. It is almost as though each were telling its own personal myth of the origins of the film art, or recreating a primal scene: the child's fantasy of its parentage, its origins.

This "originary" story is expressed with various emphases in the three films, as I shall enlarge upon, but is always articulated through a predictably racial and specifically gendered view of the erotics of artistic collaboration. Although artists' identities in terms of race, gender, and sexual orientation are obviously in fact various, these three films rely on the construct of a prototypical artistic relationship between heterosexual white men and women. Further, in each a young woman artist is apprenticed to an older male, a relationship of power and gender that is at the same time entirely realistic and profoundly mythic. Two of the films under discussion, *Artemisia* and *Camille Claudel*, are based on the stories of two "real" historical woman artists, the Italian Baroque painter Artemisia Gentileschi and the fin-de-siècle French sculptor Camille Claudel. The third, *Life Lessons*, represents a fictional relationship between contemporary artists in New York, but is based on Dostoyevsky's *The Gambler* and on the real diaries of Apollinaria (Polina) Suslova, who was Dostoyevsky's mistress when she was a young aspiring writer in her twenties and he was in his forties, already establishing a reputation.[2] Thus, each of the three films that I shall analyze as articulations of a myth of origins is in fact grounded in history, a situation that both reinforces their originary quest and entangles them with issues of historicity and fact not irrelevant to their analysis.

Dirty Pictures

Artemisia, directed by French director Agnès Merlet, should not be discussed without reference to the controversy that resulted from this film's travesty of historical justice, although it should be recognized that the historical record, like the film itself, is a construct open to analysis. The "historical" (as opposed to Merlet's fictional) Artemisia Gentileschi was the gifted daughter of a prominent Roman painter and was known in her time and subsequently not so much for the powerful talent displayed in her work—and her singular, almost unprecedented achievement as a woman painter—but, sadly, as a notorious figure at the center of an infamous trial. In 1611, when his daughter was still a teenager, Orazio Gentileschi, who had been instructing her himself, hired Agostino Tassi, with whom he was then working on several important commissions, to teach Artemisia perspective. Tassi, a fine painter, it turned out, was also a violent rogue who had been previously implicated in murder and incest and had been imprisoned on several occasions. He raped young Artemisia, then tried to quell the offense with empty promises of marriage. Orazio, who learned of the crime only later, finally took Tassi to court, suing him for the rape of his daughter, as well as for the theft of several pictures. During the trial, which lasted five months, Artemisia, cross-examined under torture—a kind of period version of the "lie detector"—persisted in her testimony that Tassi had raped her and then had tried to assuage her with promises of marriage. She is said to have shouted at him as the strings of the *sibille* were pulled tighter around her fingers, "This is the ring you give me, and these are your promises."[3]

As Mary Garrard, the foremost scholar of Artemisia Gentileschi's art and career, put it in her scathing review of Merlet's film,

> There can be no doubt that the basic facts of the story are inverted in the film. In Merlet's narrative, Artemisia begs to study under and then falls in love with . . . Tassi, is deflowered by him—an act accomplished with tender solicitude on his part and minimal resistance on hers—and is initiated by the older painter into the mysteries of love and art. When her father . . . brings suit against Tassi for rape, Artemisia testifies repeatedly, even when tortured by *sibille*, that Tassi did not rape her but gave her pleasure, and she loves him. Pained to see Artemisia suffer torment, Tassi magnanimously accepts the charge of rape and his own conviction, thus ending the trial as something of a hero.[4]

A film ought not be judged strictly according to criteria of literary or historical fidelity, but in one that touts its historical basis and its feminist heroine—and was directed by a self-professed feminist, to boot[5]—such distortions are provocative. The film's misrepresentation of Gentileschi's art is also appalling. It shows the juvenile Artemisia painting a self-portrait that actually dates from the artist's maturity, some twenty years later, and reduces it to half its actual size (and, since the picture hardly resembles the young actress who is supposed to have painted it, it even impugns, although perhaps unwittingly, Gentileschi's talent as a portraitist). The film implicitly attributes Artemisia Gentileschi's *Portrait of a Gonfaloniere* to her father, portraying her as his assistant on it; and it misrepresents Gentileschi's most famous painting, *Judith Slaying Holofernes,* as Garrard so bitingly observes, by incorporating this chilling image of tyrannicide, and of real and symbolic female power, into an erotic tableau.[6]

These offenses to art, history, and feminism, however, are less my interest in *Artemisia* than the view of art and sex it bodies forth in its scenario of artistic passion and artistic apprenticeship, its translation of these themes into images of erotic passion and involvement, and the manner in which it finally posits these as a matrix or model for cinematic origins. The film boldly sexualizes art. It constantly collapses artistic sensuality and human sexuality through scenes in which models become sexual objects, artistic compositions become sexual dramas, and visceral responses to artistic images slip into images of pornographic titillation.

One of *Artemisia*'s key images of artistic vision is a paradox. In the scene showing Artemisia's second lesson, Agostino Tassi takes his new pupil outdoors in order to have her see the world through a perspectival grid, an apparatus that assists the artist in translating objects seen receding into depth onto the two-dimensional plane of the picture. But Artemisia has barely glanced at their

Learning to see in *Artemisia* (Agnès Merlet, 1997).

putative subject, a seascape—one, significantly, that is not shown—before the lesson takes an interesting turn. He instructs her to close her eyes. Tassi teaches Artemisia to "see" through verbal seduction. He employs poetic, sensuous descriptive language to evoke a radiant image of a seascape in her mind's eye. All the while, of course, the perspective apparatus is there before her, but she neither looks nor sees through it. Rather, we view her through it. We come to occupy what is in effect a position reciprocal to hers—in the place of the object of her study. It is not the vast but inhuman vista of the sea that is situated on the other side of the perspectival divide; it is I, it is you, the viewers.

This matrix sutures the viewer to the "master's" point of view, since Tassi soon moves from a position just behind Artemisia around the grid to occupy a position comparable to ours, looking at her—as she stands in rapture, eyes shut—thus turning her forcefully from the seer, subject of the gaze, to the seen, its object. We join the seducer in effacing the spectacle of nature—or, rather, taking its place—and taking Artemisia herself as spectacle, objectifying her, as women are so often, so typically, objectified by the gaze of the painter, or the camera. Behind the supposedly disinterested and objective art and science of perspective, of course, lurked in the Renaissance and Baroque, as later, inexorable power relations between portrayer and portrayed, a fact Albrecht Dürer brilliantly illustrated in his woodcut of a draftsman using the perspective device to apprehend a recumbent nude from his "A Course in the Art of Measurement with Compass and Ruler" (1525–1527), which might be titled "where objectivity becomes objectification," so clearly does it explicate the sexualized dynamics of the perspectival gaze.

Thus, in Merlet's *Artemisia,* wherein it comes to virtually fill the frame, the grid of the perspective screen becomes an analogue to the camera frame and the cinematic screen themselves, securing our identification with Tassi, the male figure of authority, the "master," the director (so-to-speak) who directs Artemisia's performance. In this scene, the objective landscape and the subjective feminine disappear together and are replaced by fantasy: the fantastic, shimmering, rather cinematic (because temporal) image conjured by Tassi's poetic utterances and the fantastic image of the objectified feminine—accessible and receptive—eyes shut and lips glistening in passive exultation.

Another scene confirms this translation of Artemisia from viewing subject into viewed object and consummates the act that was suggested by the evident excitement, bordering on sexual arousal, associated with this first introduction of the perspective mechanism. In it, Gentileschi employs the device to draw her teacher Tassi in the position familiar to us from the figure of the Old Testament villain, Holofernes, from her later painting, *Judith Slaying Holofernes* (1615–1620). This highly unlikely scene, of a Baroque "master" posing, undressed, for his student, a female one at that, is rationalized in the film by two prior scenes. In one, Tassi, plainly attracted to his young student, consents to pose for her. In the other, just prior to this, the "master" forces himself sexually on his seemingly willing but nonetheless much pained disciple. After the rape, Artemisia is shown at home in a reverie; in a voice-over she relates her sense of a "confused mixture of forms and dreams."

Indeed, this subsequent scene is exactly a "confused mixture of forms and dreams." In it there is a complete dissolution of boundaries between subject and object, beholder and beheld, historical practice and contemporary fantasy. Again, the perspective screen is mounted, only to be traversed. Artemisia, aroused by the spectacle she beholds, puts down her instrument and inserts herself (bodily) into the composition of her scene, not as the vengeful assassin of a tyrant that we know from the Bible and from Gentileschi's magnificent canvas, but as a lover, literally lowering herself onto the supine figure of her "master." The scene, unwittingly perhaps, literalizes the ironic distance between the linguistically parallel terms "master" and "mistress." The primary definition of "master" in the second edition of the *Webster's Collegiate Dictionary* is "a male person having another being subject to his will, as a teacher, an employer, an owner of a slave or a dog, an official in a school, etc." Although gender is not specified in the seventh subdefinition ("One, esp. an artist, who has attained great skill in the use of anything"), the semantic and historical field of the term, used by the ruling classes of most cultures to legitimize and enforce the subjuga-

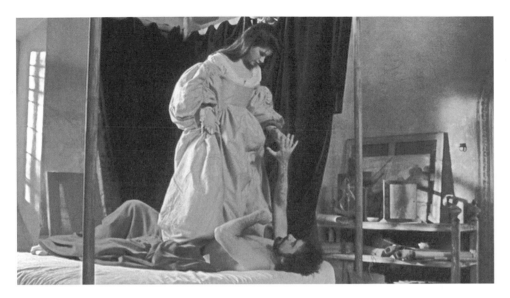

Artemisia: master + mistress = masterpiece?

tion and sometimes enslavement of animals, women, racial, and ethnic "others," narrows its perceived applicability.[7]

There is, of course, intriguing feminist potential in showing a woman artist taking a "master" as model, a conceit that is fraught with subversive possibility. But here this conceit not only inverts the meaning of Gentileschi's great picture, turning it from an eloquent image of female power and a probable reaction against Tassi and the male tyranny he embodied into a premonition of desire, but it also turns her, again, from subject of the gaze, and possessor of the pencil, into sexual object and seductress. "It is this repeated dislocation (of which the film-maker seems sublimely unconscious) between woman-as-eye and woman-as-seen, fantasising sexual receptivity," as Griselda Pollock notes, that unhinges the feminist potential of Merlet's *Artemisia*.[8]

The film conceives Artemisia as passionate looker, or voyeur: she shamelessly provokes a youthful male companion to undress for her; peeks into Tassi's windows one night and gleefully watches the orgy she espies, and generally is shown as hungry for visual pleasure. The almost demented, eroticized gaze attributed to Artemisia in this film seems to suggest a psychosexual pathology: scopophilia, sexual pleasure in looking. Interestingly, *Artemisia* attributes this usually male "perversion" to its female protagonist, even as her agency is eclipsed by the film's tendency to translate her from subject to object. The film wants to have it both ways: to imbue its heroine with (an entirely anachronistic) sexual license and visual subjectivity and at the same time to offer her up as an object of desire. Indeed, the film begins with a sequence that perfectly embodies this double project. Its credits appear over a series of striking close-ups of eyes, across the retinas of which are seen the brilliant flares of reflected candlelight. Then it dwells on the ardent visage of a young, cloistered Artemisia in a state of fervent devotion before religious paintings in a Roman church, fragments of male nudes from Michelangelo's *Last Judgement,* according to Griselda Pollock. "Thus we are introduced to the concept of the artist as a hungry eye," Pollock observes, "desiring to see, to know, to participate in the jumble of expressively naked bodies and the mysteries of representation."[9] But these are images of a lust for looking that also reveal something of the film's—and perhaps the cinema's in general—view of what you might call the erotics of cinema: the basic scopophilia ("I like to watch")[10] that may constitute a primary part of every moviegoer's and every moviemaker's passion.

Mud Lust

Camille Claudel (1988), another biopic about a woman artist, also uses its story of lust and art to posit a theory of cinematic origins. The film portrays Claudel, her passion for sculpture, her relationship with Auguste Rodin (the most important sculptor of his day—the turn of the century), its demise, and her ultimate descent into madness. In it, scopophilia, a visual pathology, is compounded by a related, more tactile, one that has in fact been called a "madness of mud."[11] The relationship between Claudel and Rodin is seen as fueled by what you might call mud lust. Their mutual calling is a "filthy" one, as they reveal in a scene early in their acquaintance (prior to their sexual relationship), when Rodin is taking Claudel home late one night by carriage. Rodin asks Camille if she is "afraid of being scolded." "No," she replies, and then, "I'm no longer a child. And my mother doesn't speak to me. . . . She doesn't like sculpture—all that filth." Rodin, smiling knowingly, responds, "Mine always said, 'Get rid of them! They're everywhere! Even under the bed! . . . Your mess . . .'"

Camille Claudel, the first directorial work of Bruno Nuytten, a cinematographer turned director, is a more honest film than *Artemisia,* both in its historical fidelity and its respect for the artistic work of its subjects. Art is again shown as the product of a sexual passion. But this is more appropriate to Rodin's and Claudel's story than it was to Gentileschi's, since the two French sculptors both did, in the period of their greatest mutual achievement, take images of sexual love as their very frequent subject and employed each other consensually as sexual and artistic partners.[12] Their works from the decade in which the two were romantically and professionally involved not only share formal and stylistic

The imagined origins of Rodin's *Crouching Woman*, in *Camille Claudel* (Bruno Nuytten, 1988).

affinities (to the extent of having sometimes caused attribution problems), but also deeply interpenetrating heteroerotic themes.[13]

But even as it plays up Rodin's and Claudel's affinities, Nuytten's film is at pains to create an image of Claudel as young, beautiful, impetuous, and obsessive to the point of indecency, much as Merlet portrayed Artemisia. The atmospheric and mysterious opening scene of the film shows Claudel's furtive nighttime venture into the streets of Paris in search of clay and her return to her cold atelier and her awaiting male model, Gigante, in a manner that at first suggests dirty, clandestine, criminal, or morally questionable activity. Rodin, like Tassi, is portrayed as older, wiser, more worldly than Claudel, inspired and stimulated by the joy and rejuvenation such youthful company affords. In the scene where Rodin first takes Claudel, who has been apprenticing at his public atelier, to his private studio, he encourages her to palpably engage with his nude (female) model, whose awkward crouching pose he manipulates. Claudel then takes over, adjusting the pose in a way that finally corresponds to an actual Rodin study from the period, the caryatid-like *Crouching Woman* of 1880–1882. This date in fact suggests that the film's "attribution" of this figure to Claudel is unlikely, since it is thought she first met Rodin in 1883. In the film, Claudel discovers the pose that works (although one wonders how well it worked from the model's point of view), adjusting Rodin's model, achieving the successful posture and an almost carnal mutual excitement, an excitement suggested by a precipitous cut from the image of the sculptors eagerly examining the three-dimensional effects of the pose at the spinning platform to that of the head of a rushing horse, always an image of erotic force.

It is rather bold of *Camille Claudel* to portray this and other well-known

Discovering the melancholy eroticism of Rodin's *Danaïd*, in *Camille Claudel*.

works by the "master," Rodin, as at least in part the result of Claudel's eye (if not hand). Where *Artemisia* effectively deattributed works long known to belong to Gentileschi's, *Camille Claudel* does the opposite. Inspiration for poses of a number of Rodin's major works are implicitly attributed in the film to Claudel. But, ironically, such seemingly feminist and historically generous cinematic gestures can have problematic double meanings, here often turning Claudel herself into an erotic object.

This is the case with another scene in which Claudel visits Rodin's private atelier. Set on the afternoon of Victor Hugo's funeral, this scene moves the relationship to a more sexual plane. The model is dismissed by a dispirited Rodin and Claudel herself adopts the pose that achieves the melancholy eroticism of Rodin's beautiful *Danaïd* (1885), exposing her shoulders and the nape of her neck to Rodin, who approaches and kisses her there. The historical record confirms that Claudel was the model for this piece—probably when the relationship was well under way, however—but not that she conceived it. Yet the moment perfectly illustrates both the strangely symbiotic process through which a work of erotic power can come into being and the ease with which the female figure slips from a position of subject to that of object. It is that slippage, as well as enduring cultural assumptions about masculine priority, that contribute to the atmosphere of madness and persecution that beset Claudel later in the film and indeed in her life.

In two rather parallel scenes, in which Rodin's and Claudel's portrait busts of each other come into being, gender and passion become entangled in a web of prejudice. While Rodin—in one scene—molds her head in a blind, sensual fervor, passionately alternating between (with his eyes shut) palpating her living head and the soft, giving clay, Claudel—in a later scene—has reproduced his head from memory in Rodin's absence, a feat that the film treats with awe and not a little horror, expressed in reactions that relate it to her gender. "She did it in your absence?!" asks one of a group of (male) visitors to whom Rodin is displaying Claudel's bust of him. "Mlle. Claudel has become a master," Rodin admiringly exclaims. "She has the talent of a man," replies a visitor. "She's a witch!" pronounces another. The notion that such virtuosity is unnatural in a woman is reinforced by the strangeness of the appellation "master," when Rodin bestows it upon Claudel, his "mistress" (here again "master" and "mistress" are as close sexually as the two words are remote semantically), as well as by the charge of witchery that betrays a less admiring position. Such attitudes combined with real madness (clinical paranoia probably) must have contributed much to the nightmare into which (the historical) Claudel descended after her relationship with Rodin came to an end in 1893. After years of struggling in an atmosphere of squalor, isolation, and increasing delusions of persecution, she was committed by her brother, the poet Paul Claudel, in 1913 and spent the last thirty years of her life institutionalized.[14]

But prior to revealing itself as something we now call psychosis, Claudel's madness was called a madness of mud and the film portrays it as a sculptural perversion, if you will: a passion for touching, feeling, and making that is tactile and dirty, virtually scatological and highly eroticized. This "dirtiness" was alluded to in the dialogue between Rodin and Claudel in the carriage. It is illustrated beautifully by a scene of Claudel at work—a scene situated chronologically in the narrative at the very juncture between life with Rodin and descent into madness—in which, stripped down to her underclothes, she is shown passionately engaged with a huge mound of clay, pulling and tearing at it, embracing it and covering herself in it, breathing heavily—indeed panting—ending up covered in brown smears of clay. This is a very ambivalent scene. There is no mistaking the explicit eroticism of it (if you listen without watching, it sounds exactly like a sex scene). But, at the same time, its place in the trajectory of the story and its inherently disturbing imagery place *Camille Claudel*'s viewers at an intersection where the allure of a dangerously passionate woman threatens to give way to the horror of madness.

Thus, from a "clinical" point of view, the psychosexual pathology revealed in *Camille Claudel* is not *Artemisia*'s scopophilia—love of looking. Instead, it is the more disturbing coprophilia—love of excrement, which suggests a fixation at the infantile "smearing" stage. Indeed, this film's sense of its subject necessarily holds at a distance this very tangible, visceral, sensory engagement with the material. Even as it approximates the sculptor's spatial and textural sensibility through imaginative use of cinematic technique—camera movement and sound especially (both of which are intensely descriptive and atmospheric in this film)—*Camille Claudel* finally will not go so far as to equate its own voyeurism

Mud lust: *Camille Claudel.*

and love of craft, even fetishism of technique, with its subject's mud lust and madness. As a possible component of the cinematic psyche, coprophilia is certainly too threatening an explanation for the filmmaker's interest in "making." The shame associated with the repression of excremental pleasures infects this portrait of Claudel with ambivalence and an anxiety that attaches to gender.

This ambivalence contributes to the film's oscillation between mythic images of a productive "madness of mud" and more realist yet sensitive images of a destructive, paranoid madness. This realist, seemingly almost justified, madness reflects an inequity that has been bitterly repeated throughout art history to the extent it retains any memory at all of women artists. Their stories, especially those of women who worked in the shadow of a great male mentor or "peer," are all too often tragic. Claudel's life ended in madness. Constance Mayer—apprentice, mistress, and model to Pierre-Paul Prud'hon—slit her own throat with his razor in 1821. Elizabeth Siddall—wife and model of Dante Gabriel Rossetti—died of a laudanum overdose in 1862. Ana Mendieta—wife of Carl Andre—died in 1985 after a "fall" from the window of their SoHo loft. And Frida Kahlo—wife of Diego Rivera—died after unspeakable sufferings of pneumonia and pulmonary embolism in 1954, only emerging from the shadow of Rivera and achieving recognition, along with her singular iconic status, decades after her death.

The grief Kahlo endured in her relationship with Rivera is one theme in the vivid and poignant, if uneven, *Frida* (Julie Taymor, 2002). Directed by a woman, and motivated by Salma Hayek's financial and artistic investment in creating a fitting portrayal of the complex Kahlo and her work, this artist biopic strikes an interesting contrast with another, its contemporary, *Pollock* (Ed Harris, 2001). As a necessary corollary to its portrayal of the painfully masculine, tortured, alcoholic genius, Jackson Pollock, Harris's film paints a strange portrait indeed of the artist's wife and fellow painter, Lee Krasner (1908–1984). One of modern art history's only women artists to both retain her sanity and survive her more famous spouse, Krasner, an accomplished artist (arguably the equal of her husband), relative to him or any of the exemplars named above, suffered from mere obscurity. That is, until *Pollock*, a film that constructs her as a pushy, pedantic, controlling shrew. Anne M. Wagner has well deconstructed this tendency to prop up the image of the paradigmatically macho, intuitive, inarticulate, Protestant, Western-born genius Pollock with a Krasner of straw, defined antithetically, and in terms of sexist and ethnic stereotypes: an Easterner, pretentious and urban, but also a wily, homely, and suffocatingly Jewish-mother type.[15]

Abject Desire

The figure of the hard-drinking Jackson Pollock and the big, fierce, muscular action paintings for which he became famous—along with latter-day followers, such as the egotistical, macho, neo-expressionist painters of huge ambitious canvases who were dominant in the 1980s (e.g., Julien Schnabel, Francesco Clemente, or Anselm Kiefer)—are prototypes for the character and work of Lionel Dobie, played by Nick Nolte in Martin Scorsese's short but stunning 1989 film, *Life Lessons* (his contribution to the *New York Stories* anthology). Pollock is tacitly (and punningly) acknowledged as Dobie's original in the film's credit sequence, where the New York School's most famous painter's characteristic "splatter" is the background to the film's opening titles. The story, like that of *Artemisia* and *Camille Claudel*, concerns a relationship between an older male master and a younger female pupil, but here the student neither rises to nor surpasses the master's genius. She is an insecure and indifferent painter.

It is not Paulette's vision or talent that inspire Dobie, but, as is probably more realistic, her youth and beauty, and his desire for her. She is to him that improbably mythic and old-fashioned object—a muse. Though eloquent about the experience of being such a mythic creature (late in the film, Paulette cries out, "Sometimes I feel like a human sacrifice!"), *Life Lessons* focuses less on the muse and more on the master and the means by which he creates. And this film is the most explicit of the three in its visual focus on artistic facture. It features sustained and repeated scenes of art making, equating art making with filmmaking and offering a cinematic equivalent for virtually every painterly flourish (bold,

"Life Lessons" (Martin Scorsese, from *New York Stories,* 1989; photo courtesy of Jerry Ohlinger's Movie Material Store).

up-front use of handheld camera; panning and tilting; iris shots; slow motion; jump cuts; filtered shots, to name a few) and suggesting a parallel between the progress (or "action") of the big painting that Dobie creates in the course of the film and the film narrative itself.

At the film's outset, the sexual relationship has already ended: Paulette, who has evidently been Lionel Dobie's live-in apprentice-*cum*-mistress for some time, informs him that it's over and she's moving out, possibly away from New York, which has not been nice to her (she's just been thrown over by an up-and-coming performance artist for whom she harbors a debilitating passion). Lionel persuades Paulette to stay in New York, in his loft, as his assistant, assuring her that he respects her decision to end their relationship. But he harbors a passion for her that makes hers look like a schoolgirl crush. And while Paulette's desire disables her artistically, Lionel's fuels his work. He is catapulted from a state of artistic inertia by lust. The more abject he becomes, the more energetically he paints.

Much of the film illustrates this as Lionel alternates between pathetic, humiliating encounters with Paulette and ever more vigorous work on his big canvas, as in the scene where he cannot, for the second time in one evening, resist entering her room, and uses an excuse both feeble and obvious in its sexual symbolism: "I think I left my sable brush in here," he insists when she chides him for entering unbidden. The scene is framed by scenes of Dobie at work, which are noteworthy in several respects. First, in a couple of big, sweeping pans, the power and the glory of Dobie's art and reputation is established (the accompanying song is about power: it's Cream's "Politician"), along with the vast scale and ambition of his work and his thick, *creamy*, painterly virtuosity. Big, passionate, athletic gestures, in the expressionist vernacular, suggest deep psychosexual forces at work.

That Dobie's is essentially a sexual energy (and a highly gendered sexual energy at that) is implied by the image of the painter glancing at, then stepping upon, a black-and-white photo of a female nude in a magazine—shown in striking jump-cut close-ups—followed by a quick cut to viscous yellow paint squirting out of a tube. Then it is confirmed by his almost demented behavior, his silly lost sable brush gambit, and his fetishistic focus on Paulette's foot. "I just wanted to kiss your foot. I'm sorry. It's nothing personal," Dobie quite improbably insists. "Do you want me to get you anything?" The scene then succinctly evokes, in the little "blue" movie this question conjures in Paulette's mind's eye, and the dialogue that follows, her ambivalent sense of erotic power over Lionel. First she remembers (or imagines) him as a tender, confident, clean romantic partner (in a monochromatic sequence shot in shades of blue to Procol Harum's "A Whiter Shade of Pale"). Or does she? The song has already been associated strongly with him. As Ronald Librach puts it, relating the scene to the opening sequence of Godard's *Une Femme Mariée*, "Here, too, stylization signals an ironic supremacy of images over reality: that is, of the pathos of fulfilled desire as the theme of an interpretive pantomime all about the consummation of a relationship between an artist/lover and the object of his aesthetics and desire (palette/Paulette). The comic irony of the sequence is ensured by a simple deflection in continuity: the expressly described look of desire on *her* face establishes *his* point of view."[16]

Paulette sends the soiled, emotionally exposed, abject Lionel on his way: "Do you love me?" she asks. "Love you? I said I did. Yes," replies Dobie. "What would you do if I left?" she probes. "What would I do? . . . I'd go up on the roof and howl like a gut-shot dog." "Well, I don't love you," Paulette rejoins. "So what?" says Dobie. He departs her room and resumes painting with renewed vigor; this time, in a rather intriguing and symmetrical conceit (shot/reverse shot), the process is shown from the painting's point of view (when the screen looks back at him, though—cf. *Artemisia*—he is no mere object; he is very much a subject; he retains the brush/phallus and his agency).

Abject, Dobie is in fact powerful, converting his misery into the action that produces the huge, virile, violent paintings so valued by society. That his passion for Paulette—for whom he'll do almost anything, he claims (kiss a New York City cop on the lips; even stretch her canvases)—not only cannot take precedence over his work but actually fuels it, is evident in a scene where Dobie fails even to notice her. Paulette has come down from her room (visible from the floor

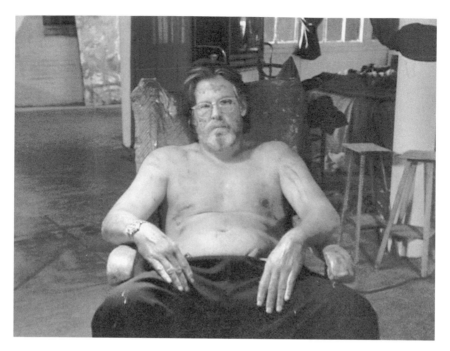

Abject desire: "Life Lessons."

of Lionel's loft as a hole in the wall upon which he repeatedly fixates) to ask him to turn down the music, but he neither hears nor sees her as she stands, at first bemused, and then plainly bedazzled by his display of creative force.

Here, too, one sees the explicit erotic force of Dobie's painting, both in terms of his thrusting and lunging libidinous energy and sensual engagement with the work and in terms of Paulette's reaction, which betrays evidence, in successively tighter close-ups, of not only admiration but seduction, past and present. The cutting between the impression his work registers on her face, the process, and the work itself, the matching of cinematic gesture with painterly flourish, the choreography of the entire piece to Bob Dylan's live "action" version (with The Dead) of "Like a Rolling Stone"—all achieves a thrilling vision of creative force, a tour de force (really a perfect term to describe the cumulative effect of Scorsese's film, Nolte's performance, and the production of the painting).

Another scene demonstrates conclusively the irony of Dobie's degradation and the function of his desperate lust. He returns from an event at which he witnessed Paulette leaving with a younger, very handsome painter and discovers that she's brought the guy home: he sees movement and hears voices from his vantage point below her little hole in the wall. In this scene, again, Scorsese's use of music is notable: the handsome Latin rival is named Toro; the song is

Procol Harum's "Conquistador." Dobie looks—disheartened and long—up at Paulette's window, then strips off his shirt and paints like a house on fire. He goes over to the radio to tune the dial and, as the sound segues from "Conquistador" to "Nessum Dorma," a dissolve cuts to him seated, glazed, sweaty, exhausted, with paint in his beard. Never, perhaps, has the abject been more poignantly realized on film than here, where Nick Nolte sits, seemingly in ruins—lumpish, inert, and filthy—as Puccini's aria (from *Turandot*) throbs. As this "lament for both unrelieved fatigue and unfulfilled love" reinforces, Dobie is the very picture of pathos and defeat.[17] But no, after a shower and a cup of coffee he is ready for a confrontation with the "bull." Toro comes down and asks him for a cup of coffee; Dobie pours him one, and in a revealing, supercilious, racist quip, asks him if he's a graffiti artist. Then a sudden burst of music shocks, as Dobie adopts his pose before the big canvas and performs the coup de grâce. The phallic thrust of the paintbrush signifies. The grin on his face says it all. Toro may have slept with Paulette but he, Dobie, is the better painter (he knows it). Toro's sexual conquest is nothing to his artistic one. He, not Toro, is the conquistador. Dobie's sense of superiority derives from his success but, the details of the film's script and setting suggest implicitly, also from the very privileges that attend to his sex, age, and race.

Coup de grâce: "Life Lessons."

The film ends with Paulette leaving as Dobie is completing his grand picture—a canvas as big as a movie screen, filled with action. (The painting is actually *The Bridge to Nowhere* by Chuck Connelly. Paulette's paintings are by Susan Hambleton.) "You think I just use people," he charges. "Well, you don't know anything about me. You don't know how involved I get, or how far down I go. Hell, I was married four times since before you were even born, so don't you tell me." She leaves. He is stricken. At the gallery opening where the product of Dobie's passion is displayed with other recent work, the lovely young bartender (an aspiring painter) practically throws herself at Dobie's feet and his next "human sacrifice" is in place—more grist for the mill.

The story of Lionel Dobie and Paulette, finally, is a remake of an ancient story, or is it a myth?—the story of the genius and his muse. Scorsese sees Dobie's accomplishment as the gift of genius and the grace of sublimation, what Freud described as "the process through which the excessive excitations from individual sexual sources are discharged and utilized in other spheres, so that no small enhancement of mental capacity results from a predisposition which is dangerous as such."[18] Although Dobie's excessive sexual sources are hardly described in *Life Lessons* as unconscious, they are plainly "utilized in other spheres," much along Freud's model. Indeed, in describing the basic nature of the urges that can be sublimated into higher, cultural aims, Freud employs a term peculiarly evocative of the fine arts: "We therefore have to conclude that the sexual impulse-excitations are exceptionally 'plastic,' if I may use the word."[19] And Freud identifies art as the most privileged product of sublimation, describing the artist, in a now immortal passage that delimits the reader's picture of an artist's race, sexual orientation, and gender as much as does the term "master," as "urged on by instinctual needs which are too clamorous; he longs to attain to honour, power, riches, fame, and the love of women."[20] With consummate irony and self-consciousness and not a little immodesty, Scorsese exposes in *Life Lessons* the sordid side of this gift of sublimation, its psychic cost to both "genius" and, especially "muse," as the artistic process consumes the "relationship."

Myths of Origin and the Cinematic Object

And Scorsese knows of what he speaks. He is, after all, portraying himself (in this case, quite self-consciously, I think) in Lionel Dobie: the mature, celebrated, oft-married artist, renowned for his big, colorful, violent, action-packed, gestural, almost baroque tours de force. Likewise (whether he knows it or not) is Bruno Nuytten, the cameraman turned director, at some level portraying himself in *Camille Claudel*, his film about artists whose work is shown as craft as well as art: tactile, manual, and in the case of Rodin's big projects like *The Gates of Hell* or *The Burghers of Calais,* also big productions, created by large teams of specialists. And so, naturally, is Agnès Merlet involved in self-portraiture in her image of Artemisia Gentileschi, shown as a woman so turned on by looking at art that she must make it and make it hot. In Merlet's mind's eye, the baroque studio becomes the modern film studio, the painting the cinematic tableau. It's a simple substitution of one kind of machinery for another.

Despite their titular female protagonists, *Artemisia* and *Camille Claudel* ultimately propose a view of artistic or cinematic origins hardly empowering to women, since each constructs art as a product of a female imagination deformed by pathology (scopophilia, coprophilia). "The conflation of an artist's biography and works of art functions very differently if the artist is a man or a woman," Griselda Pollock notes of the biographical background to films such as these. "*His* art appears to give us access to the mystery of genius; *hers* merely confirms the pathology of the feminine, saturated by her sex, of which she becomes both emblem and symptom. And while a female artist's paintings are read with the knowledge of her 'deviant' femininity firmly in mind, her biography is usually twisted to hinge on a powerfully sexual male figure."[21] *Life Lessons,* no gem of feminist filmmaking either, only reiterates the more common view of female artistic imagination as feeble, insecure, and distracted by more immanent concerns.

But in all three films, the passionate commitment to art is seen not only as inherently and originally sexual in its underlying energies but also as explicitly bound up in sexual forces. In them, the heterosexual artist couple embodies the cinema's love affair with love, erotic and sublime. The art that seems to issue from this love, product of the erotic engagement, becomes the film itself. The narrative is a mythic one of cinematic origins — the couples personifying the ultimately erotic act of filmmaking — that touches upon the peculiar sensibility of the film and its maker(s), be those involved with the quasi-pornographic experience of looking, the almost fetishistic interest in technique and handling, or heroic passions and the valorization of gesture and production. It's a narrative that articulates the erotic nature of energies that flow into the production of any art. But by reiterating an ancient and mythic scenario of genius and muse, of master and subject, by focusing (as is usual) on the normative, white, heterosexual couple of older man and younger woman, and by entangling its female protagonists' artistic passions with images of pathological desire, the narrative finally offers an exclusive myth that aims only to explain — indeed to naturalize — the achievement of those already "known" to be great or potentially great. You might call it the primal scene of canon formation.

Notes

Introduction: Baring the Device

1. Erwin Panofsky, "Iconography and Iconology: An Introduction to the Study of Renaissance Art," in *Meaning in the Visual Arts* (Garden City, NY: Doubleday Anchor, 1955), 26–54. Originally published as "Introductory" in *Studies in Iconology: Humanistic Themes in the Art of the Renaissance* (New York: Oxford University Press, 1939).

2. First published in 1934, and written in support of the foundation of the Museum of Modern Art's film department, Panofsky's "Style and Medium in the Motion Pictures" was revised and given its definitive form in *Critique* 1, no. 3 (January-February 1947): 5–28. On Panofsky and film, see Thomas Y. Levin, "Iconology at the Movies: Panofsky's Film Theory," *Yale Journal of Criticism* 9, no. 1 (1996): 27–55.

3. MPAA statistics, published in "The 1980s: A Reference Guide to Motion Pictures, Television, VCR, and Cable," "Appendix B: Top 10 Films," *Velvet Light Trap*, no. 27 (Spring 1991, special number on the 1980s): 81.

4. First verse of "Artists and Models," title song of film written by Jack Brooks and Harry Warren.

5. The intuitive relationship between this embedded kind of "animation" and the kind at which Tashlin got his start in pictures—a cartoonist and comic artist, he became an animator for RKO, Warner Brothers (*Merrie Melodies* and *Looney Tunes*), and MGM in the 1930s—has been noted elsewhere, for instance by Robert Mundy, "Frank Tashlin: A Tribute," in *Frank Tashlin*, ed. Claire Johnston and Paul Willemen (Edinburgh: Edinburgh Film Festival, in assoc. with *Screen*, 1973), 10. Among the cartoon-like gags that Mundy does not mention is the opening gag of the animated (blowing) billboard mouth.

6. Paul Willemen, "Tashlin's Method: An Hypothesis," in *Frank Tashlin*, 117–129.

7. Henry Jenkins and Kristine Brunovska Karnick, "Acting Funny," in *Classical Hollywood Comedy*, ed. Kristine Brunovska Karnick and Henry Jenkins (London: Routledge, 1995), 161.

8. "zetes," Madison, WI, Internet Movie Database (www.imdb.com) user comment for *Artists and Models*, September 14, 2002.

9. Frank Krutnik, "A Spanner in the Works: Genre, Narrative and the Hollywood Comedian," in *Classical Hollywood Comedy*, 354, n. 34.

10. Ibid., 37.

11. Molly Haskell, *From Reverence to Rape: The Treatment of Women in the Movies* (New York: Holt, Rinehart and Winston, 1974), 66.

12. Krutnik, "A Spanner in the Works," 37.

1. The Moving Picture Gallery

A much earlier, somewhat shorter, version of this chapter originally appeared in the journal *Iris*, nos. 14–15 (Fall 1992). It appears here with permission.

1. When earlier versions of this chapter were written, first as a conference paper, then as an article for a special number of the journal *Iris*, Greta Garbo and Bette Davis were the stars whose rather recent deaths I recalled. As I revise "The Moving Picture Gallery" in the summer of 2003, it is Peck and Hepburn whose passings are still uncannily fresh.

2. Leon Battista Alberti, excerpts from "On Painting" (Della pittura), in *A Documentary History of Art*, vol. 1, ed. Elizabeth Gilmore Holt (Garden City, NY: Doubleday Anchor, 1957), 211.

3. The painted portrait in film was the subject of a Louvre conference and, subsequently, a special number of the journal *Iris*, nos. 14–15 (Fall 1992), edited by Dominique Païni and Marc Vernet, in which an earlier version of this chapter appeared (191–200). Other pertinent essays in that volume, not cited elsewhere, are Vernet's "Dictatures du pignoché: Les fictions du portrait," 45–54; and Thomas Elsaesser's "Mirror, Muse, Medusa: *Experiment Perilous*," 147–159. Kent Minturn's absorbing essay, "Peinture Noire: Abstract Expressionism and Film Noir," in *Film Noir Reader 2*, ed. Alain Silver and James Ursini (New York: Limelight, 1999), 271–309, makes a strong case for the influence of film noir on the development of abstract expressionism, in formal, cultural-historical, and structural terms. It also includes a useful appendix that lists films noir in which art and artists figure.

4. Roland Barthes, *Camera Lucida*, trans. Richard Howard (New York: Farrar, Straus and Giroux, 1981), 96.

5. Specifically the painted portrait; see ibid., e.g., 11, 30–32, 79, 89–90.

6. Michael Fried, *Absorption and Theatricality: Painting and Beholder in the Age of Diderot* (Berkeley: University of California Press, 1980), 109.

7. Jacques Lacan, *The Four Fundamental Concepts of Psychoanalysis*, trans. Alan Sheridan (New York: Norton, 1981).

8. Peter Brunette and David Wills, *Screen/Play: Derrida and Film Theory* (Princeton, NJ: Princeton University Press, 1989), 117.

9. Tania Modleski, *The Women Who Knew Too Much: Hitchcock and Feminist Theory* (New York: Methuen, 1988), 49.

10. Ibid., 55.

11. Stephen Heath, "Narrative Space," in *Narrative, Apparatus, Ideology*, ed. Philip Rosen (New York: Columbia University Press, 1986), 378.

12. Reynold Humphries, *Fritz Lang: Genre and Representation in His American Films* (Baltimore: Johns Hopkins University Press, 1989), 116.

13. As J. P. Telotte notes, "Film noir has often been described as the most consciously arty of popular genres" and "perhaps our most direct confrontation with noir's arty nature occurs in the films that focus on modern art." See Telotte, "Self Portrait: Painting and the Film Noir," *Smithsonian Studies in American Art* 3, no. 1 (Winter 1989): 3–17.

14. Mary Ann Doane, *The Desire to Desire: The Woman's Film of the 1940s* (Bloomington: Indiana University Press, 1987), 143.

15. Ibid., 123. Doane is not the first critic of *The Two Mrs. Carrolls* to mistakenly (I think) describe Mr. Carroll's pictures as abstracted. She follows the lead of Diane Waldman, who, in her landmark article, "The Childish, the Insane and the Ugly: The Representation of Modern Art in Popular Film and Fiction of the Forties," *Wide Angle* 5, no. 2 (1982): 52–65, claimed that "the artist-husband's nonrepresentational style is actually presented as a sign of his mental derangement" (56). "Nonrepresentational" is really not an apt adjective for the distortions evident in the canvas shown.

16. *Really* abstract portraits are featured, however, to comedic effect in at least two films of the 1940s. In both Ernst Lubitsch's *That Uncertain Feeling* (1941) and John Farrow's *The Big Clock* (1948), surrealistically abstract portraits intentionally confound. In these instances, misrepresentation and misrecognition are concertedly the point.

17. The image of the secreted canvas, hidden away in the garret, and its degraded representation, is comparable not only to *The Picture of Dorian Gray*, but also to Balzac's *The Unknown Masterpiece*, the literary source for Jacques Rivette's *La Belle Noiseuse*, discussed in my chapter 4.

18. Edgar Allan Poe, "The Oval Portrait," in *Selected Writings*, ed. David Galloway (Harmondsworth, England: Penguin, 1967), 250–253.

19. Elisabeth Bronfen, *Over Her Dead Body: Death, Femininity, and the Aesthetic* (New York: Routledge, 1992), 112.

20. For a compelling discussion of the element of the portrait in Epstein's film, see Jacques Aumont, "Le Portrait absent," *Iris*, nos. 14–15 (Fall 1992): 135–145.

21. Françoise Meltzer, *Salome and the Dance of Writing: Portraits of Mimesis in Literature* (Chicago: University of Chicago, 1987), 106. In the story, Meltzer continues, "death and life are exchanged, and this through the power of art. This parallels Hawthorne's formulation: 'Others, frightened at the art which could raise phantoms at will, and keep the form of the dead among the living'" (109). Nathaniel Hawthorne's "Prophetic Pictures" and Poe's "Oval Portrait," thus, according to Meltzer, derive their thrilling discomfort from a Mosaic taboo against image making. "The taboo itself is a mark of the power of art: for despite its frame, art cannot be contained; but it is the attempt to contain it which generates the taboo" (110–111).

22. Sigmund Freud, "The Uncanny" (1919), in *Studies in Parapsychology*, ed. Philip Rieff (New York: MacMillan/Collier, 1963), 53–54.

23. Parker Tyler, "Dorian Gray: Last of the Movie Draculas," *View* (New York) 7, no. 2 (October 1946): 22.

24. Lewin repeated this effect in his subsequent film, *The Private Affairs of Bel Ami* (1947), based on the Maupassant novel *Bel-Ami*, in which he inserted, again in Technicolor, a "decalcomaniacal" Max Ernst painting, *The Temptation of Saint Anthony*. Again, an intensely formalized black-and-white, fin-de-siècle mise-en-scène is ruptured by a gruesome twentieth-century painting. Ivan Albright was one of the eleven artists (mostly surrealists or magic realists), in addition to Ernst, who were invited by Lewin to submit a painting on this theme to "The Bel Ami Competition." The judges of the competition—Alfred Barr, Marcel Duchamp, and Sidney Janis—selected the Ernst. See Susan Felleman, *Botticelli in Hollywood: The Films of Albert Lewin* (New York: Twayne, 1997), 63–79.

25. For a fascinating discussion of reception and the barely suppressed representations of lesbian relationships in these two films, see Rhona J. Bernstein, "Adaptation, Censor-

ship, and Audiences of Questionable Type: Lesbian Sightings in *Rebecca* (1940) and *The Uninvited* (1944)," *Cinema Journal* 37, no. 3 (Spring 1998): 16–37.

26. Dana Polan, *Power and Paranoia: History, Narrative, and the American Cinema, 1940–1950* (New York: Columbia University Press, 1986), 20. The historical movement Polan describes is interesting, though, relative to the progressive "disenchantment" charted by Theodore Ziolkowski in *Disenchanted Images: A Literary Iconology* (Princeton, NJ: Princeton University Press, 1977) and central to my analysis in chapter 3.

27. Polan, *Power and Paranoia*, 188–189.

28. Joseph Mankiewicz, "Measure for Measure," interview with Jacques Bontemps and Richard Overstreet, *Cahiers du Cinema (English)* 8 (February 1967): 32.

29. For a thorough discussion of this iconology, see chapter 3 of Ziolkowski's invaluable *Disenchanted Images*.

30. Cocteau's film was actually the impetus for Ziolkowski's literary iconology. See his introduction. On the Italian and Russian silent cinematic use of portraiture, see two essays in the special issue of *Iris*, nos. 14–15 (Fall 1992): Ivo L. Blom's "*Il Fuoco* or the Fatal Portrait: The Nineteenth Century in the Italian Silent Cinema," 55–66; and Yuri Tsivian's "Portraits, Mirrors, Death: On Some Decadent Clichés in Early Russian Films," 67–83.

31. At least two films I have neglected employ portraits in morbid melodramas of almost Gothic proportions: in Curtis Bernhardt's *A Stolen Life* and John Brahm's *The Locket* (both 1946), male portraitists (Dane Clark and Robert Mitchum, respectively) produce images that symptomatize the deceits of their female subjects (Bette Davis's character's substitution of herself for her dead twin is evidenced by the mimetic record of the portrait; Laraine Day's character's pathological lying and its roots in a trauma of innocence are echoed in the portraits of her as Cassandra).

32. Thomas Elsaesser, "Rivette and the End of Cinema," *Sight and Sound* (new series) 1, no. 12 (April 1992): 20.

2. A Form of Necrophilia (The Moving Picture Gallery Revisited)

1. François Truffaut, *Hitchcock* (New York: Simon and Schuster, 1967), 186.

2. I am grateful to Sara Netzley for bringing the last of these to my attention. She delivered a version of her excellent consideration of *Dellamorte*, written for my fall 2002 graduate seminar on feminism and film theory, to the Midwest Popular Culture Association's meeting in Minneapolis in October 2003.

3. Bronfen, *Over Her Dead Body*, 326. It should be noted that Albert Lewin worked briefly on a film adaptation of *Bruges la Morte*. See Felleman, *Botticelli in Hollywood*, 157.

4. Heinrich Heine, *Aus den Memoiren des herren von Schnabelwopski, Heines Werk*, vol. 2 (East Berlin: Aufbau-Verlag, 1981), 310 (my translation).

5. Ibid., 311. Lewin's screenplay and film include this line almost verbatim in the Dutchman's memoir/recitation.

6. See, e.g., Robin Wood, "Male Desire, Male Anxiety: The Essential Hitchcock," *A Hitchcock Reader*, Marshall Deutelbaum and Leland Poague, eds. (Ames: Iowa State University Press, 1986), 219–230; Modleski, *The Women Who Knew Too Much*, 87–100; and Ayako Saito, "Hitchcock's Trilogy: A Logic of Mise en Scène," in *Endless Night: Cinema and Psychoanalysis, Parallel Histories*, ed. Janet Bergstrom (Berkeley: University of California Press, 1999), 200–214.

7. For an excellent treatment of melancholy and mood in Hitchcock, see Saito, "Hitchcock's Trilogy."

8. Georges Auric's score for *Corridor of Mirrors,* as William Everson has pointed out, "with its Wagnerian undertone of menace complementing the dominant romantic themes, is so like his music for the Cocteau film [*Beauty and the Beast,* 1946] that it is perhaps a more constant reminder of it." "Rediscovery: *Corridor of Mirrors,*" *Films in Review* 38 (January 1987): 39. Bernard Herrmann's score for De Palma's *Obsession* is, of course, "uncannily" like the one he had done for *Vertigo.* Rawsthorne composed the score to *Pandora and the Flying Dutchman* and Jarre, *The Last Tycoon.*

9. Bronfen, *Over Her Dead Body,* 326.

10. Sigmund Freud, "Mourning and Melancholia" (1917), in *Collected Papers,* vol. 4, trans. and ed. Joan Riviere (New York: Basic Books, 1959). Mourning, Freud maintains, arises from the struggle to detach the libido from a beloved object after its loss, while melancholia's lost objects arise from within the psyche and are obscure.

11. André Bazin, "The Ontology of the Photographic Image," in *What Is Cinema?* vol. 1, trans. and ed. Hugh Gray (Berkeley: University of California Press, 1967), 9.

12. I am indebted to Tony Williams, who in his book *Structures of Desire: British Cinema, 1939–1955* (Albany: State University of New York Press, 2000), 120–121, first brought this film to my attention.

13. William Everson astutely observes that this detail, along with the framing narration on the railway carriage, are rather direct borrowings from a very successful British film of a few years earlier, David Lean's *Brief Encounter.* See "Rediscovery: *Corridor of Mirrors,*" in which Young's film is characterized as "heavily influenced" by both Lean's film and Cocteau's *Beauty and the Beast* (39). I would add another powerful influence among recent films: Albert Lewin's *Picture of Dorian Gray* (1945). Among other similarities, this film concerns comparably eerie, supernatural goings-on. The protagonist secretly keeps an uncanny portrait and meets his love interest, Sibyl Vane, in a club (where she performs), causing a temporary disturbance as he enters in his lordly, caped costume; he moves around his grandiose home—a virtual museum, full of obscure collections and antiquities—like a somnambule; the film also employs a mannequin or dummy in a way that is echoed variously in *Corridor.* See Felleman, *Botticelli in Hollywood,* 40–61.

14. On the relationship to Cocteau, see Everson, "Rediscovery"; also see Alain Mitjaville, "Un Etrange rendez-vous, ou *Le Corridor des Miroirs,*" *Les Cahiers de la Cinématheque* 30/31, no. 1 (Summer/Fall 1980): 129–131, who notes the surrealist aspects of the scenario. Mitjaville describes Mifanwy as "the faithful living reproduction of the adored image. At first, she plays this anachronistic game. But isn't it, from a surrealist point of view, the most authentic manifestation of love: the recognition in the beloved object of the always already desired, in other words, the one already encountered in a bygone era, in the depths of one's heart!" (129, translated by Virginie Lamarche and the author).

15. Lacan, *Psychoanalysis,* 205.

16. See, e.g., Freud, "The Uncanny"; Otto Rank, "The Double as Immortal Self," in *Beyond Psychology* (New York: Dover, 1958), 62–101; and, for a literary explanation, Meltzer, *Salome,* 105–111.

17. Barthes, *Camera Lucida,* 79.

18. I devote less description of narrative and plot to the four later films because they are generally better known, having been described elsewhere (for *Pandora,* see chapter 4 of my *Botticelli in Hollywood*).

19. Mankiewicz's film is discussed further in the next chapter. Mankind itself is eradicated permanently, of course, in *On the Beach*, a story of nuclear annihilation.

20. This painting was originally to be a commission by Man Ray, but Lewin did not like the results and substituted one by British artist, set designer, and art director Ferdie Bellan. See Felleman, *Botticelli in Hollywood*, 87–88.

21. See, e.g., Sarah Boxer, "Paintings Too Perfect? The Great Optics Debate," *New York Times*, December 4, 2001, Sec. E, 1.

22. See Felleman, *Botticelli in Hollywood*, 85–96.

23. Poe, "The Oval Portrait," 250–253. The other authors are quoted and cited elsewhere.

24. Bronfen, *Over Her Dead Body*, 59–75.

25. The film was adapted by Alec Coppel and Samuel Taylor from the novel *D'entre les morts*, by Pierre Boileau and Thomas Narcejac, which does not include the "corridor of mirrors" metaphor in its dialogue. Of the various authors who have read *Vertigo* as allegory, a foremost example is William Rothman, in *Hitchcock: The Murderous Gaze* (Cambridge, MA: Harvard University Press, 1982). A hugely influential reading is that of Robin Wood in *Hitchcock's Films Revisited* (New York: Columbia University Press, 1989), as well as his "Male Desire, Male Anxiety." An indispensable summary of much relevant feminist work on *Vertigo* is Susan White's "*Vertigo* and Problems of Knowledge in Feminist Film Theory," in *Alfred Hitchcock: Centenary Essays*, ed. Richard Allen and S. Ishii-Gonzales (London: BFI, 1999), 279–298. See also her "Allegory and Referentiality: *Vertigo* and Feminist Film Criticism," *MLN* 106, no. 5 (1991): 310–332. Two authors who have preceded me in focusing on the role of art in the film are Barbara Odabashian in "Portrait of an Artist: Hitchcock's *Vertigo*," *Hitchcock Annual* (1999–2000), 93–99; and Brigitte Peucker, whose "The Cut of Representation: Painting and Sculpture in Hitchcock," in *Alfred Hitchcock: Centenary Essays*, ed. Richard Allen and S. Ishii-Gonzales (London: BFI, 1999), 141–156, is incisive. See also the exhibition catalogue edited by Dominique Païni and Guy Cogeval, *Hitchcock and Art: Fatal Coincidences* (Montreal: Montreal Museum of Fine Arts, 2000). As mentioned previously, Elisabeth Bronfen, in *Over Her Dead Body*, discusses *Vertigo* in the context of two literary works with a similar trope, in her chapter 15, "Risky Resemblances."

26. Midge defaces her self-portrait as Carlotta, making her, with Veronica in *Corridor of Mirrors* and Pandora in Lewin's film, the third of three female iconoclasts in as many films.

27. Modleski, *The Women Who Knew Too Much*; and Peucker, "The Cut of Representation."

28. This parable is central to Jean Epstein's (1928) beautiful adaptation of Poe's *The Fall of the House of Usher*, into which narrative the director folds two other Poe stories in which life and death are exchanged, "The Oval Portrait" and "Ligeia."

29. Barthes, *Camera Lucida*, 79.

30. Robert C. Cumbow and Grace A. Cumbow, "The New Life Begins: Dantean Obsession in *Obsession*," *Movietone News*, no. 53 (January 16, 1977): 25.

31. Jonathan Rosenbaum, review of "*Obsession*," *Monthly Film Bulletin* 43, no. 513 (October 1976): 217.

32. The portraits are credited to one Barton De Palma.

33. Robin Wood, *Hollywood from Vietnam to Reagan* (New York: Columbia University Press, 1986), 144.

34. Cumbow and Cumbow, "The New Life Begins," 26.

35. Susan Sontag, *On Photography* (New York: Delta, 1973), 70.

36. Harold Pinter, *The Last Tycoon*, in *"The French Lieutenant's Woman" and Other Screenplays* (London: Methuen, 1982), 227–229.

37. Jeff Young, *Kazan: The Master Director Discusses His Films* (New York: Newmarket, 1999), 320.

38. Pinter, *The Last Tycoon*, 241, scene 85.

39. Ibid., 275–276.

40. Freud, "The Uncanny," 40.

41. Tom Gunning, "Phantom Images and Modern Manifestations: Spirit Photography, Magic Theater, Trick Films, and Photography's Uncanny," in *Fugitive Images: From Photography to Video*, ed. Patrice Petro (Bloomington: Indiana University Press, 1995), 68.

42. On the closeness of cinephilia to necrophilia, "relating to something that is dead, past, but alive in memory," see Paul Willemen, "Through the Glass Darkly: Cinephilia Reconsidered," chapter 12 of his *Looks and Frictions* (Bloomington: Indiana University Press/BFI, 1994), 227.

43. It should be noted here that the 1948 Young film is an obvious, if heretofore unheralded, influence on the plot of *Dead Again*. The basic story and many other similarities suggest that Branagh and his screenwriter relied heavily on the then quite obscure *Corridor of Mirrors* in piecing together their pastiche: a contemporary man and woman who are reincarnations of a prior couple in which one was accused of murdering the other; the surprise ending, in which a household servant (or son thereof) turns out to be responsible for a murder for which his/her employer was executed; the characters Paul Mangin and Roman Strauss—both arrogant, severe, rather tyrannical figures; the gifts of antique jewels; the extravagant costume ball.

44. Marcia Landy and Lucy Fischer, "*Dead Again* or A-Live Again: Postmodern or Postmortem?" *Cinema Journal* 33, no. 4 (Summer 1994): 18.

45. *The Majestic*'s Adele asks the question, "You remember movies, but you don't remember your life?" of Luke/Appleton when she discovers that he can recite plotlines and dialogue from *The Life of Emile Zola*, but remembers nothing of his own or (obviously) Luke's life.

46. Varda often conspicuously plays with gender in her travesties of cinematic monuments. Her protagonist, the ancient Simon Cinema (Michel Piccoli in an outrageous wig), has not a little in common with Norma Desmond, for instance, and hires the young, attractive master's student Camille (Julie Gayet) in an inversion of *Sunset Boulevard*'s gender scheme.

47. Helen Schulman, *P.S.* (New York and London: Bloomsbury, 2001).

48. For an interview with the artist, see Danielle Sonnenberg, "Inner Thoughts of an Artist . . . Bryan LeBoeuf," *NY Arts Magazine* 9, no. 9/10 (September–October, 2004), available on the web: http://nyartsmagazine.com.

3. The Birth, Death, and Apotheosis of a Hollywood Love Goddess

1. Richard Lippe, "Ava Gardner," *International Dictionary of Films and Filmmakers*, 4th ed., vol. 3, *Actors and Actresses* (Detroit: St. James, 2000), 468.

2. In addition to Gauteur, cited above, other exemplars include *Cahiers du Cinéma*, which describes Gardner, as Pandora, with delirious admiration, under G in "F comme

femme," an alphabetical compendium in its special issue, "La femme et le cinéma" (vol. 5, no. 30, December 1953: 32–33); Jacques Siclier, *Le Mythe de la femme dans le cinéma américain* (Paris: Les éditions du Cerf, 1956), which devotes an entire chapter (163–171) to Gardner; Ado Kyrou, *Amour, érotisme et cinéma* (Paris: Terrain Vague, 1957), 242–243, 405–407, 502–503; and, from later, Jean Domarchi, "Pour Ava, beau monstre touché par la grace," in the special number of *Cinema d'Aujourd'hui*, "L'Amérique des stars" (no. 8, May–June 1976: 101–103); and Gilles Dagneau, *Ava Gardner*, a hefty monographic tome on the actress and her films (Paris: Editions Pac, 1984).

3. Felleman, *Botticelli in Hollywood*, 84–85. Mason was interviewed by Rui Nogueira in *Focus on Film*, no. 2 (March–April 1970): 25.

4. Albert Lewin, letter to Yves Kovacs, July 1, 1964 (Albert Lewin Papers, University of Southern California Cinema-Television Library and Archives of Performing Arts). The substantive portions of this letter, written in response to a request for a statement for a special double number ("Surréalisme et cinéma") of *Études Cinématographiques*, appeared in French in the journal's second volume on this subject, no. 40–42 (1965): 167–169.

5. Ava Gardner, *Ava: My Story* (New York: Bantam, 1990), 115–116. I have no reason to doubt Gardner's account, but I have not independently verified that Nicolosi in fact executed a prior, nude version of the statue. This anecdote is repeated elsewhere, however.

6. Even though Peikov sculpted two statues — one for the graveyard scene that "had to be made to withstand the rain" and another for the scene in which the sculpture is in progress — and also served as technical advisor to the actor who played the sculptor in that scene, he is not credited on the film. Peikov is identified as the sculptor in Mankiewicz's papers, which are not public. Cheryl Bray Lower, of the Joseph L. Mankiewicz Project, who has access to the papers, was kind enough to locate this information for me.

7. Peikov emigrated to Rome in 1938 and spent the rest of his career there. He married Emilia Boccanegra, a marquise well connected to the Italian nobility and, as a singer, actress, poet, and journalist, to artistic circles, among which two societies he found many of his subjects. See *Ritratti di Assen Peikov* (Rome: Canesi, 1964); and Atana Bozhkov, "On the Trails of the Colossi," in *Bulgarian Contributions to European Civilization* (Sofia: Bulvest, 2000), 403–421.

8. Charles Godfrey Leland (as Hans Breitmann), "Venus and the Ring," in *Legends of Florence, Collected from the People, and Retold*, 2nd series (Florence: B. Seeber; London: David Nutt, 1896; Detroit: Singing Tree Press, Book Tower, 1969), 242.

9. Gardner, *Ava*, 114.

10. François Truffaut, "*The Barefoot Contessa*," In *The Films in My Life*, trans. Leonard Mayhew (New York: Simon and Schuster, 1978), 130.

11. Maureen Turim, *Flashbacks in Film: Memory and History* (New York and London: Routledge, 1989), 138.

12. Cheryl Bray Lower, "The Mankiewicz Woman," in *Joseph L. Mankiewicz: Critical Essays with an Annotated Bibliography and a Filmography*, by Cheryl Bray Lower and R. Barton Palmer (Jefferson, NC, and London: McFarland, 2001), 102.

13. Coincidentally — or not — Gardner as Pandora was characterized by Ado Kyrou, a late surrealist film critic, as "avec Lya Lys (de *L'âge d'or*) . . . la seule femme farouchement surréaliste de tout le cinéma" (the only fiercely surrealist woman in all cinema). *Amour-Érotisme et Cinéma* (Paris: Le Terrain Vague, 1957), 406.

14. Gardner, *Ava*, 114.

15. Only a decade after Hayworth's and Gardner's "descents" from on high, Ado Kyrou claimed that these two performances, with their "érotisme destructeur," describe or anticipate an era of "grands films d'amour merveilleux." *Amour, érotisme et cinéma,* 242–243.

16. Lower, "The Mankiewicz Woman," 107–108.

17. Domarchi, "Pour Ava," 102–103.

18. Gauteur, "Portrait d'Ava Gardner," 30–31.

19. Lena Horne, testimonial in Gardner, *Ava,* 146–147. Interesting in terms of the racial difference one would expect to be meaningful between two southerners, Horne also said, "Ava was like my younger sister; she and I were spiritually akin."

20. Molly Haskell, *From Reverence to Rape: The Treatment of Women in the Movies* (New York: Holt, Rinehart and Winston, 1974), 260. To Haskell's half-caste category, one must add Gardner's role as Julie Laverne in *Showboat* (1951). It should also be added that Gardner did play her share of American women, although she was also often cast as a darkly exotic European-Russian (*The Great Sinner, 55 Days in Peking*) or Spanish (*The Angel Wore Red, The Naked Maja*). Perhaps the most common typecasting of Gardner, though, was as nobility—ironic given her humble origins. After playing the queen of goddesses in *One Touch of Venus,* she was or became titled in *Knights of the Round Table, The Barefoot Contessa, The Little Hut, The Sun Also Rises, The Naked Maja, 55 Days in Peking,* and *Mayerling.*

21. David Shipman, "A Conversation with Joseph L. Mankiewicz," *Films and Filming* (November 1982): 11.

22. Gilles Deleuze, *Cinema I: The Movement-Image,* trans. Hugh Tomlinson and Barbara Habberjam (Minneapolis: University of Minnesota, 1986), 134.

23. Henry James, "The Last of the Valerii," in *Tales of Art and Life,* ed. Henry Terrie (Schenectady: Union College Press, 1984), 37.

24. Theodore Ziolkowski, *Disenchanted Images: A Literary Iconology* (Princeton, NJ: Princeton University Press, 1977), 34–35.

25. Ibid., 232.

26. Ibid., 233.

27. Ibid., 25.

28. Sigmund Freud, *Delusion and Dream and Other Essays,* ed. Philip Rieff (Boston: Beacon Press, 1956), includes as an appendix a translation of Wilhelm Jensen's *Gradiva: A Pompeiian Fancy.*

29. Ziolkowski, *Disenchanted Images,* 46.

4. Survivors of the Shipwreck of Modernity

1. Among others to observe this is James Monaco, who calls the Hollywood film a "particular mode of discourse (which was dying at the time; *Le Mépris* is a kind of eulogy)." *The New Wave* (New York: Oxford University Press, 1976), 136.

2. Freud, "Mourning and Melancholia," 154.

3. Godard, interviewed by Jean Collet (September 12, 1963), in Jean Collet, *Jean-Luc Godard: An Investigation into His Films and Philosophy,* trans. Ciba Vaughan (New York: Crown, 1970), 95.

4. Lewin, letter to Yves Kovacs.

5. Bardot's previous credits included *And God Created Woman* (Vadim, 1956).

6. Heine, *Aus den Memoiren*, 10.

7. Jean-Paul Török, in his ecstatic reconsideration of *Pandora*, wrote: "En passant de ses brumes wagnériennes à la pleine lumière du midi, la légende nordique s'allie à la fable grecque, et le Hollandais, Ulysse du septentrion, met le pied sur la terre des dieux." "Eva Prima Pandora," *L'Avant-Scène du Cinéma*, no. 245 (April 1, 1980): 4.

8. *Cahiers du Cinéma* (December 1957); see Jean-Luc Godard, *Godard on Godard*, trans. and ed. Tom Milne (New York: Da Capo, 1972/1986), 64.

9. Statement in Cinémathèque Française, *Hommage à Albert Lewin* (Paris: Cinémathèque Française, 1958). My translation.

10. Catherine Russell, *Narrative Mortality: Death, Closure, and New Wave Cinemas* (Minneapolis: University of Minnesota, 1995), 147.

11. Ibid., 157.

12. Collet, *Jean-Luc Godard*, 48.

13. Ibid., 68.

14. Richard Combs, "Retrospective: *The Picture of Dorian Gray*," *Monthly Film Bulletin* 52, no. 622 (November 1985): 355.

15. Collet, *Jean-Luc Godard*, 93–94.

16. For an interesting discussion of the "Lang" rushes, see Kaja Silverman and Harun Farocki, *Speaking about Godard* (New York: New York University Press, 1998), 37–38. According to Wheeler Winston Dixon (introduction to a screening of *Contempt* at conference, "Hollywood and Its Discontents," University of Arizona, Tucson, May 18, 2001), Cocteau was the original actor/director in the Lang role in *Contempt*, but became ill and the part was recast, while the images, conceived as "his," were not.

17. Although it is not a focus of this chapter, *Contempt*'s affinity to *Viaggio in Italia* cannot be overstated. What Rossellini said of his films is almost a mirror image of what Godard said of his: "It was very important for me to show Italy, Naples, that strange atmosphere which is mingled with a very real, very immediate, very deep feeling, the sense of eternal life. It is something that has completely disappeared from the world." Interview with Eric Rohmer (pseud. of Maurice Schérer) and François Truffaut, *Cahiers du Cinéma* 37 (July 1954), translated by Liz Heron and reprinted in *Cahiers du Cinéma: The 1950s*, ed. Jim Hillier (Cambridge: Harvard University Press, 1985), 211.

18. Russell, *Narrative Mortality*, 148.

19. Jonathan Glancey, "House of the Spirit," *The Guardian* (Manchester), February 7, 1998.

20. Ibid.

21. Francesco Garofalo and Luca Veresani, *Adalberto Libera* (New York: Princeton Architectural Press, 1992), 114.

22. The morphological affinity with images from *Un Chien Andalou* cannot be coincidental. Lewin's setting is in the very Catalan landscape from which the two Spaniards came and that was the backdrop to Dalí's hallucinatory paintings. And the period in which *Pandora* is set, around 1930, was the period of Dalí's and Buñuel's prestige among Breton and the surrealist movement.

23. Deleuze, *Cinema I*, 71.

24. Collet, *Jean-Luc Godard*, 92.

25. Gregg M. Horowitz, "Death after Contempt," paper presented in the session "Godard's *Contempt*: Before and After," College Art Association annual meeting, Los Angeles, February 12, 1999.

26. For a penetrating exploration of this connection between narrative and death, see Russell, *Narrative Mortality*.

27. Simone de Beauvoir, *The Second Sex*, trans. H. M. Parshley (New York: Random House/Vintage, 1989), 143.

28. See Joan Riviere, "Hate, Greed, and Aggression," in *Love, Hate, and Reparation*, by Melanie Klein and Joan Riviere (New York: Norton, 1964), 19–25.

29. "Godard elicits a mesmerizing performance from Bardot, who imbues her sex kitten persona with romantic agony and savage bitterness." Derek Malcom in *The Guardian*, quoted on the Film Forum website: http://www.filmforum.com/contempt.html.

30. Geneviève Sellier, "Gender, Modernism and Mass Culture in the New Wave," in *Gender and French Cinema*, ed. Alex Hughes and James S. Williams (Oxford and New York: Berg, 2001), 135. Huyssen's "Mass Culture as Woman" is from his *After the Great Divide: Modernism, Mass Culture and Postmodernism* (Bloomington and Indianapolis: Indiana University Press, 1986), 17. For further analysis of Bardot's signification in French cinema, and for the New Wave, see Ginette Vincendeau, *Stars and Stardom in French Cinema* (London: Continuum, 2002), 102–107.

31. It must be noted that Bama Dillert, Dean Martin's character in *Some Came Running* (Minnelli, 1959), is one of the Hollywood cinema's great misogynists, typically referring to women as "pigs." Not only his character (who never takes off his hat, putatively for reasons having to do with gambling luck), but the film generally, which is based on a James Jones novel, is remarkably sexist, even for its day.

32. Sellier, "Gender," 135.

33. Godard, *Godard on Godard*, 200.

34. Alberto Moravia, *Contempt (Il Disprezzo)*, trans. Angus Davidson (New York: New York Review Books, 1999), 79–80.

35. Marsha Kinder, "A Thrice-Told Tale: Godard's *Le Mépris* (1963), from the Novel *A Ghost at Noon* by Alberto Moravia," in *Modern European Filmmakers and the Art of Adaptation*, ed. Andrew Horton and Joan Magretta (New York: Frederick Ungar, 1981), 102.

36. Moravia, *Contempt*, 21.

37. Ibid., 29.

38. Sarah Kofman, *The Enigma of Woman: Woman in Freud's Writings*, trans. Catherine Porter (Ithaca, NY: Cornell University Press, 1980), 43.

39. Ibid., 44.

40. Moravia, *Contempt*, 230.

41. Ibid., 321.

42. Ibid., 233.

43. Janice M. Kozma, "Say It with Flowers: Imagistic Representations of Women in Alberto Moravia's Prose," *Italica* 70, no. 3 (Fall 1993): 376–387.

44. For more in-depth discussion of these intercut images, see Silverman and Farocki, *Speaking about Godard*, 40–46.

45. Edgar Morin, *The Stars*, trans. Richard Howard (New York: Grove, 1960), 30–31.

46. Collet, *Jean-Luc Godard*, 20–21.

47. Silverman and Farocki, *Speaking about Godard*, 34.

48. Ibid., 42.

49. Laura Mulvey, "The Hole and the Zero: The Janus Face of the Feminine in Godard," in *Jean-Luc Godard: Son + Image, 1974–1991*, ed. Raymond Bellour with Mary

Lea Bandy (New York: Museum of Modern Art and Abrams, 1992), 81. Godard is quoted from an interview with Gideon Bachman: "In the cinema, it is never Monday"; *Sight and Sound* 52, no. 2 (Spring 1983): 118.

50. Laura Mulvey and Colin MacCabe, "Images of Woman, Images of Sexuality," chapter 4 of *Godard: Images, Sounds, Politics*, ed. Colin MacCabe (London: BFI, 1980), 87.

51. Ibid., 89.

52. Mulvey, "The Hole and the Zero," 87.

53. Jean-Luc Godard, "Godard Makes [Hi]stories: Interview with Serge Daney," in *Jean-Luc Godard*, 167. This Dostoyevsky novel, loosely adapted, along with his biography, was a source for Martin Scorsese's *Life Lessons*, a film written by Richard Prince and discussed in chapter 7.

54. Balzac, quoted by Beauvoir, *The Second Sex*, 669.

55. Time and duration, characteristically Rivettian aspects of *La Belle Noiseuse*, although not focal issues herein, are discussed vis-à-vis process, portraiture, and the performative ambience of the film in Anne-Marie Faux, "Portraits d'artistes en noiseurs," *Iris*, nos. 14–15 (Fall 1992): 187–190.

56. Anne-Marie Faux (188) notes the uncanniness the film imputes to the mimetic effort, comparing the characters to apprentice-vampires, or sorcerers, invoking Poe ("The Oval Portrait," *The Fall of the House of Usher*), and the undead progenitors of Mary Shelley (*Frankenstein*) and Bram Stoker (*Dracula*).

57. Thomas Elsaesser, in "Rivette and the End of Cinema," 22, observes that "Rivette makes of Frenhofer the Minotaur, a creature both powerful and baffled, half man, half beast. It brings the Frenhofer figure once more close to Picasso, for whom the Minotaur was a central reference point." Elsaesser elaborates, comparing Marianne to Ariadne and Nicolas to Theseus, describing her as a sacrificial offering "to appease the man-god/man-beast of artistic genius." The Minotaur analogy is apt in other ways, too, though. Picasso was one of a number of modern artists fascinated with Balzac's legendary painter. Like Cézanne, he identified deeply with the passionate Frenhofer, who struggled, suffered, and died for truth in art. Picasso illustrated a 1931 edition of *Le chef-d'oeuvre inconnu*. See Dore Ashton, *A Fable of Modern Art* (London: Thames and Hudson, 1980), and René Guise et al., *Autour du "Chef-d'oeuvre inconnu" de Balzac* (Paris: ENSAD, 1985). Bernard Dufour, a painter of Rivette's and Piccoli's generation who executed all the Frenhofer work for *La Belle Noiseuse*, is clearly a figurative artist in the long shadow of Picasso.

58. Elsaesser, "Rivette and the End of Cinema," 22.

59. Mulvey and MacCabe, "Images of Woman," 87.

60. Sidney Peterson, *The Dark of the Screen* (New York: Anthology Film Archives and New York University Press, 1980), 103. Peterson played explicitly with the Picasso connection, intercutting "elements taken from Picasso's *Minotauromachy* . . . by way of contrast to the modification of Balzac's rather simple acceptance of the worship of painting as consisting of a devotion to naturalism and of deviation from the veneration as being a form of madness" (104). See also P. Adams Sitney, *Visionary Film: The American Avant-Garde, 1943–1978* (New York: Oxford University Press, 1979), 69–74.

61. For an excellent assessment of the role of sound in relationship to the cinematic focus on process in Rivette's film and Henri-Georges Clouzot's *Le Mystère Picasso* (1956), see Lynda Nead, "Seductive Canvases: Visual Mythologies of the Artist and Artistic

Creativity," *Oxford Art Journal* 18, no. 2 (1995): 59–69. Nead's article also considers gender and myth.

62. On *Contempt*, see Monaco, *The New Wave*, 137.

63. Michel Piccoli, interview with Herbert Lottman, "Cinéma vérité: Jean-Luc Godard," *Columbia University Forum*, Spring 1968, quoted in Monaco, *The New Wave*, 135. Elsewhere Piccoli was quoted as saying that Godard is represented by both characters, Paul and Lang, as a kind of "two headed monster, Godard's double." Sellier, "Gender," 133, quoting the actor as cited in P. Vimenet, *Le Mépris* (Paris: Hatier, 1991), 104.

64. Honoré de Balzac, *The Unknown Masterpiece* (*Le Chef-d'oeuvre inconnu*), trans. Richard Howard (New York: New York Review Books, 2001), 24.

65. Ashton, *Fable*, 29.

66. Alexandra K. Wettlaufer, *Pen vs. Paintbrush: Girodet, Balzac and the Myth of Pygmalion in Postrevolutionary France* (New York: Palgrave, 2001), 215. In this discussion, Wettlaufer cites and incorporates the work of a number of feminist visual theorists, including Laura Mulvey, Linda Nochlin, Lynda Nead, Marcia Pointen, and Carol Duncan.

67. For a lucid picture of the economic attitudes and practices of New Wave filmmakers generally, and Rivette's hostility to the corrupting influences of big budgets, see Michel Marie, *The French New Wave: An Artistic School*, trans. Richard Neupert (Oxford: Blackwell, 2003), esp. chapter 3 and p. 56.

68. Wettlaufer, *Pen vs. Paintbrush*, 217.

69. Elsaesser, "Rivette and the End of Cinema," 22.

70. Balzac, *The Unknown Masterpiece*, 40–41.

71. See Maurice Merleau-Ponty, "Cézanne's Doubt," in *The Essential Writings of Merleau-Ponty*, ed. Alden L. Fisher (New York: Harcourt, Brace and World, 1969), 233–251.

72. See Rosalind Krauss and Jane Livingston, *L'Amour fou: Photography and Surrealism* (New York: Abbeville, 1985), and Rosalind Krauss, "Louise Bourgeois: Portrait of the Artist as *Fillette*," in *Bachelors* (Cambridge, MA: October/MIT Press, 1999), 50–74.

73. See, on Dufour's work of the 1950s and 1960s, e.g., *Bernard Dufour: Paintings, 1954–1963* (New York: Albert Loeb Gallery, 1963); his recent photographic nudes are collected in Bernard Dufour, *Mes Modèles: Femmes-nues-à-l'atelier* (Paris: La Musardine, 2001). See also Dufour works illustrated on-line at www.le-rire-bleu.org/artistes/dufour/10.htm.

On his participation in *La Belle Noiseuse*, see Bernard Dufour, "Questions au peintre," *Cahiers du Cinéma*, no. 447 (September 1991): 25–29; for critiques of the film's representation of the art process, see Philip Pearlstein, "Modeling the Soul," *Art in America* 80, no. 1 (January 1992): 61–63; and Dore Ashton, "The Death of Frenhofer: *La Belle Noiseuse* according to Jacques Rivette," *Arts Magazine* 66 (February 1992): 47–49, in which Ashton—an expert on Balzac's fable—also faults the film as adaptation.

74. This suggestive phrase is from *Passion*. As Laura Mulvey aptly describes the scene in which it is uttered: "The image consists of a beautiful young and naked girl, who, at the director's request, floats in an Oriental pool and spreads her arms and legs into the shape of a star . . . As the camera moves closer to the director, his friend asks him what he is looking at. He answers, 'The wound of the world . . .'" "The Hole and the Zero," 86.

5. Out of Her Element

This chapter is a revised version of what was initially written as a paper for Linda Nochlin's graduate seminar in feminism and visual theory at CUNY Graduate Center, then revised as an article, "Fluid Fantasies: *Splash* and *Children of a Lesser God*," for *Camera Obscura* 19 (January 1989): 108–133. It appears here with permission. I have introduced references to only a few of the many more recent publications that are pertinent to the discussion. Those that really add depth or breadth to my argument are by Barbara Creed, Susan White, and Lauren Dundes and Alan Dundes.

1. Barbara Creed, *The Monstrous-Feminine: Film, Feminism, Psychoanalysis* (London: Routledge, 1993), 1.

2. For more on mermaids, see Beatrice Phillpotts, *Mermaids* (New York: Ballantine, 1980).

3. Susan White, "Split Skins: Female Agency and Bodily Mutilation in *The Little Mermaid*," in *Film Theory Goes to the Movies*, ed. Jim Collins, Hilary Radner, and Ava Preacher Collins (New York and London: Routledge, 1993), 185.

4. White, "Split Skins"; and Alan Dundes with Lauren Dundes, "The Trident and the Fork: Disney's 'The Little Mermaid' as a Male Construction of an Electral Fantasy," in Alan Dundes, *Bloody Mary in the Mirror: Essays in Psychoanalytic Folkloristics* (Jackson: University Press of Mississippi, 2002).

5. Teresa de Lauretis, *Alice Doesn't: Feminism, Semiotics, Cinema* (Bloomington: Indiana University Press, 1984), 45.

6. Klaus Theweleit, *Male Fantasies, Volume. I: Women, Floods, Bodies, History*, trans. Stephen Conway (Minneapolis: University of Minnesota Press, 1987), 283.

7. From the caption to Paramount publicity photograph no. CLG-5040-10A.

8. Sandor Ferenczi, *Thalassa: A Theory of Genitality* (New York: Norton, 1968), 48.

9. Sigmund Freud, *Introductory Lectures on Psychoanalysis*, trans. James Strachey (New York: Norton, 1977), 160–161.

10. "We must not forget that this symbol is able to appeal in two ways to evolutionary truth. Not only are all terrestrial mammals, including man's ancestors, descended from aquatic creatures (this is the more remote of the two facts), but every individual mammal, every human being, spent the first phase of its existence in water—namely as an embryo in the amniotic fluid of its mother's uterus, and came out of that water when it was born." Ibid., 160.

11. Ferenczi, *Thalassa*, 48.

12. Interestingly, Ferenczi's theory is cited by Theweleit in support of his reading of male aggression. Theweleit employs both Ferenczi's understanding of human genitality as a result of primeval trauma and Elaine Morgan's related, though anthropologically and historically different, theory of human physiology and human sexuality as adaptations to a largely aquatic existence and subsequent re-adaptation to land, wherein the female of the species initiates and preserves the aquatic episode, her anatomy therefore reflecting it more profoundly (thicker subcutaneous fat layer; longer head hair—not only to protect the exposed head from sun, but also to be grasped by infants; larger breasts—with fur lost, the infant had to be held in the arms to nurse, etc.), while the male more readily preserves and re-initiates the land-based existence. See Elaine Morgan, *The Aquatic Ape: A Theory of Human Evolution* (London: Stein and Day, 1982). As Theweleit concludes his section, "Very Early History: The Woman from the Water" (288–294): "The ocean and the mother-child relationship produced the female body, just as the male body acquired

its heavier musculature, strength, and speed through subsequent involvement in hunting and warfare." Seductive and fascinating though such biologically based theories may be, they cannot fully account for culturally specific mythologies of femininity, nor, more importantly, do such explanations of physiological evolution adequately inform questions of why the male's fantastic relationship to the primal mother should be differently phrased from that of the female.

13. Sigmund Freud, *Delusion and Dream.*

14. Kofman, *Enigma,* 48.

15. Ibid., 44. Lea Jacobs describes just such a reaction to feminine "silence" operative in *Now Voyager:* "Charlotte's enunciating stance is silence, a silence which refers to the private realm figured by her room, where body, image and language itself exist for Charlotte alone . . . Jerry puts Charlotte into a position of enunciation . . . her cure is completed when her silence is converted into this man's language, when through him, her ambiguous and private relation to her own desire becomes public, representable . . . Jerry's 'I wish I understood you' is the expression of his fascination before the enigma, an effort to penetrate Charlotte's silence and to know her desire." The parallel to *Children*'s discourse and to Kofman's understanding of the psychoanalytic project is striking. "*Now Voyager:* Some Problems of Enunciation and Sexual Difference," *Camera Obscura,* no. 7 (Spring 1981): 97 99.

16. With regard to the problem of communicating with both deaf and hearing audiences, I must note a stage production I saw, directed by the playwright, of David Rush's electrifying drama *Police Deaf Near Far,* about a tragic encounter between hearing and deaf people. The play grew out of a workshop with deaf actors and found a challenging and intriguing solution to the problem of communicating in two languages simultaneously: each role was performed simultaneously by two actors, one signing, one speaking. This effective theatrical solution dispenses with naturalism, at least as regards staging and casting (McLeod Theater, Southern Illinois University–Carbondale, spring 2003).

17. Doane, *The Desire to Desire,* 10.

18. When Sarah learns from James that he went to see her mother, she becomes furious. James, in turn, expresses dismay: "Let me help you, damn it!" he yells at her. Sarah's response (as it is signed by her but enunciated by James—he substitutes his "you" for her "I") is dramatic: "How? By showing you the joys of sex with a hearing man?" He responds to that charge by angrily (and revealingly) saying, "I think that is one language that you don't speak!" In Sarah's subsequent "monologue" there is a shift in James's assignment of personal pronouns as he speaks her signed language. He begins, "You have more than enough communication skills; I don't." (Presumably, Sarah has said, "*I* have more than enough communication skills; *you* don't!") She/He continued (James, for the first time in the film, using the word "I" for Sarah's "I"): "They never did . . . they could never be bothered to learn my language, I was always expected to learn to speak. Sex was always something I could do as well as hearing girls . . . better! At first I let them have me because they wanted to. Before long, the boys were lined up on a waiting list. My sister pimped for me. No introduction. No talk. We just went to a dark place and . . . (she makes a dramatic sign—clearly that for "fuck," three times; James does not "say" it) . . . They didn't even take me out for a Coke first." Sarah then turns to James and signs something. "No, that is *not* what I wanted to know about you!" he responds. "I thought I was such a big deal coming on to the deaf girl, giving her a thrill," he translates Sarah's further remarks, again substituting his "I" for her "you," and then, "and all the time you were laughing at me. I was thinking poor, little, deaf virgin . . . who spread her

legs for every . . ." James then violently interrupts his repetition of Sarah's insults and yells at her, "Do you think I'm threatened by that? You think that I give a god damn that you fucked every pimply faced teenager . . . I don't. I don't give a shit!" (He clearly does). Sarah storms out again. The shifting of pronouns in this scene is confusing and telling.

19. Mary Ann Doane, "Film and the Masquerade: Theorising the Female Spectator," *Screen* 23, nos. 3–4 (September/October 1982): 75–76.

20. Sigmund Freud, "On Narcissism: An Introduction" (1914), in *General Psychological Theory*, ed. Philip Rieff (New York: Collier, 1963), 69–70.

21. Hans Christian Andersen, "The Little Mermaid," in *Hans Christian Andersen's Fairy Tales: A Selection*, trans. L. W. Kingsland (Oxford: Oxford University Press, 1984), 94–95.

22. The mermaid's interactions in the story are with her grandmother and her sisters. She has a father, king of her underworld realm, who is never directly engaged in the narrative, but her mother is never mentioned. Nina Auerbach discusses "The Little Mermaid" as "a guide to a vital Victorian mythology whose lovable woman is a silent and self-disinherited mutilate, the fullness of whose extraordinary and dangerous being might at any moment return through violence," in *Woman and the Demon: The Life of a Victorian Myth* (Cambridge, MA: Harvard University Press, 1982), 8.

23. For enlightening discussion of how Disney's adaptation dispatches with many of the more disturbing implications of Andersen's tale, see White, "Allegory and Referentiality."

24. Andersen, "The Little Mermaid," 98.

25. Karen Horney, "The Dread of Woman: Observations on a Specific Difference in the Dread Felt by Men and Women Respectively for the Opposite Sex," in *Feminine Psychology* (New York: Norton, 1967), 134.

26. Other important applied psychoanalytic studies of the cultural manifestations of the dread of woman, in addition to the indispensable relatively recent books by Barbara Creed and Klaus Theweleit, include Oliver Brachfeld, "Die Furcht vor der Frau, in Sage, Märchen und Literatur," *Internationale Zeitschrift individual Psychologie*, no. 6 (1928): 442–456; and Wolfgang Lederer, *The Fear of Women* (New York: Harcourt Brace Jovanovich, 1968). It must be noted that Karen Horney, whose observations cited herein are consistent with Freudian ones, came to reject the central Freudian articulation of the Oedipal moment. She argued that innate sexual differences are psychically experienced and "known" by infants from birth. Male and female infants' pre-Oedipal relationships to the mother are seen as inherently different; the male infant has an instinct for penetration; the female for reception. Thus, like Ferenczi, Theweleit, and Elaine Morgan, she privileges biology. The essentialism of Horney's position has been critiqued by, among others, Janet Sayers, *Sexual Contradictions* (London: Tavistock Publications, 1986), 36–42, 62–63, and 79–80; and Juliet Mitchell, *Psychoanalysis and Feminism* (New York: Vintage, 1974), 125–131.

27. Auerbach, *Woman and the Demon*, 8. See n. 23, above.

28. Horney, "Dread," 141.

29. Constance Penley, "Time Travel, Primal Scene, and the Critical Dystopia," *Camera Obscura* 15 (Fall 1986): 76.

30. Simon Frith, discussing the theories of musicologist Zofia Lissa, in "Hearing Secret Harmonies," in *High Theory/Low Culture: Analysing Popular Television and Film*, ed. Colin MacCabe (New York: St. Martin's Press, 1986), 53.

31. Beauvoir, *The Second Sex,* 148.

32. Lacan, *Psychoanalysis,* 205.

33. Jacqueline Rose, "Julia Kristeva—Take Two," in *Sexuality in the Field of Vision* (London: Verso, 1986), 155–156.

6. Playing with Fire

This chapter originated as a paper delivered at the "Violence, Cinema, and American Culture" conference, held at the University of Missouri–St. Louis, April 7, 2001. A previous version of it was published in Steven Schneider, ed., *New Hollywood Violence* (Manchester: Manchester University Press, 2004), 230–246. It is reprinted here with permission.

1. The sculpture is actually by Nora Chavooshian. Kiki, whose name may invoke the famous Kiki of Montparnasse, who modeled for Man Ray and many of the other avant-gardistes of Paris in the 1920s, may also reference Kiki Smith, who, though certainly not yet well known, was already active in the downtown New York scene of the early 1980s. Her works of that period included figures in plaster and probably papier-mâché, too.

2. In his classic 1922 essay "Medusa's Head," Freud analyzes how that ancient apotropaic image isolates the "horrifying effects" of the female genitals from the "pleasure-giving ones." *Collected Papers,* vol. 5, ed. James Strachey (London: Hogarth Press, 1950), 106.

3. Steve Reinke, "Desire in Scorsese's *After Hours*," *CineAction!* (Summer/Fall 1986): 32–34.

4. See, for instance, Bryan Bruce, "Scorsese: *After Hours*," *CineAction!* (Summer/Fall 1986): 28.

5. Martin Scorsese, *Scorsese on Scorsese,* ed. David Thompson and Ian Christie (London: Faber and Faber, 1989), 100.

6. In three of Hannah's roles of this era—this one, in *Splash* (1984), and in *Clan of the Cave Bear* (1986)—her character is introduced as a child, with primal-scene overtones. These prefaces underscore the narcissistic, childlike qualities of the grown character. The elements of the *Legal Eagles* plot relating to the fraudulent handling of the Deardon estate were inspired by and loosely based on aspects of the Rothko case. See Lee Seldes, *The Legacy of Mark Rothko,* rev. ed. (New York: Da Capo Press, 1996).

7. See Amelia Jones, *Body Art: Performing the Subject* (Minneapolis: University of Minnesota Press, 1998), esp. chapter 4, "The Rhetoric of the Pose: Hannah Wilke and the Radical Narcissism of Feminist Body Art," 151–195.

8. According to the film's credits, the performance was created by Arne Glimcher, Daryl Hannah, and Lin Hixson, the last of whom is in fact an established performance artist. The performance was accompanied by the song "Put Out the Fire," written by Hannah with Michael Monteliere.

9. Gaston Bachelard, *The Psychoanalysis of Fire,* trans. Alan C. M. Ross (Boston: Beacon Press, 1964).

10. The film's associate producer, gallerist Arne Glimcher, ran Pace Gallery—the basis for the gallery in the film—one of the 1980s' bluest of blue-chip venues.

11. Quoted in Jones, *Body Art,* 151.

12. The European release of *Backtrack* (titled *Catchfire*) was recut by the producers, disowned by Hopper, and credited to Alan Smithee.

13. For a synoptic view of Holzer's career, see David Joselit, Joan Simon, and Renata Salecl, *Jenny Holzer* (London: Phaidon Press Limited, 1998).

14. Steven Schneider points out (correspondence with author) that in *The Apostate* (a.k.a. *Michael Angel*, 1998), Hopper would play the role of an artist-murderer.

15. Stephen Holden, in his *New York Times* review of *Addicted to Love* (May 23, 1997), anticipated scholarly interest in these reflexive aspects of the film. Due to the use of the camera obscura, he predicted, a future "scholar might interpret the movie "as a mocking cinematic allegory about movies, voyeurism and spying in an age when electronic surveillance and the inquiring media have eroded personal privacy."

7. Dirty Pictures, Mud Lust, and Abject Desire: Myths of Origin and the Cinematic Object

An earlier version of this chapter was published in *Film Quarterly* 55, no. 1 (Fall 2001): 27–40. It is reprinted here with permission.

1. André Breton, "As in a Wood," in *The Shadow and Its Shadow*, ed. Paul Hammond (Edinburgh: Polygon, 1991), 82. This piece originally appeared as "Comme dans un bois," in *L'Age du Cinéma* 4–5 (August–November 1951).

2. Scorsese, *Scorsese*, 147–150; and Ronald Librach, "A Nice Little Irony: *Life Lessons*," *Literature/Film Quarterly* 24 (1996): 128–144.

3. My sources on Gentileschi and her ordeal are Mary D. Garrard, "Artemisia's Trial by Cinema," *Art in America* 86, no. 10 (October 1998): 65–69, in which the author draws on the findings published in her larger study, *Artemisia Gentileschi: The Image of the Female Hero in Italian Baroque Art* (Princeton: Princeton University Press, 1989); Ann Sutherland Harris and Linda Nochlin, *Women Artists, 1550–1950* (Los Angeles: Los Angeles County Museum of Art and New York: Knopf, 1984), 118–124; and Rudolf Wittkower and Margot Wittkower, *Born under Saturn: The Character and Conduct of Artists* (New York: Norton, 1969), 162–164.

4. Garrard, "Artemisia's Trial," 65.

5. "The true story of the first female painter in art history," according to advertisements for *Artemisia*. See Garrard, "Artemisia's Trial" 65. As for Merlet's avowed feminism, Garrard cites a newspaper article by Kristine McKenna, "'Artemisia': Artistic License with an Artist," *Los Angeles Times*, May 27, 1998.

6. Garrard, "Artemisia's Trial," 67.

7. More recent editions, although they do not specify gender in their primary definitions, do not avoid it entirely, for obvious historical reasons. *Webster's New Collegiate Dictionary*, 2nd ed. (Springfield, MA: Merriam, 1951), 517.

8. Griselda Pollock, "A Hungry Eye," *Sight and Sound* (new series) 8, no. 11 (November 1998): 28.

9. Ibid.

10. This line and the psychosexual ambiguities that relate to looking were employed with pointed insight and scathing humor by Hal Ashby's 1979 film, *Being There*, in which Peter Sellers played a naïf who meant by "I like to watch" that he liked to watch television, and Shirley MacLaine played a sophisticate who understood him to mean something rather kinkier.

11. Leonard Maltin's *1999 Movie and Video Guide* (New York: Penguin/Signet, 1998), 199, for instance, describes *Camille Claudel* as an "overblown biography of the French

sculptress (Adjani), who has a 'madness of mud' and who single-mindedly pursues her art."

12. An excellent short discussion of Rodin's and Claudel's relationship and impact on each other's careers—one that supports assumptions of my argument—is Anne Higgonet's "Myths of Creation: Camille Claudel and Auguste Rodin," in *Significant Others: Creativity and Intimate Partnership,* ed. Whitney Chadwick and Isabelle de Courtivron (London: Thames and Hudson, 1993), 15–29.

13. Assessing the full stylistic and thematic scope of Claudel's work from the period is very difficult, as she later destroyed most of it. See Reine-Marie Paris, *Camille: The Life of Camille Claudel,* trans. Liliane Emery Tuck (New York: Arcade, 1988).

14. For more biographical and historical background on Claudel, see Higgonet, "Myths of Creation," or Paris, *Camille.*

15. The most significant book on the subject of artist couples is Chadwick and de Courtivron, *Significant Others.* "Artistic Coupling" was the title of a session organized by Susan Felleman and Peter Chametzky at the 82nd annual College Art Association (CAA) meeting, held in New York, February 17–19, 1994. The session included an introduction by Felleman and papers by Beth Harris, "'Either Sex Alone Is Half Itself': Elizabeth Siddall and Dante Gabriel Rossetti"; Renée Riese Hubert, "Surrealist Artist Couples"; and Robert Hobbs, "Lee and Jackson: Symbiosis and Critique"; and as discussants, contemporary artist-couple Nancy Spero and Leon Golub. Abstracts and audiotapes available through CAA. On Pollock and Krasner, in addition to Hobbs's work, see Anne M. Wagner, "Krasner's Presence, Pollock's Absence," in *Significant Others,* 222–243.

16. Librach, "A Nice Little Irony," 138.

17. Ibid., 136.

18. Sigmund Freud, *Dictionary of Psychoanalysis,* ed. Nandor Fodor and Frank Gaynor (New York: Philosophical Library, 1948), 178.

19. Freud, *A General Introduction to Psychoanalysis,* trans. Joan Riviere (Garden City, NY: Garden City Books, 1952), 302.

20. Freud, *A General Introduction to Psychoanalysis,* 327.

21. Pollock, "A Hungry Eye," 27.

Bibliography

Alberti, Leon Battista. "On Painting" (Della pittura). In *A Documentary History of Art*. Vol. 1. Edited by Elizabeth Gilmore Holt, 203–243. Garden City, NY: Doubleday Anchor, 1957.

Andersen, Hans Christian. "The Little Mermaid." In *Hans Christian Andersen's Fairy Tales: A Selection*. Translated by L. W. Kingsland, 76–106. Oxford: Oxford University Press, 1984.

Andrew, Dudley, ed. *The Image in Dispute: Art and Cinema in the Age of Photography*. Austin: University of Texas Press, 1997.

Ashton, Dore. "The Death of Frenhofer: *La Belle Noiseuse* according to Jacques Rivette." *Arts Magazine* 66 (February 1992): 47–49.

———. *A Fable of Modern Art*. London: Thames and Hudson, 1980.

Auerbach, Nina. *Woman and the Demon: The Life of a Victorian Myth*. Cambridge, MA: Harvard University Press, 1982.

Aumont, Jacques. "Le Portrait absent." *Iris*, nos. 14–15 (Fall 1992): 135–145.

Bachelard, Gaston. *The Psychoanalysis of Fire*. Translated by Alan C. M. Ross. Boston: Beacon, 1964.

Balzac, Honoré de. *The Unknown Masterpiece (Le Chef-d'oeuvre inconnu)*. Translated by Richard Howard. New York: New York Review Books, 2001.

Barthes, Roland. *Camera Lucida*. Translated by Richard Howard. New York: Farrar, Straus, and Giroux, 1981.

Bazin, André. "The Ontology of the Photographic Image." In *What Is Cinema?* Vol. 1. Translated and edited by Hugh Gray, 9–16. Berkeley: University of California Press, 1967.

Beauvoir, Simone de. *The Second Sex*. Translated by H. M. Parshley. New York: Random House/Vintage, 1989.

Bernard Dufour: Paintings, 1954–1963. New York: Albert Loeb Gallery, 1963.

Bernstein, Rhona J. "Adaptation, Censorship, and Audiences of Questionable Type: Lesbian Sightings in *Rebecca* (1940) and *The Uninvited* (1944)." *Cinema Journal* 37, no. 3 (Spring 1998): 16–37.

Blom, Ivo L. "*Il Fuoco* or the Fatal Portrait: The Nineteenth Century in the Italian Silent Cinema." *Iris*, nos. 14–15 (Fall 1992): 55–66.

Boileau, Pierre, and Thomas Narcejac. *The Living and the Dead (D'entre les morts)*. Translated by Geoffrey Sainsbury. New York: Ives Washburn, 1957.

Bozhkov, Atana. "On the Trails of the Colossi." In *Bulgarian Contributions to European Civilization*, 403–421. Sofia: Bulvest, 2000.

Brachfeld, Oliver. "Die Furcht vor der Frau, in Sage, Märchen und Literatur." *Internationale Zeitschrift für individual Psychologie*, no. 6 (1928): 442–456.

Breton, André. "As in a Wood." In *The Shadow and Its Shadow*. Edited by Paul Hammond, 80–85. Edinburgh: Polygon, 1991.

Bronfen, Elisabeth. *Over Her Dead Body: Death, Femininity, and the Aesthetic*. New York: Routledge, 1992.

Bruce, Bryan. "Scorsese: *After Hours*." *CineAction!* (Summer/Fall 1986): 28.

Brunette, Peter, and David Wills. *Screen/Play: Derrida and Film Theory*. Princeton, NJ: Princeton University Press, 1989.

Chadwick, Whitney, and Isabelle de Courtivron, eds. *Significant Others: Creativity and Intimate Partnership*. London: Thames and Hudson, 1993.

Cinémathèque Française. *Hommage à Albert Lewin*. Paris: Cinémathèque Française, 1958.

Collet, Jean. *Jean-Luc Godard: An Investigation into His Films and Philosophy*. Translated by Ciba Vaughan. New York: Crown, 1970.

Combs, Richard. "Retrospective: *The Picture of Dorian Gray*." *Monthly Film Bulletin* 52, no. 622 (November 1985): 355.

Creed, Barbara. *The Monstrous-Feminine: Film, Feminism, Psychoanalysis*. London: Routledge, 1993.

Cumbow, Robert C., and Grace A. Cumbow. "The New Life Begins: Dantean Obsession in *Obsession*." *Movietone News*, no. 53 (January 16, 1977): 25.

Dagneau, Gilles. *Ava Gardner*. Paris: Éditions Pac, 1984.

Dalle Vacche, Angela. *Cinema and Painting: How Art Is Used in Film*. Austin: University of Texas Press, 1996.

———, ed. *The Visual Turn: Classical Film Theory and Art History*. New Brunswick, NJ: Rutgers University Press, 2003.

Deleuze, Gilles. *Cinema I: The Movement-Image*. Translated by Hugh Tomlinson and Barbara Habberjam. Minneapolis: University of Minnesota Press, 1986.

Doane, Mary Ann. *The Desire to Desire: The Woman's Film of the 1940s*. Bloomington: Indiana University Press, 1987.

———. "Film and the Masquerade: Theorising the Female Spectator." *Screen* 23, nos. 3–4 (September/October 1982): 74–88.

Domarchi, Jean. "Pour Ava, beau monstre touché par la grace." *Cinema d'Aujourd'hui*, no. 8 (May–June 1976): 101–103.

Dufour, Bernard. *Mes Modèles: Femmes-nues-à-l'atelier*. Paris: La Musardine, 2001.

———. "Questions au peintre." *Cahiers du Cinéma*, no. 447 (September 1991): 25–29.

Dundes, Alan. *Bloody Mary in the Mirror: Essays in Psychoanalytic Folkloristics*. Jackson: University Press of Mississippi, 2002.

Dundes, Alan, with Lauren Dundes. "The Trident and the Fork: Disney's 'The Little Mermaid' as a Male Construction of an Electral Fantasy," In *Bloody Mary in the Mirror: Essays in Psychoanalytic Folkloristics*, 55–75. Jackson: University Press of Mississippi, 2002.

Ehrlich, Linda, and David Desser, eds. *Cinematic Landscapes: Observations on the Visual Arts and Cinema of China and Japan*. Austin: University of Texas Press, 1999.

Elsaesser, Thomas. "Mirror, Muse, Medusa: *Experiment Perilous*." *Iris*, nos. 14–15 (Fall 1992): 147–159.

————. "Rivette and the End of Cinema." *Sight and Sound* (new series) 1, no. 12 (April 1992): 20–23.

Everson, William. "Rediscovery: *Corridor of Mirrors.*" *Films in Review* 38 (January 1987): 39.

"F comme femme." *Cahiers du Cinéma* 5, no. 30 (December 1953): 32–33.

Faux, Anne-Marie. "Portraits d'artistes en noiseurs." *Iris*, nos. 14–15 (Fall 1992): 187–190.

Felleman, Susan. *Botticelli in Hollywood: The Films of Albert Lewin.* New York: Twayne, 1997.

Ferenczi, Sandor. *Thalassa: A Theory of Genitality.* New York: Norton, 1968.

Frazer, Sir James George. *Myths of the Origin of Fire: An Essay.* London: Macmillan, 1930.

Freud, Sigmund. *Delusion and Dream and Other Essays.* Edited by Philip Rieff. Boston: Beacon, 1956.

————. *Dictionary of Psychoanalysis.* Edited by Nandor Fodor and Frank Gaynor. New York: Philosophical Library, 1948.

————. *A General Introduction to Psychoanalysis.* Translated by Joan Riviere. Garden City, NY: Garden City Books, 1952.

————. *Introductory Lectures on Psychoanalysis.* Translated by James Strachey. New York: Norton, 1977.

————. "Medusa's Head" (1922). In *Collected Papers.* Vol. 5. Edited by James Strachey, 105–106. London: Hogarth Press, 1950.

————. "Mourning and Melancholia" (1917). In *Collected Papers.* Vol. 4. Translated and edited by Joan Riviere, 152–170. New York: Basic Books, 1959.

————. "On Narcissism: An Introduction" (1914). In *General Psychological Theory.* Edited by Philip Rieff, 56–82. New York: Collier, 1963.

————. "The Uncanny" (1919). In *Studies in Parapsychology.* Edited by Philip Rieff, 19–60. New York: Macmillan/Collier, 1963.

Fried, Michael. *Absorption and Theatricality: Painting and Beholder in the Age of Diderot.* Berkeley. University of California Press, 1980.

Frith, Simon. "Hearing Secret Harmonies." In *High Theory/Low Culture: Analysing Popular Television and Film.* Edited by Colin MacCabe, 53–70. New York: St. Martin's, 1986.

Gardner, Ava. *Ava: My Story.* New York: Bantam, 1990.

Garofalo, Francesco, and Luca Veresani. *Adalberto Libera.* New York: Princeton Architectural Press, 1992.

Garrard, Mary D. *Artemisia Gentileschi: The Image of the Female Hero in Italian Baroque Art.* Princeton, NJ: Princeton University Press, 1989.

————. "Artemisia's Trial by Cinema." *Art in America* 86, no. 10 (October 1998): 65–69.

Gauteur, Claude. "Portrait d'Ava Gardner." *Cahiers du Cinéma*, no. 88 (October 1958): 29.

Glancey, Jonathan. "House of the Spirit." *The Guardian* (Manchester), February 7, 1998.

Godard, Jean-Luc. "Godard Makes [Hi]stories: Interview with Serge Daney." In *Jean-Luc Godard: Son + Image.* Edited by Raymond Bellour with Mary Lea Bandy, 159–167. New York: Museum of Modern Art and Abrams, 1992.

————. *Godard on Godard.* Translated and edited by Tom Milne. New York: Da Capo, 1972/1986.

Guise, René, et al. *Autour du "Chef-d'oeuvre inconnu" de Balzac.* Paris: ENSAD, 1985.

Gunning, Tom. "Phantom Images and Modern Manifestations: Spirit Photography, Magic Theater, Trick Films, and Photography's Uncanny." In *Fugitive Images: From Photography to Video*. Edited by Patrice Petro, 42–71. Bloomington: Indiana University Press, 1995.

Harris, Ann Sutherland, and Linda Nochlin. *Women Artists, 1550–1950*. Los Angeles: Los Angeles County Museum of Art and New York: Knopf, 1984.

Haskell, Molly. *From Reverence to Rape: The Treatment of Women in the Movies*. New York: Holt, Rinehart and Winston, 1974.

Heath, Stephen. "Narrative Space." In *Narrative, Apparatus, Ideology*. Edited by Philip Rosen, 379–420. New York: Columbia University Press, 1986.

Heine, Heinrich. *Aus den Memoiren des herren von Schnabelwopski, Heines Werk*. Vol. 2. East Berlin: Aufbau-Verlag, 1981.

Higgonet, Anne. "Myths of Creation: Camille Claudel and Auguste Rodin." In *Significant Others: Creativity and Intimate Partnership*. Edited by Whitney Chadwick and Isabelle de Courtivron, 15–29. London: Thames and Hudson, 1993.

Horney, Karen. "The Dread of Woman: Observations on a Specific Difference in the Dread Felt by Men and Women Respectively for the Opposite Sex." In *Feminine Psychology*, 133–146. New York: Norton, 1967.

Horowitz, Gregg M. H. "Death after Contempt." Paper read at "Godard's *Contempt*: Before and After" session, College Art Association annual meeting, Los Angeles, February 12, 1999.

Humphries, Reynold. *Fritz Lang: Genre and Representation in His American Films*. Baltimore: Johns Hopkins University Press, 1989.

Huyssen, Andreas. "Mass Culture as Woman." In *After the Great Divide: Modernism, Mass Culture and Postmodernism*, 44–62. Bloomington: Indiana University Press, 1986.

Iris, nos. 14–15 (Fall 1992). Special number: "Le portrait peint au cinéma/The Painted Portrait in Film."

Jacobs, Lea. "*Now Voyager:* Some Problems of Enunciation and Sexual Difference." *Camera Obscura*, no. 7 (Spring 1981): 97–99.

James, Henry. "The Last of the Valerii." In *Tales of Art and Life*. Edited by Henry Terrie, 17–43. Schenectady: Union College Press, 1984.

Jardine, Alice. "Death Sentences: Writing Couples and Ideology." In *The Female Body in Western Culture*. Edited by Susan Suleiman, 84–96. Cambridge, MA: Harvard University Press, 1986.

Jenkins, Henry, and Kristine Brunovska Karnick. "Acting Funny." In *Classical Hollywood Comedy*. Edited by Kristine Brunovska Karnick and Henry Jenkins, 149–167. London: Routledge, 1995.

Jones, Amelia. *Body Art: Performing the Subject*. Minneapolis: University of Minnesota Press, 1998.

Joselit, David, Joan Simon, and Renata Salecl. *Jenny Holzer*. London: Phaidon Press Limited, 1998.

Kinder, Marsha. "A Thrice-Told Tale: Godard's *Le Mépris* (1963), from the Novel *A Ghost at Noon* by Alberto Moravia." In *Modern European Filmmakers and the Art of Adaptation*. Edited by Andrew Horton and Joan Magretta, 100–114. New York: Frederick Ungar, 1981.

Kofman, Sarah. *The Enigma of Woman: Woman in Freud's Writings*. Translated by Catherine Porter. Ithaca, NY: Cornell University Press, 1980.

Kozma, Janice M. "Say It with Flowers: Imagistic Representations of Women in Alberto Moravia's Prose." *Italica* 70, no. 3 (Fall 1993): 376–387.

Krauss, Rosalind. "Louise Bourgeois: Portrait of the Artist as *Fillette*." In *Bachelors*, 50–74. Cambridge, MA: October/MIT Press, 1999.

Krauss, Rosalind, and Jane Livingston. *L'Amour fou: Photography and Surrealism*. New York: Abbeville, 1985.

Krutnik, Frank. "A Spanner in the Works: Genre, Narrative and the Hollywood Comedian." In *Classical Hollywood Comedy*. Edited by Kristine Brunovska Karnick and Henry Jenkins, 17–38. London: Routledge, 1995.

Kyrou, Ado. *Amour, érotisme et cinéma*. Paris: Terrain Vague, 1957.

Lacan, Jacques. *The Four Fundamental Concepts of Psychoanalysis*. Translated by Alan Sheridan. New York: Norton, 1981.

Landy, Marcia, and Lucy Fischer. "*Dead Again* or A-Live Again: Postmodern or Postmortem?" *Cinema Journal* 33, no. 4 (Summer 1994): 3–22.

Lauretis, Teresa de. *Alice Doesn't: Feminism, Semiotics, Cinema*. Bloomington: Indiana University Press, 1984.

Lederer, Wolfgang. *The Fear of Women*. New York: Harcourt Brace Jovanovich, 1968.

Leland, Charles Godfrey (as Hans Breitmann). "Venus and the Ring." In *Legends of Florence, Collected from the People, and Retold*. 2nd series, 242–247. Florence: B. Seeber; London: David Nutt, 1896; Detroit: Singing Tree Press, Book Tower, 1969.

Levin, Thomas Y. "Iconology at the Movies: Panofsky's Film Theory." *Yale Journal of Criticism* 9, no. 1 (1996): 27–55.

Librach, Ronald. "A Nice Little Irony: *Life Lessons*." *Literature/Film Quarterly* 24 (1996): 128–144.

Lower, Cheryl Bray. "The Mankiewicz Woman." In *Joseph L. Mankiewicz: Critical Essays with an Annotated Bibliography and a Filmography*, by Cheryl Bray Lower and R. Barton Palmer, 73–124. Jefferson, NC, and London: McFarland, 2001.

Lower, Cheryl Bray, and R. Barton Palmer. *Joseph L. Mankiewicz: Critical Essays with an Annotated Bibliography and a Filmography*. Jefferson, NC, and London: McFarland, 2001.

Mankiewicz, Joseph. "Measure for Measure." *Cahiers du Cinema* (English) 8 (February 1967): 32.

Marie, Michel. *The French New Wave: An Artistic School*. Translated by Richard Neupert. Oxford: Blackwell, 2003.

Meltzer, Françoise. *Salome and the Dance of Writing: Portraits of Mimesis in Literature*. Chicago: University of Chicago Press, 1987.

Merleau-Ponty, Maurice. "Cézanne's Doubt." In *The Essential Writings of Merleau-Ponty*. Edited by Alden L. Fisher, 233–251. New York: Harcourt Brace and World, 1969.

Minturn, Kent. "Peinture noire: Abstract Expressionism and Film Noir." In *Film Noir Reader 2*. Edited by Alain Silver and James Ursini, 271–309. New York: Limelight, 1999.

Mitchell, Juliet. *Psychoanalysis and Feminism*. New York: Vintage, 1974.

Mitjaville, Alain. "Un Etrange rendez-vous, ou *Le Corridor des Miroirs*." *Les Cahiers de la Cinémathèque* 30/31, no. 1 (Summer/Fall 1980): 129–131.

Modleski, Tania. *The Women Who Knew Too Much: Hitchcock and Feminist Theory*. New York: Methuen, 1988.

Monaco, James. *The New Wave*. New York: Oxford University Press, 1976.

Moravia, Alberto. *Contempt (Il Disprezzo).* Translated by Angus Davidson. New York: New York Review Books, 1999.

Morgan, Elaine. *The Aquatic Ape: A Theory of Human Evolution.* London: Stein and Day, 1982.

Morin, Edgar. *The Stars.* Translated by Richard Howard. New York: Grove Press, 1960.

Mulvey, Laura. "The Hole and the Zero: The Janus Face of the Feminine in Godard." In *Jean-Luc Godard: Son + Image, 1974–1991.* Edited by Raymond Bellour with Mary Lea Bandy, 75–88. New York: Museum of Modern Art and Abrams, 1992.

Mulvey, Laura, and Colin MacCabe. "Images of Woman, Images of Sexuality." In *Godard: Images, Sounds, Politics.* Edited by Colin MacCabe, 79–104. London: BFI, 1980.

Mundy, Robert. "Frank Tashlin: A Tribute." In *Frank Tashlin.* Edited by Claire Johnston and Paul Willemen, 9–16. Edinburgh: Edinburgh Film Festival, in assoc. with *Screen,* 1973.

Nead, Lynda. "Seductive Canvases: Visual Mythologies of the Artist and Artistic Creativity." *Oxford Art Journal* 18, no. 2 (1995): 59–69.

Neumann, Dietrich, ed. *Film Architecture: From "Metropolis" to "Blade Runner."* Munich and New York: Prestel, 1996.

Odabashian, Barbara. "Portrait of an Artist: Hitchcock's *Vertigo.*" *Hitchcock Annual* (1999–2000), 93–99.

Païni, Dominique, and Guy Cogeval, eds. *Hitchcock and Art: Fatal Coincidences.* Montreal: Montreal Museum of Fine Arts, 2000.

Panofsky, Erwin. "Iconography and Iconology: An Introduction to the Study of Renaissance Art." In *Meaning in the Visual Arts,* 26–54. Garden City, NY: Doubleday Anchor, 1955.

———. "Style and Medium in the Motion Pictures." *Critique* 1, no. 3 (January–February 1947): 5–28.

Paris, Reine-Marie. *Camille: The Life of Camille Claudel.* Translated by Liliane Emery Tuck. New York: Arcade, 1988.

Pearlstein, Philip. "Modeling the Soul." *Art in America* 80, no. 1 (January 1992): 61–63.

Penley, Constance. "Time Travel, Primal Scene, and the Critical Dystopia." *Camera Obscura* 15 (Fall 1986): 67–84.

Peterson, Sidney. *The Dark of the Screen.* New York: Anthology Film Archives and New York University Press, 1980.

Petro, Patrice, ed. *Fugitive Images: From Photography to Video.* Bloomington: Indiana University Press, 1995.

Peucker, Brigitte. "The Cut of Representation: Painting and Sculpture in Hitchcock." In *Alfred Hitchcock: Centenary Essays.* Edited by Richard Allen and S. Ishii-Gonzales, 141–156. London: BFI, 1999.

———. *Incorporating Images: Film and the Rival Arts.* Princeton, NJ: Princeton University Press, 1995.

Phillpotts, Beatrice. *Mermaids.* New York: Ballantine, 1980.

Pinter, Harold. "The Last Tycoon." In *"The French Lieutenant's Woman" and Other Screenplays,* 192–277. London: Methuen, 1982.

Poe, Edgar Allan. "The Oval Portrait." In *Selected Writings.* Edited by David Galloway, 250–253. Harmondsworth, England: Penguin, 1967.

Polan, Dana. *Power and Paranoia: History, Narrative, and the American Cinema, 1940–1950.* New York: Columbia University Press, 1986.

Pollock, Griselda. "A Hungry Eye." *Sight and Sound* (new series) 8, no. 11 (November 1998): 26–28.

Rank, Otto. "The Double as Immortal Self." In *Beyond Psychology*, 62–101. New York: Dover, 1958.

Reinke, Steve. "Desire in Scorsese's *After Hours*." *CineAction!* (Summer/Fall 1986): 32–34.

Ritratti di Assen Peikov. Rome: Canesi, 1964.

Riviere, Joan. "Hate, Greed, and Aggression." In *Love, Hate, and Reparation*, by Melanie Klein and Joan Riviere, 19–25. New York: Norton, 1964.

Romer, Eric (pseud. of Maurice Schérer), and François Truffaut. Interview with Roberto Rossellini. *Cahiers du Cinéma* 37 (July 1954). Translated by Liz Heron and reprinted in *Cahiers du Cinéma: The 1950s*. Edited by Jim Hillier, 211. Cambridge, MA: Harvard University Press, 1985.

Rose, Jacqueline. "Julia Kristeva—Take Two." In *Sexuality in the Field of Vision*, 141–164. London: Verso, 1986.

Rosenbaum, Jonathan. Review of *Obsession*. *Monthly Film Bulletin* 43, no. 513 (October 1976): 217.

Rothman, William. *Hitchcock: The Murderous Gaze*. Cambridge, MA: Harvard University Press, 1982.

Russell, Catherine. *Narrative Mortality: Death, Closure, and New Wave Cinemas*. Minneapolis: University of Minnesota Press, 1995.

Saito, Ayako. "Hitchcock's Trilogy: A Logic of Mise en Scène." In *Endless Night: Cinema and Psychoanalysis, Parallel Histories*. Edited by Janet Bergstrom, 200–214. Berkeley: University of California Press, 1999.

Sayers, Janet. *Sexual Contradictions*. London: Tavistock, 1986.

Schulman, Helen. *P.S.* New York and London: Bloomsbury, 2001.

Scorsese, Martin. *Scorsese on Scorsese*. Edited by David Thompson and Ian Christie. London: Faber and Faber, 1989.

Seldes, Lee. *The Legacy of Mark Rothko*. Rev. ed. New York: Da Capo Press, 1996.

Sellier, Geneviève. "Gender, Modernism and Mass Culture in the New Wave." In *Gender and French Cinema*. Edited by Alex Hughes and James S. Williams, 125–137. Oxford and New York: Berg, 2001.

Shipman, David. "A Conversation with Joseph L. Mankiewicz." *Films and Filming* (November 1982): 11.

Siclier, Jacques. *Le Mythe de la femme dans le cinéma américain*. Paris: Les éditions du Cerf, 1956.

Silverman, Kaja, and Harun Farocki. *Speaking about Godard*. New York: New York University Press, 1998.

Sitney, P. Adams. *Visionary Film: The American Avant-Garde, 1943–1978*. New York: Oxford University Press, 1979.

Sontag, Susan. *On Photography*. New York: Delta, 1973.

Surréalisme et cinéma." *Études cinématographiques*, nos. 40–42 (1965): 167–169.

Sykora, Katharina. *As You Desire Me: Das Bildnis in Film*. Köln: Verlag der Buchandlung König, 2003.

Telotte, J. P. "Self Portrait: Painting and the Film Noir." *Smithsonian Studies in American Art* 3, no. 1 (Winter 1989): 3–17.

Theweleit, Klaus. *Male Fantasies*. Vol. 1. *Women, Floods, Bodies, History*. Translated by Stephen Conway. Minneapolis: University of Minnesota Press, 1987.

Török, Jean-Paul. "Eva Prima Pandora." *L'Avant-Scène du Cinéma*, no. 245 (April 1, 1980): 4.

Truffaut, François. "The Barefoot Contessa." In *The Films in My Life*. Translated by Leonard Mayhew, 129–132. New York: Simon and Schuster, 1978.

————. *Hitchcock*. New York: Simon and Schuster, 1967.

Tsivian, Yuri. "Portraits, Mirrors, Death: On Some Decadent Clichés in Early Russian Films." *Iris*, nos. 14–15 (Fall 1992): 67–83.

Turim, Maureen. *Flashbacks in Film: Memory and History*. New York and London: Routledge, 1989.

Tyler, Parker. "Dorian Gray: Last of the Movie Draculas." *View* (New York) 7, no. 2 (October 1946): 22.

Vernet, Marc. "Dictatures du pignoché: Les fictions du portrait." *Iris*, nos. 14–15 (Fall 1992): 45–54.

Vimenet, P. *Le Mépris*. Paris: Hatier, 1991.

Vincendeau, Ginette. *Stars and Stardom in French Cinema*. London: Continuum, 2002.

Wagner, Anne M. "Krasner's Presence, Pollock's Absence." In *Significant Others: Creativity and Intimate Partnership*. Edited by Whitney Chadwick and Isabelle de Courtivron, 222–243. London: Thames and Hudson, 1993.

Waldman, Diane. "The Childish, the Insane, and the Ugly: The Representation of Modern Art in Popular Film and Fiction of the Forties." *Wide Angle* 5, no. 2 (1982): 52–65.

Walker, John. *Art and Artists on Screen*. Manchester, England: Manchester University Press, 1993.

Wettlaufer, Alexandra K. *Pen vs. Paintbrush: Girodet, Balzac and the Myth of Pygmalion in Postrevolutionary France*. New York: Palgrave, 2001.

White, Susan. "Allegory and Referentiality: *Vertigo* and Feminist Film Criticism." *MLN* 106, no. 5 (1991): 310–332.

————. "Split Skins: Female Agency and Bodily Mutilation in *The Little Mermaid*." In *Film Theory Goes to the Movies*. Edited by Jim Collins, Hilary Radner, and Ava Preacher Collins, 182–195. New York and London: Routledge, 1993.

————. "*Vertigo* and Problems of Knowledge in Feminist Film Theory." In *Alfred Hitchcock: Centenary Essays*. Edited by Richard Allen and S. Ishii-Gonzales, 279–298. London: BFI, 1999.

Willemen, Paul. "Tashlin's Method: An Hypothesis." In *Frank Tashlin*. Edited by Claire Johnston and Paul Willemen, 117–129. Edinburgh: Edinburgh Film Festival, in assoc. with *Screen*, 1973.

————. "Through the Glass Darkly: Cinephilia Reconsidered." In *Looks and Frictions*, 223–257. Bloomington: Indiana University Press/BFI, 1994.

Williams, Linda. *Figures of Desire: A Theory and Analysis of Surrealist Film*. Urbana: University of Illinois Press, 1981.

Williams, Tony. *Structures of Desire: British Cinema, 1939–1955*. Albany: State University of New York Press, 2000.

Wittkower, Rudolf, and Margot Wittkower. *Born under Saturn: The Character and Conduct of Artists*. New York: Norton, 1969.

Wood, Robin. *Hitchcock's Films Revisited*. New York: Columbia University Press, 1989.

————. *Hollywood from Vietnam to Reagan*. New York: Columbia University Press, 1986.

————. "Male Desire, Male Anxiety: The Essential Hitchcock." In *A Hitchcock Reader*.

Edited by Marshall Deutelbaum and Leland Poague, 219–230. Ames: Iowa State University Press, 1986.

Young, Jeff. *Kazan: The Master Director Discusses His Films.* New York: Newmarket Press, 1999.

Ziolkowski, Theodore. *Disenchanted Images: A Literary Iconology.* Princeton, NJ: Princeton University Press, 1977.

Index

Boldface page numbers indicate illustrations